NEPAL HIMALAYA

H. W. TILMAN

Everest from due west

NEPAL HIMALAYA

H. W. TILMAN

TILMAN

First published 1952 by Cambridge University Press
This edition published 2017 by Tilman Books
www.tilmanbooks.com
a joint venture by
Lodestar Books www.lodestarbooks.com
and Vertebrate Publishing www.v-publishing.co.uk

Original text copyright © Simon Heyworth Davis 1974
Foreword copyright © Ed Douglas 2017

Cover design by Jane Beagley
Vertebrate Graphics Ltd. www.v-graphics.co.uk

Lodestar Books has asserted their right
to be identified as the Editor of this Work

Series editor Dick Wynne
Series researcher Bob Comlay

The publisher has made reasonable effort to locate
the holders of copyright in the illustrations in this book,
and will be pleased to hear from them regarding
correct attribution in future editions

All rights reserved

A CIP catalogue record for this book
is available from the British Library

ISBN 978-1-909461-38-3

Typeset in Baskerville from Storm Type Foundry
Printed and bound by Pulsio, Bulgaria
All papers used by Tilman Books are sourced responsibly

Contents

	Foreword – *Ed Douglas*	9
	Preface	13
	PART ONE: THE LANGTANG HIMAL, 1949	
I	To Nepal	17
II	Katmandu	30
III	To the Langtang	41
IV	The Langtang	52
V	Rasua Garhi	68
VI	The Ganesh Himal	80
VII	The Langtang Again	93
VIII	The Jugal Himal	106
	PART TWO: ANNAPURNA HIMAL, 1950	
IX	The Start	121
X	The Marsyandi	133
XI	Manangbhot	144
XII	To the Mountain	155
XIII	On the Mountain	168
XIV	A Change of Scene	180
XV	Mustangbhot	191
XVI	Muktinath	204
XVII	Bimtakhoti and Himal Chuli	214
XVIII	A Fresh Start	226
XIX	Approach to Mt Everest	241
	The Natural History of the Langtang Valley – *O. Polunin*	258

Photographs

Everest from due west	2
Bodnath temple	23
...in Katmandu near the Kot	24
A temple door in Patan	24
...the temple of the Five Stages at Bhatgaon	35
Temure village in the upper Trisuli	36
Outside the Langtang gompa	36
...gompa of Kyangin	47
...the Kyangin gompa	47
...view eastwards across the hidden Langtang glacier	48
The view from Langsisa up the East glacier	48
Our camp at Rasua Garhi	61
'...a stout, affable official in Homburg hat...'	61
A flailing fatigue at Langtang village	62
In Chilime village	62
View of the range in Tibet	73
'A big snow peak filling the head of the valley'	73
Looking across the East Langtang glacier	74
The Jugal side of the pass	85
Three of the five desolate tarns at Panch Pokhara	86
A distant view of the Jugal Himal	86
A quiet corner in Patan	97
At Baleji water garden	97
Coolies resting at a chautara	98
A village on the route to the Marsyandi valley	98
...occasional glimpses of Manaslu...	109
The north ridge of Manaslu	110
Braga village	123
...across the valley to Annapurna IV	124
Looking north across the Marsyandi valley	135
A similar view from below Camp III	135
The 'Fishtail' (Macha Puchare) floating on a sea of cloud	136
Lieut. S. B. Malla skins a bird	147
Three generations at Tange	147
Phugaon	148
Tange	148
Looking north up the wide basin of the Kali river	159

A good example of 'organ-pipe' erosion on the cliffs	159
Muktinath temple	160
The Naur Khola bridge	160
Some of the 108 spouts...	171
Off-loading bags of salt from zos at Bimtakhoti	172
Our camp on the Bahara Pokhara Lekh	172
Bimtakhoti against a background of rock spires	183
Looking across the big moraine at Bimtakhoti	183
...a Saussurea growing at about 16,000 ft.	184
Rice fields in the lower Marsyandi valley	197
A last glimpse of the snows on the way home	197
Dhankhuta is an immaculately clean little place	198
A family group in Bung	198
An oil press in a village in the Arm valley	209
The village cobbler of Panga	209
Prayer flags ...in the Dudh Kosi valley	210
Namche Bazar	221
On the march to Thyangboche	222
The snow disappeared next day	222
Looking at Everest, north-west of the monastery	233
Looking north up the Chola Khola	234
A view of Everest from due west	245
A party outside the monastery	246
Sonam Tensing & Prometheus Danu	246
The young abbot	255

Maps

1	General Map of Nepal	19
2	Map to illustrate 1949 journey	55
3	Langtang Glaciers	58
4	Journey to Manangbhot	127
5	Journey to Mustangbhot	194
6	Journey to Nepal side of Everest	229
7	Sketch-map of Everest region	249

Foreword

Ed Douglas

'I FELT I COULD GO ON LIKE THIS FOR EVER, that life had little better to offer than to march day after day in an unknown country to an unattainable goal.' Bill Tilman wrote these words in *Two Mountains and a River*, published in early 1949, the year he went to Nepal for the first time. They capture so much of his appeal as an adventurer, in fact, *the* adventurer, a man whose extraordinary and unrepeatable life has achieved a sort of mythological status. He is a modernist Odysseus, crossing a fractured ocean, the old world no more than smoking ruins, his hand firmly on the tiller. Odysseus, of course, had a home to aim for: Ithaca, where Penelope waited oh-so-patiently. Tilman had no one waiting for him. Only one thing held his attention: the horizon.

The impact his experiences in the Great War had on Tilman were visceral and permanent. He went to war a month before his eighteenth birthday and was soon wounded, in the thigh, but recovered and went back to the front in time for the Somme. 'When one took stock,' he wrote decades later, 'shame mingled with satisfaction at finding oneself still alive. One felt a bit like the Ancient Mariner; so many better men, a few of them friends, were dead.' And then he quotes Coleridge: 'And a thousand thousand slimy things / Lived on; and so did I.'

Odysseus too found himself washed in gore and horror, but he came from an honour culture that saw such bloody outcomes as affirmation. For Tilman, the Great War was a cultural catastrophe, one he felt guilty to have survived. He clung to great literature as one would to wreckage after a storm rather than regarding it as foundations for a new order. Jim Perrin recalled Tilman quoting the war poet Max Plowman's *When It's Over*: 'I shall lie on the beach / Of a shore where the rippling waves just sigh, / And listen and dream and sleep and lie / Forgetting what I've had to learn and teach / And attack and defend.'

That is principally what Tilman spent the rest of his life doing, except during the fight against fascism, which he might have avoided but didn't, serving once more with distinction.

So there are hints of the bitter past as well as romance in Tilman's wanderlust. And there is sadness too in the notion that he could go on marching day after day forever, because, as he well knew, he could not. *Nepal Himalaya* was his last mountain book, before the great shift to life afloat and another quarter century of astonishing adventures. He arrived at a moment of immense upheaval, both political and cultural, across the Himalaya. In Nepal, the consequences of Indian independence were fast unwinding: the Rana regime, preserved like a mosquito in amber, sucking the blood of its own people from beyond the grave, was about to fall. The old order was changing, yielding place to something Tilman regarded with some horror: the modern world. Nepal, he knew, was the largest inhabited space left that remained unexplored to European travellers. He was entering the endgame.

Starting in the monsoon of 1949, Tilman made three journeys to Nepal, at the front of a mad rush of explorers wanting to 'discover' this beautiful, complex and accommodating country. As he explains in his book, that complexity and cultural depth was well understood in the region; it was the West that remained in ignorance. He was wary of projecting the Western desire for some untouched Eden onto a people who always greeted you with a smile. On the third of those journeys, to the Khumbu region below Everest with the American climber Charles Houston and his father Oscar, Tilman reached Namche Bazaar, the quasi-capital of this corner of Sherpa country. Houston saw the Himalayan equivalent of the noble savage, as though Sherpas were a lost North American tribe with the wisdom of the earth still in their veins. Tilman noticed that some of the windows had glass in them, and understood the impact remittances from migrant workers in Darjeeling were having on this paradise.

On the first journey, to Langtang, Tilman overcame his allergy to science so the expedition would have some higher purpose and so have a greater chance of being allowed in. He took along a geologist and a botanist, both of whom did useful work. Tilman himself got into the swing of things, promising to collect a certain species of beetle. 'Not knowing much about beetles,' his biographer J.R.L. Anderson wrote, 'he interpreted this as collecting any beetle that came his way, which he did conscientiously, one of his beetles turning out to be new to science.' You can almost hear him cursing in disappointment.

In Khumbu, Tilman faced another challenge that set his teeth on edge: the presence of a woman. A fair bit is made of Tilman's supposed misogyny but his relationship with Betsy Cowles, an old climbing friend of Charlie Houston's who joined them in 1950, suggests at least an alternative view. Tilman sulked when he realised she was sharing their adventure, but Cowles promised to win him round and soon did, the pair becoming inseparable, prompting a small burst of jealousy in Oscar. Cowles was then in her late forties, Tilman fifty-two; there is something in their friendship of the road not travelled, an unusual experience for Tilman, who travelled most of them.

The concluding lines of the book have a quiet but noble melancholy, the old soldier finally bowing before his greatest adversary: time. 'The best attainable should be good enough for any man, but the mountaineer who finds his best gradually sinking is not satisfied.' Tilman then quotes Beowulf's stern demand that in old age the heart should be bolder, the spirit harder, and suggests that because he can't achieve such a high standard, he will withdraw. Breezy self-deprecation was his literary signature, the bathetic always just around the corner. In his diaries he was almost darkly hard on his himself. I think Beowulf would have approved of his shift to the ever-restless oceans.

'He was a deep and private man,' Charles Houston wrote, 'with an immense willpower and strength and an incredible sense of humour which he reserved for greatest effect, and one of the toughest men I ever knew. One sometimes felt that he courted disaster, longed for trauma, and he never did things the easy way if with a little effort they could be made to be impossible.'

That he is still read, when so much of mid-twentieth-century travel literature is not, says a great deal about his ability as a writer. He was shrewd enough not to strain too hard in his prose, which often reads like a translation from Latin, old-fashioned even when it was written, but often charming. He understood what his readers loved about him, twinkled with humour and mastered the English habit of self-mockery. And despite all that he suffered, was never quite overtaken by the deep shadows he ran from, to the ends of the earth.

Preface

A WRITER OF TRAVELS, by the title he gives his book, should not promise more than he performs. But titles must be brief and, if possible, striking. The brief and rather too all-embracing title of this book may conjure up visions of the author stepping lightly from one Nepal peak to the next, or surveying the whole from the top of one stupendous giant. In the course of three journeys herein described, only one mountain, a modest one, was successfully climbed, a fact which may account for any wordy pomposity, not unlike the style of a White Paper put out to cover up some appalling blunder on the part of Authority. Moreover, two of the three journeys had a serious purpose, which may account for the comparatively few occasions on which cheerfulness manages to break in. I am glad that the learned will benefit from the report on the Natural History of the Langtang valley specially contributed by Mr O. Polunin in an appendix.

Again I have to thank Dr R. J. Perring for criticism and help; and R. T. Sneyd, Esq., for attending to the reading of proofs in my absence.

H. W. TILMAN
Barmouth
September 1951

PART ONE

The Langtang Himal

1949

CHAPTER I

TO NEPAL

There can be no other country so rich in mountains as Nepal. This narrow strip of territory, lying between Sikkim and Garhwal, occupies 500 miles of India's northern border; and since this border coincides roughly with the 1500-mile-long Himalayan chain, it follows that approximately a third of this vast range lies within or upon the confines of Nepal. Moreover, besides being numerous, the peaks of the Nepal Himalaya are outstandingly high. Apart from Everest and Kangchenjunga and their two 27,000 ft. satellites, there are six peaks over 26,000 ft., fourteen over 25,000 ft., and a host of what might be called slightly stunted giants of 20,000 ft. and upwards, which cannot be enumerated because they are not all shown on existing maps.

In trying to grasp the general lay-out of this mountain region it is convenient to divide it into three parts, represented—from west to east—by the basins of the Karnali, the Gandak, and the Kosi. These three important rivers, some of whose tributaries rise in Tibet north of the Himalaya, all flow into the Ganges. The Karnali drains the mountains of western Nepal between Api (23,339 ft.), near the Garhwal border, and Dhaulagiri (26,795 ft.); the basin of the Gandak occupies central Nepal between the Annapurna Himal and the Langtang Himal; and the Kosi drains the mountains of eastern Nepal from Gosainthan (26,291 ft.) to Kangchenjunga. It should be understood that, except for Everest and those peaks on the Nepal-Sikkim border, most of which (except Kangchenjunga) have been climbed, this enormous field has remained untouched, unapproached, almost unseen, until this year (1949) when the first slight scratch was made.

Nepal is an independent kingdom. Like Tibet it has always sought isolation and has secured it by excluding foreigners, of whom the most undesirable were white men. A man fortunate enough to have been admitted into Nepal is expected to be able to explain on general grounds the motives behind this invidious policy and, on personal grounds, the reason for such an unaccountable exception. But now that the advantages of the Western way of life are becoming every day less obvious no explanation should be needed. Wise men traditionally come from the East, and it is probable that to them the West and its ways were suspect long before we ourselves began to have doubts. Anyhow, for the rulers of countries like Nepal and Tibet, whose polity until very recent days was medieval feudalism, the wise and natural course was to exclude foreigners and their advanced ideas. And the poverty and remoteness of those countries made such a policy practicable. A hundred years ago the rulers of China and Japan regarded foreign devils with as much distrust and aversion, but unfortunately for them their countries had sea-coasts and ports; and, unlike Tibet and Nepal, promised to become markets which no nation that lived by trade could afford to ignore.

The Nepalese, who number about five millions, are mostly Hindus. Consequently it has been suggested that the Brahmins have been the most fervent advocates of an exclusive policy. It does not seem logical, because a thin trickle of European visitors has long been admitted to the *sanctum sanctorum* of the Katmandu valley, whereas in remote parts, where Hinduism sits lightly or merges into Buddhism as the northern border is approached, the ban has been most rigid. A simple explanation is that the early rulers of Nepal, themselves independent and warlike, having established their sway over a turbulent people, naturally wished to remain masters in their own house. With the example of India at hand, these rulers, not without reason apprehensive and suspicious of the British, concluded that the best way of remaining in power was to have as little as possible to do with Europeans. And since this avowed policy was approved and respected by the Indian Government, it could be strictly maintained.

Writing in 1928 Perceval Landon (*Nepal*, two vols.) estimated that only some 120 English and ten other Europeans had been permitted to enter the Katmandu valley; while from the time of Brian Hodgson (British Resident from 1833 to 1843) onwards not even the British Resident has been allowed to set foot outside the valley. Since 1928 the number of visitors to Katmandu must have increased considerably but the mesh is still fine. However, in 1948 a party of Indian scientists had been allowed to investigate the upper basin of the Kosi river in

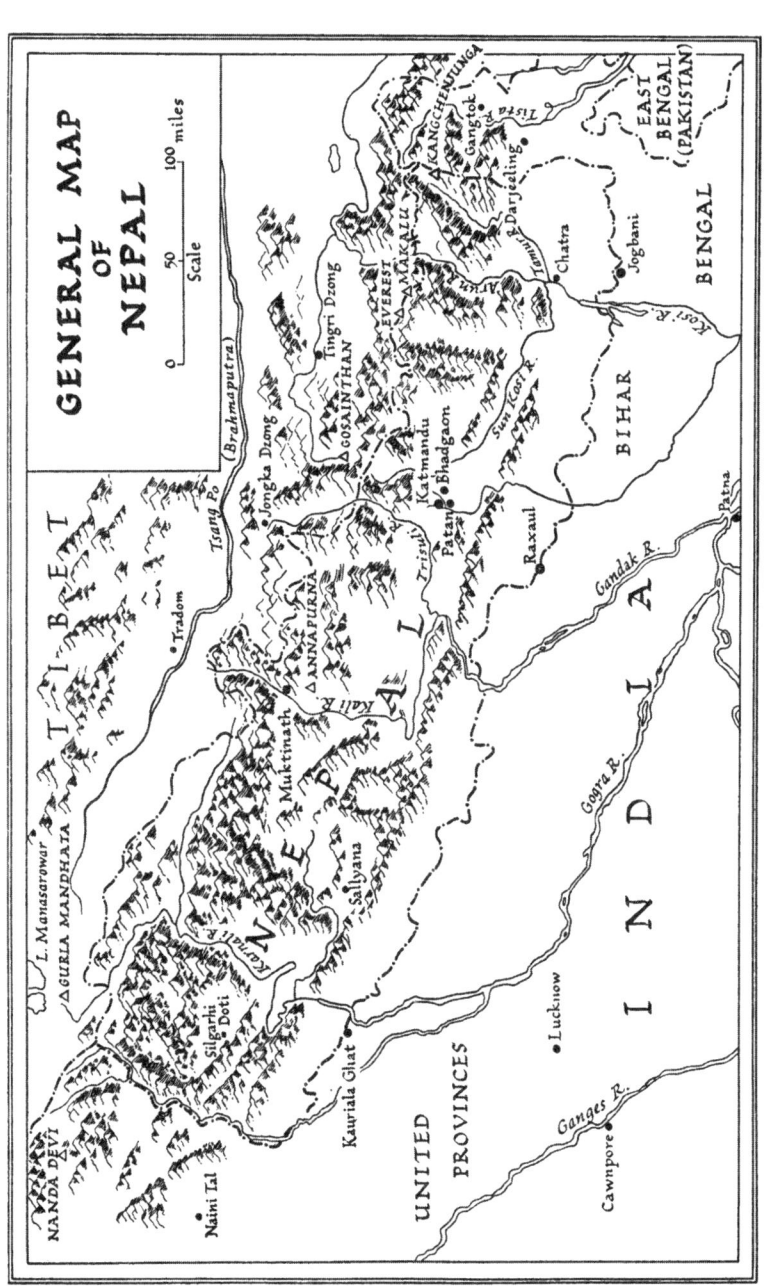

Map 1: General Map of Nepal

eastern Nepal where they climbed to the Nangpa La, a 19,000 ft. pass west of Everest; and in the winter of 1948-9 an American party led by Dr Dillon Ripley was busy collecting birds in the foothills of central and eastern Nepal.

Thus encouraged, at the end of 1948 the British Ambassador at Katmandu (Sir George Falconer) sought permission for a climbing party to visit the Nepal Himalaya; and the Prime Minister, when he understood that the project had the blessing of the President of a small band of harmless eccentrics who had no other axe to grind than an ice axe, readily consented. There were, however, conditions attached. Instead of going as we had hoped to the vicinity of Gauri Sankar (23,440 ft.), whence we could also have had a look at the south side of Everest, we were to confine ourselves to the Langtang Himal; and instead of merely gambolling upon the mountains we had to undertake some serious scientific work. Science, of course, is no laughing matter, but I use the word serious advisedly so that there may be no mistake.

Except for the Nepal side of Kangchenjunga, which Hooker, Freshfield, and Dyhrenfurth's party had visited, the Nepal Himalaya is unknown to Europeans. No one part was less interesting or exciting for us than another; but the second of these conditions meant not only a change in the composition of the party but a change, almost a *volte face*, on the part of a leader who had hitherto refused to mingle art with science. To be too stiff in opinion is a grave fault; a man should be sure of more than his principles before deciding never to break them. Benedick, when he swore he would die a bachelor, did not expect to live until he was married; and just as the great Henry once deemed Paris worth a Mass, so I thought a glimpse of the Nepal Himalaya worth the swallowing of a strong prejudice.

The party finally consisted of four, two scientists, or embryo scientists and two very mature climbers. Botany and geology were two obvious fields in which all that a first visit demanded were the collecting of specimens and the noting of data—tasks more suited to the embryo than to the full-blown professor. A botanist was quickly forthcoming in Mr O. Polunin, a master at Charterhouse, who was acceptable to the British Museum for whom most of the collecting was to be done. Blotting-paper and a love of flowers is not enough for the disciple of

Linnaeus. Finding a geologist gave some trouble. The number of them who do anything so vulgar as battering the living rock in the field is extraordinarily minute. As weathering agents they can be dismissed. I worked steadily through a list of twenty of the older practitioners, none of whom seemed eager to pluck his rusting hammer from the wall to strike a blow for his faith. Nor would they detail a subordinate for the job. Research, setting and answering examination papers, kept the whole geological strata of England firmly *in situ*. A very willing victim was at last found in J. S. Scott, and his University, St Andrews, came to our aid with a handsome grant.

Having no wish to be bound too tightly to the wheel of science Mr Peter Lloyd, who was my fellow climber, and myself were prepared to pay for our own amusement. There was little difficulty in raising what money was needed for the others; for I have remarked elsewhere upon the readiness of some learned bodies to support and encourage minor enterprises of this sort, provided that among those who go upon them are men able and willing, as our Russian friend put it,* to tear a few more rents in Nature's veil. Breathing this rarefied air of high purpose must have gone to my head. Encouraged by the impreciseness of the map of our area, I found myself suggesting to Lloyd that we, or rather he, should undertake to improve it. This would be of benefit to future mountaineers, and would put all four members of our party on the same high intellectual plane. Lloyd, to whom theodolites were strange but who was familiar with much more recondite instruments, welcomed the idea.

Nepal is usually referred to as 'unknown'. Possibly the reader has already mistakenly inferred that the whole country, including the Nepal Himalaya, is unexplored, whereas there are maps of the whole country on a ¼-in. scale. One of the pleasing traits of the Westerner or Paleface is to assume that what is not known to him cannot be known to anyone. 'Unexplored' country means country unexplored by him, rather in the grand manner of Mrs Elton who had never been to Box Hill and talked ardently of conducting an exploring party there. Unknown Nepal must have become thoroughly well known to the fourteen Indian surveyors (European officers of the Indian Survey

---

* See *China to Chitral*, p. 111.

Department were excluded) who in three seasons, 1924–7, surveyed the whole 55,000 sq. miles from the 'terai' along the Indian border to the Himalaya. Even before this, Nepal must have been tolerably familiar to its inhabitants, and some of the remote valleys were made known to the outside world by a few of the devoted 'pundit' explorers sent out by the Survey of India. 'M.H.', for example, who in 1885 travelled up the valley of the Dudh Kosi west of Everest to Tingri in Tibet, whence he returned to India by Kyerong and the Trisuli valley, thus traversing Nepal twice; while in 1873 Hari Ram, another Indian explorer, followed the valley of the Kali river to Tradom in Tibet. Two Jesuit missionaries are also believed to have returned from Shigatse in Tibet to Katmandu in 1629, probably by Nyenam, but unfortunately they left no record of their journey. Moreover, the various British Residents at Katmandu from 1802 onwards have collected from native sources a mass of information?—in particular, Hodgson, who for ten years made it his principal task. He never moved out of the valley, but he knew fairly accurately, for example, the drainage system of the Gandak river and much of the natural history of the country. In short, Nepal is by no means *terra incognita*, but it is true to say that it is the largest inhabited country still unexplored by Europeans.

The area we were to visit had thus been surveyed (of which more hereafter), but a glance at the relevant map sheet (71 H ¼-in.), showed a tract of country immediately north of the Langtang Himal in Tibet that bore the magic word 'unsurveyed'; this was the more interesting because in it lay Gosainthan (26,291 ft.) some ten miles north of the main Himalayan crest-line. Tibet was out of bounds but it occurred to me that by lugging a photo-theodolite up to several points on the frontier ridge we might with luck get enough data for the mapping of this stretch of country of which not even the drainage system was known. Gosainthan probably lies on the watershed between the Trisuli Gandak and the Kosi system, but the ¼-in. map shows an intervening ridge to the west of the mountain, the whole of which is thus made to lie in the Kosi basin.

Gosainthan, meaning the Place of the Saint, is the Sanskrit name for the peak the Tibetans call Shisha Pungma. Kailas and Gurla Mandhata are two other Sanskrit names for very famous mountains, both in Tibet, given by Hindu pilgrims visiting the sacred shrines in the

Bodnath temple, the largest and one of the oldest in Nepal; in the low wall surrounding the dome hundreds of prayer wheels wait to be turned by anyone who treads the lustral path; the object on legs is a stack of maize in the cob

This fierce apparition of the four-armed Kola Bhaibar, painted black, yellow, and vermilion, stands in Katmandu near the Kot

A temple door in Patan and one of a pair of colossal stone dragons guarding it

vicinity of the peak. With the spread of Buddhism the same places became the goals of Buddhist pilgrims who gave the peaks Tibetan names. Kailas (22,028 ft.) lying to the north of Lake Manasarowar was Siva's paradise, and still is the resort of Hindu pilgrims who walk right round the mountain prostrating themselves as they go, a journey which under these arduous conditions takes three weeks. No Hindu pilgrim visits Gosainthan; were it not for the evidence of the name it would be difficult to believe they had even seen it. They do, however, visit in large numbers the sacred lake of Gosainkund situated high on a long southerly spur of the Langtang Himal on the east side of the Trisuli valley. Possibly some confusion exists between this lake and the mountain; for in the Nepalese map published in Landon's *Nepal*, the frontier is so drawn as to include the mountain, implying that it is of importance to Hindus.

It is not often possible to visit the Himalaya at the best time. West of the central Himalaya there is probably not much to choose between any of the summer months, but in the eastern Himalaya from the end of June to the end of September the prevalence of monsoon conditions is a serious handicap to climbing and to comfort. Comfort must not be expected by folks that go a-pleasuring, but the first consideration would persuade the mountaineer, if he could, to climb in May and June, to lie at earth during July and August, and to return refreshed in October for a final fling. For those who visit the Himalaya for less serious reasons the weather is of less account, the only exception being the surveyor for whom weather is all important. In order to see the first flowers a botanist should be in the field by early May, remain throughout the summer (having much trouble drying his specimens) for successively later ones, and stay until the end of October when most of the seeds have ripened. Generally such nice considerations of the ideal time have to be omitted; the party goes out when it can and returns when it must, which in our case was late May and early September respectively. Thus only our geologist could view with indifference our arrival in the field only a week or two before the expected breaking of the monsoon.

It did not take long to collect the necessary stores and equipment, to sketch a rough plan, an even rougher estimate of cost, and to arrange for the assembly of the motley party in Katmandu towards the end of May. Lloyd and I, coming from opposite directions, met in Calcutta, while the other two travelled via Bombay. The four Sherpas I had engaged met us safely in Calcutta, in spite of the fact that in coming from Darjeeling they had had to pass from India to Pakistan and then back again to India.

Travelling north across the great flat alluvial plain of Bengal and Bihar, where for hundreds of miles a man may lift his eyes no higher than a mango tree, is a salutary but fortunately short-lived experience for a mountaineer. In twenty-four hours, after a steamer voyage across the Ganges, when we were nearly separated from our nineteen bulky packages, we reached Raxaul near the frontier of India and Nepal. From here a narrow gauge railway, opened in 1927, runs to Amlekhganj, the railhead twenty-nine miles away. Shortly after crossing the frontier at Birgunj the line enters the terai. This is a peculiar strip of jungle, twelve to twenty miles wide, stretching more or less continuously along the whole southern border. The thin gravel soil is of little use for cultivation, but the terai is of value on account of its flourishing growth of sal trees, which are in great demand for railway sleepers; it is also a big-game reserve, where tiger, panther, the one-horned Indian rhino (found also in Assam), wild elephant, wild buffalo, and smaller game abound. In the cold weather, H.H.the Maharajah and members of the ruling family, many of whom are keen shikaris, organise shoots to which privileged guests are sometimes invited. The renowned Jang Bahadur, Prime Minister from 1846 to his death in 1877, the most illustrious of a distinguished line, one who is now an almost legendary character, was a very mighty hunter. Before he had settled himself firmly in the saddle, he hunted his numerous enemies as vindictively and as effectively as later he did the tigers of the terai. He became his country's greatest benefactor, and proved a very staunch friend to Britain in the critical years of the Mutiny.

Another curious denizen of the terai at one time was Nana Sahib, the leader of the Indian Mutiny, who after his final defeat at Tantia Topi fled across the Nepal frontier and took refuge in the terai. He opened negotiations with Jang Bahadur, who, refusing either to shelter him or to give him up, yet managed to acquire at a quite moderate price the Nana's principal jewel—the Naulahka, an unrivalled necklace of pearls, diamonds and emeralds. The circumstances of the

Nana's death, or even the time and place, are still a mystery; but he was reported to have died in 1859 which, if he remained in the terai, is very probable. For six months of the year it is an unhealthy, indeed, a lethal place, where anyone who spends a night unprotected is almost sure to contract the deadly local form of malaria called 'awal'. Deadly malaria is not a monopoly of the Nepal terai. The belt of country between the Himalayan foothills and the plain of India is unhealthy everywhere from central India eastwards. In 1939, after one night in the Assam terai, three Sherpas and myself all contracted different forms of malaria, all of which were serious and one fatal.

From Amlekhganj the journey is continued by car or lorry, and the dejected traveller soon perceives from the frightful grinding of gears, that the world is not so flat as he had feared. In the journey of twenty-seven miles to road-head at Bhimpedi (3650 ft.) the road rises a hundred feet in every mile. This country of the Siwalik foothills is well wooded and well watered, but sparsely inhabited and probably fever-ridden. The Siwalik is a remarkable range; though never rising above 5000 ft. it stretches almost unbroken, parallel to the Himalaya, from the Brahmaputra to the Indus. The ancient Aryans called it, very appropriately, 'the edge of the roof of Siva's Himalayan abode'.

The motor-road passes under the crest of the Siwaliks by a tunnel 300 yd. long; the old road crossed by the Churia pass, which is a place of some military interest. In the Nepalese war of 1816 a British column 13,000 strong under General Ochterlony, advancing on Katmandu, outflanked the defended pass by means of a goat-track to the west, thus turning the main Gurkha position based on the fortress of Makwanpur. Two higher passes and much difficult country still lay between Ochterlony's force and their objective, while the Gurkha army was still intact, but the Nepalese, fearful for the hitherto inviolate Katmandu valley, made terms. Ochterlony, from whom the suggestion must have come with double force, was the first to suggest, during this very war, that Gurkha troops should be enlisted in the Indian Army.

Beyond the Siwalik range the road enters and ascends the valley of the Rapti, on the north side of which forest-clad hills rise to over 8000 ft. The motor-road ends at the head of the valley at Bhimpedi, a straggling corrugated-iron bazaar. We turned off two miles short of this to the ropeway station, Dhusing. The electrically driven ropeway, opened in 1925, is fourteen miles long and rises to a height of 4500 ft. above Dhusing; each sling carries about 5cwt. and travels at four and a half miles an hour. The mountaineer who allows himself and his load to be hauled uphill attached to the endless rope of a ski-lift should feel a slight sense of guilt, much as an anchorite would who changed his hair shirt for a silk one; but in consigning our nineteen packages to the care of this invaluable machine we experienced nothing but relief. At much less cost than the hire of coolies and with no worry on our part, the baggage would be in Katmandu before we arrived. The ropeway can deliver fifty or sixty tons a day, the equivalent of 1500 coolies working for two days. The goods shed was overflowing with bags of grain, salt and general merchandise, waiting to go up; but since very little comes down these imports must be paid for by 'invisible' exports of which the major one, no doubt, is the Gurkha soldier.

Having arranged this matter we drove on to Bhimpedi where we were decanted at three o'clock of a hot afternoon at the foot of a formidable hill quite devoid, so far as one could see, of anything in the nature of a lift. True the pylons of the ropeway could be seen marching up in giant strides, but on that no passengers are carried. So far, thanks to the admirable arrangements made by the Nepalese authorities and the British embassy, no effort, physical or mental, had been required of us until now, when for the next eighteen miles we had to put foot to ground. Even that we might have spared ourselves had we wished, H.H. the Maharajah having sent two ponies for us.

Between Bhimpedi and Thankot in the valley itself there are two passes, the Sisagarhi (6225 ft.) and the Chandragiri (7700 ft.). A night is spent at a rest-house below the first pass whence the journey to Thankot can be done in six or seven hours. Our early arrival on the pass having gone unrewarded—for on a clear day the Himalaya can be seen—we dropped 2500 ft. to a valley across which the ropeway swings in one enormous span of 1300 yd. Crossing the clear rippling Kuli, a tributary stream of the sacred Bagmati river which alone drains the Katmandu valley, we continued up an open valley to Chitlong at the foot of the steep rise to the Chandragiri, where, in company with the coolie traffic, we paused to brace ourselves for the serious business of the day. As the ropeway cannot deal with very heavy or bulky loads there is the opportunity for coolies to prove the superiority of man over machine by dealing with things like brass cannons and motor cars, for which there seemed to be a steady demand in the valley.

A team of thirty coolies handled a brass cannon easily, almost running in fact, while seventy, or perhaps ninety, if it is a Rolls Royce, are needed for a car. Two long poles which project well fore-and-aft are lashed under the car as it stands. To these wooden shoulder pieces are attached, each of which is supported by two men, one each side of the pole. On level ground this works well, but the Chandragiri pass is steep, particularly so on the Katmandu side, and a load carried thus on a thirty degree slope must set up some curious stresses. We met several car-carrying parties but the coolies each time were taking a rest, of which, no doubt, they need a lot.

As he looks from the Chandragiri pass upon the fair and spacious valley below, the most jaded traveller must feel his imagination stirred by its secluded position, its turbulent past, and by the mystery and sanctity attending this most ancient shrine of Hindu and Buddhist tradition, with its temples and stupas of Asoka, sacred groves and burning ghats. Even the traveller who views it upon a cloudy day, without seeing the sublime background of the Himalaya which are the source of these religious traditions, cannot but be charmed by the pattern of green and yellow fields, the terra-cotta houses, the gleaming white palaces and the dark roofs of the city, the whole ringed with gentle, wooded hills. Since almost the whole valley, only some twenty by fifteen miles, is in view, he may well say he is looking at Nepal: for to those who live outside the valley this is Nepal. And in a sense it is true enough; for in this small arena has been enacted and recorded in brick, wood, and stone, nearly all the ancient and modern history of what we call Nepal; and within it is concentrated nearly half a million people and nearly all the power, art, prosperity, commerce—in short everything appertaining to the life of the country.

Pursued and finally overtaken by a thunderstorm we reached Thankot in the afternoon, where we were picked up by the waiting embassy car and wafted the remaining nine miles to Katmandu.

CHAPTER II

KATMANDU

Arriving on 24 May we planned to leave on the 29th provided the Bombay party joined us in time. Had there been less to attend to we might have spent four very tranquil days, for at Katmandu tranquillity is the key-note. This was not so a hundred years ago, when intrigue and faction were the rule; when incidents like the throwing of Jang Bahadur down a well, his shooting of his uncle, and the imprisonment and suicide of a Prime Minister, were but mild preludes to the scene in the Kot courtyard when anything from fifty to five hundred notables and officials were massacred. Perhaps it was these scenes as described by Laurence Oliphant (*Journey to Katmandu*, 1850) and particularly that of a royal review which 'surpassed even the wildest notions of our highly civilized community' which gave Kipling a hint:

> And the wildest dreams of Kew are the facts of Katmandu,
> And the crimes of Clapham chaste in Martaban.

But times have changed. Now the uninhibited life of surburbia might astonish the natives of Katmandu where propriety is the rule, and where landaus, visiting cards and formality set the tone.

Our baggage having been collected from the ropeway station had now to be made up into man-loads for the journey up the Trisuli valley where animal transport, we were told, was not used. It is only a matter of seven or eight days to the Langtang by a well-used trade route about which, however, little or no information could be had. The question of whether we could buy food at Langtang had to be resolved, for obviously if we had to carry all the atta and rice we needed for three and a half months many more coolies must be engaged. Maize, and not much of that, was thought to be all we might obtain, so we compromised by taking food for a month and after that, if the worst happened, we could send back for more. There are few places in the Himalaya where the food arrangements can be left in such a conveniently fluid state; where having once arrived at one's base the question of sending back for anything is worth considering. Apparently this trip was to be another example of one 'with no transport difficulties', where each item in each load has not to be jealously weighed and where comfort has not to be sacrificed to mobility.

The rules of haggling having been sufficiently observed, we contracted with a coolie agent for forty men to go to Rasua Garhi and to find their own food. Dealing with one man who will make himself responsible for all, instead of forty, is probably more satisfactory from the point of view of the traveller and the contractor than it is from that of the coolies. It may cost a little more, but the saving of trouble is as worth buying as silence. The coolie agent—known as the 'baria naik'—receives a lump sum, half at the start and half later, but how much of this is received by the men is another matter, one which, we may hope, is attended to by that device known to economists as 'the price mechanism'. Apart from the ropeway, coolie transport is used everywhere, so that it is an organized business; it would probably be quite impossible to collect men except through such an agent, whom the traveller is free either to respect as an essential cog in the machine or to abuse as a parasite according to his political views.

This difficult business was managed with the advice and help of Col. R. R. Proud, First Secretary to the Embassy, in whose house we were staying. Besides this kindness he arranged our official visits, modified the size of the escort which the goodwill of H.H. the Maharajah would have wished larger, lent us cars for sightseeing and an orderly to see fair play in our dealings in the bazaar. Were it not for the restriction on movement outside the valley, there could hardly be a more pleasant place for a British official than Katmandu, provided he has other than social interests. Our host had plenty of these, among them an interest in mountains, but it must have been galling for him to think that even had he been free his official position would have prevented his accompanying us.

After the heavy thunderstorm of the previous day our second evening was so clear that Col. Proud took us—rather too quickly we thought—up one of the local hills for a view of the Himalaya. We went by car to the foot of the hill at Baleji where, surrounded by woods, there is a water-garden of green lawns and grey stone tanks in which monster black and green carp ogle the visitors for food. From the tanks the water is led to a long castellated wall below the terrace through which it flows by twenty carved and vermilion-painted dragon spouts. Submerged in another tank is a stone carving of Narain (Brahma the Creator) on a bed of snakes, the face alone, wreathed with cobra heads, showing above the water. This submerged symbol of Vishnu is supposed to be a replica of that which the worshippers of Shiva see in the sacred lake of Gosainkund. I offer the legend with some diffidence because, in my opinion, Hindu mythology is too much addicted to what Fowler calls 'elegant variation'—the attentive reader will have noticed that four names have already been used for the same god. But as these legends usually lead sooner or later to the Himalaya they must be respected.

When three hundred and thirty million gods—very early officials or planners of some kind, one fears—churned the ocean in search of the water of immortality, they stirred up a poison which threatened to destroy the world. In this extremity their only resource was a petition, a monster bearing three hundred and thirty million signatures, which they presented to Mahadeo. Upon receiving this strong hint the god obligingly drank the poison. The poison burning his throat blue, he acquired thereby yet another name—Nila Khanta or Blue Neck—and a raging thirst. In order to cool off he repaired at once to the Himalaya, but aware of the futility of eating snow to quench thirst, he struck his trident against a rock from which three streams immediately burst forth. In their waters he enjoyed what must have been a memorable bathe; and so exquisite did he find the icy water flowing round his head that he has remained there to this day; the waters meanwhile gathering themselves to form what is now the Gosainkund lake. The peak Nilkhanta (21,640 ft.), a strikingly beautiful and still unclimbed peak in Garhwal, is named after the god.

Climbing through the forest above Baleji, where we disturbed some barking deer, we reached an open glade just before the sun went down. From the Ganesh Himal to somewhere in the region of Everest, a hundred miles of snow mountains sparkled in its last rays. Several of the groups which the Nepalese call Himal—the Ganesh, Langtang, Jugal, and the Rolwaling Himal—could be identified; but the only *peaks* we could be sure of were Langtang Lirung (23,771 ft.), the highest of the Langtang group, and Gauri Sankar (23,440 ft.) in the Rolwaling. Everest, had it been clear, would have appeared as an inconspicuous bump just to the east of Gauri Sankar, a peak which has often been mistaken for the monarch itself. The identification of very distant peaks is a harmless and fascinating amusement so long as the results are not taken seriously—a proviso that is borne out by the Everest-Gauri Sankar controversy which will bear retelling.

The triangulation of the Everest region from stations in the plains was completed in 1850, and two years later, when the results had been worked out, that peak was found to be the highest then known. In 1855, as no local name for it could be found, Sir Andrew Waugh, the Surveyor General, suggested the name of 'Everest' after Sir George Everest who was his predecessor at the time when the triangulations were made. Hodgson, then Resident at Katmandu, who besides being a great naturalist was also a learned philologist, affirmed that the mountain had a local name, Devadhunga, which he had apparently come across in Nepalese literature. Although he had seen neither Devadhunga, which nowhere existed, nor Everest, he stuck to his point, and assured Sir Andrew Waugh that if he (Waugh) would give him the bearing and distance of any Nepal peak, he (Hodgson) would tell him the name of it. In the same year Hermann de Schlagintweit, brother of Adolph who was later murdered in Kashgar, made observations of the newly discovered peak from two directions, Sikkim and Nepal, with the unluckiest results. From Sikkim he observed and drew a panorama of Makalu, which obscured Everest, and from the 7000 ft. Kaulia hill in Nepal (a few miles west of where we sat) he mistook the prominent Gauri Sankar for the insignificant looking Everest. However, his observations and drawings were sufficiently accurate for the Survey of India to show by calculations the error he had made. In 1859 a committee decided from the available evidence that the two mountains were not the same; and this was later confirmed by Capt. Wood who, from observations made from Kaulia, proved that the two mountains were thirty-six miles apart.

The Embassy grounds, known to the natives as the 'Lines', are a mile from the centre of Katmandu. On the left on the way in, behind a high brick wall of great length, lies the palace of the King of Nepal; one of several similar buildings which are palaces in very fact as well as name. The Singha Darbar, the residence of the Prime Minister, is a vast white colonnaded palace, fronted by a formal garden, carriage drives and wrought-iron gates under a white arched gateway. The homes of other Ranas, the Commander-in-Chief (who is head of civil, not military affairs), the Senior Commanding General, and General Kaiser, G.B.E., lately Nepalese Ambassador in London, are on a correspondingly spacious scale. The centre of the town is the wide, tree-bordered, grass 'maidan' which is used as a parade ground. On one side are modern office buildings, the Chaudra College, and a clock-tower, and on the other the old and new bazaars and the old town. The whole town is lit by electric light from two hydro-electric stations.

The narrow streets of the old bazaar are lined with two-storied houses of brick and wood. The lower parts of these form open shops, interspersed with shrines, idols and brass grotesques, around which surges a flood of warm humanity. Fortunately, unlike the Kashgar market, the flood carries with it no scurrying droves of donkeys to overwhelm the idle onlooker who can, therefore, stand and admire a scene less imposing than the palaces but far more rewarding. Helped by Tensing, a Sherpa who doubled the role of cook and headman, we bought a glorious miscellany of soap (largely symbolic), nests of aluminium cooking pots, chillies, enamel pint mugs, candles, tea, paraffin, ghee, umbrellas, lentils, 'ghums' (mats for protecting loads), sugar, matches, cheap cigarettes, spices, onions, atta and rice. In addition to six maunds (480 lb.) of rice, which took a long time to weigh and bag, we wanted two of 'satu' or parched barley flour. This commodity was unknown to the Newars of Katmandu but Tensing buttonholed a passing youth in the maroon gown of a lama who directed him to a place where Tibetan tastes were catered for.

Having done all this we went on to the bank to collect 2500 silver Nepali rupees (a load in itself), pausing on the way to admire the oasis of comparative quiet of the Darbar square of the old town. Here are the old wooden pagoda-roofed house from which Katmandu takes its name, the five-storied Taleju temple overlooking the Kot of sinister memory, and an horrific four-armed figure of Kala Bhaibar, painted black, yellow and vermilion, flourishing a great sword in the attitude of a pantomime dame at bay with a poker.

Entrance to the temple of the Five Stages at Bhatgaon; the lowest statues are of two wrestlers, historic giants of the Newars, credited with the strength of ten

Temure village in the upper Trisuli; the five big chortens are those upon which some land-hungry villager has encroached with his maize field

Outside the Langtang gompa; on the left is the Rev. Nima Lama who filled the dual role of headman and lama; the other is a Tibetan lama from Kyerong

Nowhere in the valley is there a place without either temples or shrines. As Kirkpatrick, one of the earliest writers on Nepal, said: 'There are nearly as many temples as houses, and as many idols as inhabitants, there not being a fountain, a river, or a hill within its limits that is not consecrated to one or other of the Hindu or Buddhist deities.' But the concentrated essence of religious art is to be found in the Darbar squares which the Newar craftsmen delighted to embellish with the finest conceptions of their artists; and the richest squares are those of the two neighbouring towns of Bhatgaon and Patan, the ancient Newar capitals. In 1768 the Gurkhas completed their conquest of the valley by the taking and sacking of Patan, from which the town seems never to have recovered. Except for the Darbar square there broods over it an air of melancholy decay. But dilapidation and decay are thought by some to be essential to picturesque beauty, and here they do enhance the charm of the gloomy, narrow, deserted lanes, overhung with half-timbered balconied houses; especially when adorned, as we saw them, with great banners of green cloth fresh from the dyer's vat. In the square there is nothing, except perhaps the telephone wires, that is not a delight to behold; but all the sculpture and carving, down to intricate detail, is symbolic, and unless one understands the religious significance of these symbols the emotions which such art should excite is apt to be extinguished by curiosity. Instead of marvelling at the delicate carving or the airy grace of the pagoda roof, one is willingly amused by the endless repetition of elephants, peacocks, fish, rats, lions, snakes, mythical monsters and all-in wrestlers.

The plates will give some idea of these architectural wonders, but the following description of Bhatgaon from *Picturesque Nepal* (Percy Brown), conveys something of the enthusiasm of a man who understands Indian art:

> At a cross street a shrine comes into view, with crimson draperies, bright brass entrance, glittering metal pinnacle, painted woodwork, brackets of caryatid deities bristling with arms, and a large bronze bell supported by rampant dragons. From this one passes through winding streets of old wood and brick houses, each displaying some different form of ornate carving in window or doorway, and each placed at an apparently fortuitous angle. Gradually the buildings

become larger and more important and the decoration more profuse. Then a whole street of overhanging balconies and wooden colonnades comes into view, with doorways crowned by heavily carved tympanums of deities and devils, and lattice windows with peacocks cunningly carved posing in the centres, until we suddenly debouch into the main square and are confronted with the culminating effect of the combined arts of the Newars, probably the most entrancingly picturesque city scene in Nepal. Around a rambling open space of flagged pavement, temples are irregularly grouped on terraced plinths, their pagoda roofs of red tiles and golden finials climbing into the blue sky. Some of these are approached by flights of steps, flanked by stone statues of humans in elaborate costumes, elephants, horses, and rhinos, gaily caparisoned and heavily chained to their pedestals, and monstrous fauna of the nether world.

In Bhatgaon is a doorway of brick and embossed copper gilt which Percy Brown calls 'the richest piece of art work in the whole kingdom... placed like a jewel flashing innumerable facets in the handsome setting of its surroundings'.

For their spiritual needs, which I was sorry to see were not very urgent, the Sherpas had to go to one of the two famous Buddhist temples of Bodhnath and Shambu-nath. Although it stands upon no eminence Bodhnath is one of the most conspicuous objects of the valley. Surrounded by the houses and maize fields of Bodhnath, there rises from a square plinth a huge white 'stupa', in shape like an umbrella; on top is a lofty spire with a square base on each face of which is painted in crimson and black a pair of eyes, and between them a nose indicated by a '?'. In the vicinity of Bodhnath, or indeed from much farther away, there is no escape from the impassive, questioning gaze of those strange eyes. I suppose even a Buddhist who lived always in their sight might become indifferent to their mild reproach; a supposition which only an enquiry into the morals of the people of Bodhnath might decide. To a stranger they were powerful monitors, bearing an injunction more poignant than the *memento mori* of a grinning skull.

The base of the stupa is ringed with prayer wheels and a stone-flagged ambulatory round which the pilgrim walks, turning the wheels as he goes. In a building close by is a small 'gompa' in which the contents—the painted Buddhas, the banners, books, lamps and frescoed walls—seem mean and tawdry, quite out of keeping with the glory of the stupa and the fame of Bodhnath as a place of pilgrimage. We saw hardly anyone, but in winter I believe numbers of Tibetans, both lamas and laity, make their way there.

Although at Shambu-nath a smaller but similar stupa, with the same grave, all-seeing eyes, occupies a commanding position, its effect is less striking. The eyes are too far above the earth-bound mortals of the valley, so that their searching admonitory gaze is directed to the four quarters in vain. I felt I could live in the village at the foot of Shambu-nath and sin at ease. The temple stands a mile west of Katmandu on a wooded hill which is climbed by several hundreds of stone steps. The whole hill, the temple itself, and the neighbouring houses of its attendants, are the home and playground of a far too numerous colony of Rhesus monkeys, which pay even less attention than their human brothers to the unspoken question of those eyes. Instead of studying the medley of architecture, I stood fascinated by the antics of these amusing but disgusting beasts as they clambered upon and defiled the deities, and played hide-and-seek among the prayer wheels. As a climber I could only regret that if we are descended from apes, monkeys, chimpanzees, gorillas, or a blend of all four, we have not inherited their prehensile toes. I stood spellbound by the ease with which they climbed the holdless walls of the adjacent houses to poke their long arms through the carefully barred windows reaching for anything within. Living in one of these houses must be an everlasting nightmare, what with the eyes of the stupa just about level with the upper window, the sad, unblinking eyes of some damned monkey on the sill outside, and the hairy arms groping within.

In Nepal, Hinduism and Buddhism mingle and overlap; the Newar architects and craftsmen have been inspired by both, just as they have been by the art of China as well as India. In most of the temples Hinduism, Buddhism and Lamaism are represented, and in them the devotee of each will find his favourite image. Landon thus describes the surrounding of the Shambu-nath stupa:

> A multitude of smaller shrines, of guardian beasts, of chaityas, of sacred pillars crowned with images of divinities, peacocks or sarduls,

of representations of the holy footmark, fill up the rest of the sacred compound. To the west of the stupa stands a building wherein Buddhist priests tend and keep alive a sacred flame. Between are pillars crowned with exquisite gilt bronze work, and between these again are a couple of statues of which the southern is perhaps the finest piece of work ever achieved by those masters of bronze modelling, the Newars. It represents Tara, and is a reminder to the Tibetan visitor of the Nepalese woman to whom he owes the introduction of Buddhism into his country in the seventh century. Adjoining the temple of the flame is the shrine of Sitala, the dreaded goddess of smallpox. Sitala is a Hindu goddess, but Buddhists—just to make quite sure—bend the knee to her as reverently as do the followers of Vishnu or Shiva.

What with the monkeys, the squad of sweepers for whom their habits occasioned constant employment, a couple of shops, and a constant trickle of visitors, there was more liveliness at Shambu-nath than at any of the other temples. Liveliness may not be natural to the precincts of a temple, but it is better than neglect. Shambu-nath is popular because it caters for all religious tastes; it is beautiful to see, and from it great beauty can be seen. There is a variety of images for the devotee, and from its height the visitor may look down upon a glorious prospect of rich vale and meandering river. It is also close to Katmandu, which we must now leave. Having completed our preparations we might cease from viewing temples carved by man to go in search of those natural temples of rock and ice.

CHAPTER III

TO THE LANGTANG

THE GANG THAT SHUFFLED OUT of the Legation compound on 29 May was at least formidable in numbers. Besides four Europeans, four Sherpas, and forty coolies, there were Lieut. S. B. Malla with two orderlies, and a smart havildar* with two sepoys.† The military bearing of the escort so far redeemed our slovenliness that we might almost be said to have *marched* out of the compound. Gratifying as this might be, I regarded the presence of our spruce escort with some misgiving, having always a great horror of the addition of *bouches inutiles* to an expedition—of men, that is to say, who do not or will not carry loads. Such misgivings were needless. Both the lieutenant and the havildar proved their worth, without whom we should have had much difficulty and delay in our negotiations with the local people for food and transport.

Even so the party was not complete. At Bombay, Polunin had engaged a Goan, Toni Mathos, a bird-skinner, who had acted in that capacity to Dr Dillon Ripley's party the previous winter. He had been left behind to bring on a stick-gun, a small-bore gun for collecting disguised as a walking stick, which the Bombay police had removed from Polunin's care; the weapon having created some despondency among the police who regarded it as precisely the sort of thing that no good assassin would care to be without. Polunin had also a 410-bore gun, but its ammunition was packed with that of the confiscated stick-gun. The collecting of birds, upon which the British Museum set great store, was therefore more or less at a standstill until mid-August when the gun and ammunition, after a lot of trouble, at last reached us.

Of the eight stages which the baria naik allowed for the journey hardly one figured on the map; we were therefore in his hands, but a

---

*   An N.C.O. in the Indian Army, equivalent to a sergeant—Ed.
†   An infantry private—Ed.

fixed sum for the round trip having been agreed upon, the coolies were not likely to waste time. The road took us past the Baleji water-garden and out of the valley over the Sheopuri Lekh to Kaulia where we camped. ('Lekh' is the word used for a ridge or range without permanent snow.) It was warm work dragging our unaccustomed legs up the Sheopuri ridge, and we suffered all the pains of a first march. But those philosophers who assure the wretched that there is always someone who is worse off were quite right, for I would not have cared to change places with any of the labourers at work in the terraced fields. In the absence of ploughs and oxen they stretched their own backs against the stubborn glebe with an implement which would dismay the most stout-hearted digger. The handle is about two feet long, and the blade, lying parallel to and a few inches from it, is almost as long, so that as the digger strikes, his head almost touches the ground. On these less fruitful hills outside the valley everything is done by hand, from breaking the soil to threshing and grinding the corn. Nor are animals much used in the valley, where the land is too rich to spare for grazing.

Kaulia is the hill from which Wood and Schlagintweit had made their observations, whence next morning we too enjoyed, lying in our sleeping-bags in a field, a noble prospect of peaks. From this cool lodging at 6000 ft. we had now to plunge nearly 4000 ft. to the valley of the Trisuli, which is here only 2500 ft. above the sea. Instead of camping on the hill at Nawakot, the principal village of this part, we stuck to the valley. At Nawakot in 1792 the treaty of peace was signed between the defeated Gurkhas and the pursuing Chinese army which was then only two days' march from the capital. The Gurkhas had brought upon themselves this Chinese avalanche by their invasion of Tibet two years before and by the looting of Tashi-lhumpo. Provided they got their plunder away, this bold foray, 260 miles beyond the border, must have richly rewarded the raiders; for even to-day the great monastery at Tashi-lhumpo near Shigatse is reputedly crammed with jewels and precious metals. The head of the monastery, the Tashi Lama, is second only to the Dalai Lama.

In India in May, only 2000 ft. up, a march can be devilish hot. The first river we met, the Likhu, was shallow and warm—for it is not snow-fed—thus long before we reached it my hopes centred upon the Trisuli as the river for a bathe. The more I thought of it the faster I went, gradually attaining such a state of simmering exhaustion that a plunge into a warm and weedy duck-pond would have been exquisite enough to rank as a memorable bathe. At last the path met the river, surging swift, swollen, and turbid, between rocky banks—a river with which in cold blood one would prefer to have nothing to do. But just as any clothes will fit a naked man, so any water is welcome to an over-heated man provided it does not drown him. The nearest bank was mere cliff, so hurrying across the suspension bridge I turned down the other bank at full speed until at a respectful distance from the village, I stripped and plunged in. Mahadeo himself could scarcely have given such a gasp of ecstasy as the icy water closed over his head. But here there was no reclining; for having been swept helplessly down for an exhilarating minute one was glad to scramble out on to the sun-warmed rocks. Scott soon joined me, and presently the small boys of the village came along to put our timid coasting to shame by launching themselves boldly across this dangerous-looking river.

We camped in a big mango tope on the right bank of the river, some way from the bazaar but not far enough away to throw off the sight-seers. In the evening great numbers assembled round our camp, attracted less by us than by the witticisms of a wench whom I christened Trisuli Trixie, who being slightly tipsy had maintained a brisk exchange of ribaldry with the Sherpas from the moment of our arrival. But to understand all is to forgive all, and once we had sampled some of the 'raksi' which had set her alight, we forgave her from the bottom of our hearts. For the first and last time we put up our mosquito nets, less to baffle the mosquitoes, perhaps, than to protect us from Trixie. Both Europeans and Sherpas had already been taking 'Paludrin' which is not only a cure but also a preventative of malaria. In mosquito or leech-ridden country it is customary and convenient to assume that the coolies (for they are many) are either beneath the aid of science or too pachydermatous to need it.

We were astir early but dallied in the bazaar buying snacks for the road until the unwelcome rays of the sun flooded the valley. Thus warned we hurried off over the bridge, where Trixie was waiting to say farewell, sober enough to recognize us but not sober enough to cross. For two or three miles we walked easily along a terrace a little above the river. This was too pleasant to last. In my experience a Himalayan track is seldom content to follow the bank, but is always busy either climbing to escape the river or rushing down to it in order to avoid some impassable cliff. Our terrace soon petered out, and upon crossing the small Betravati stream we were faced with the choice of going high at once or clinging to the valley bottom a little longer. The Betravati stream is said to have been the scene of a vigorous action in the war of 1792 when the Gurkha rearguard cut the chains of a suspension bridge and precipitated a great many non-swimming Chinese into the river. An open debate determined for us the question of high road or low; and when in obedience to an almost unanimous vote we embarked upon a 2000 ft. climb in the heat of the day, I concluded that such grave decisions should not be left to the many-headed. Pursued by the perspiring havildar, who seldom let me out of his sight, I pushed on up the steep waterless track until we reached a small village and a gigantic pipal tree. As we sat in the grateful shade, reflecting upon the vicissitudes of life and the sweating coolies, we agreed that they would never get past this tree. I doubted if they would get so far, for in the cool of the morning along the pleasant stretch by the river they had sat down under every tree—and there were a great many—trees, too, which were far less umbrageous than this. However, soon after four o'clock they began trickling (*le mot juste*) in, dropped their loads as if they bore them some ill-will, and made a bee-line for the meagre water supply.

We were astir even earlier next morning, roused by a brisk thunderstorm from our untented beds under the pipal canopy. The track maintained its height at a couple of thousand feet above the river only by dint of striking an average, for its course resembled the line traced on a barograph in very unsettled weather. We camped outside a mean village of five houses under a great rock overhang. The shadow of a great rock, either in a thirsty land or a wet land, is the refuge of many travellers and its vicinity is consequently filthy. But a rock roof is better than a pipal tree, however gigantic or luxurious, and the dried goat dung with which the place is carpeted makes for soft lying.

We had a lucky meeting here with a Sherpa and his wife who were pleased to see our Sherpas and to hear the latest gossip from Solu Khumbu, their common home on the Nepal side of the Everest region. Driving a couple of donkeys they were on a trading venture to Kyerong, a day's march over the border to Tibet, a road they knew well. According to them atta and rice were procurable a few marches farther on, and when the man, who seemed a keen hand, offered to collect whatever we needed, I closed with him by giving a firm order for ten maunds of atta, rice, and satu, for delivery in July.

The track behaved more sedately next morning until it suddenly dropped by a staircase of stone steps nearly a thousand feet into the Trisuli nullah. This was not the main river but a small tributary descending from the Gosainkund lakes, the same sacred stream which the trident (trisul) of Mahadeo had released from its rock prison. A track, well marked with 'chortens' and 'mani' walls, leads up to Gosainkund which is sacred to Buddhists as well as Hindus. The main river, which I shall continue to call the Trisuli, rises sixty miles beyond the Tibet border within fifteen miles of the valley of the Tsangpo. Of the seven tributaries of the Gandak, of which the Trisuli is one of the biggest, four have cut through the Himalaya, while two, the Trisuli and the Kali, drain the trough beyond the Ladakh range in Tibet. Several other Nepal rivers, notably the Karnali in the west and the Arun in the east, cut through the main range in deep gorges. The Trisuli gorge is no mean cleft; a few miles south of the Tibet border, where the river crosses the main Himalayan axis, the bed of the gorge is less than 6000 ft. above sea-level, yet only six miles east lies the 23,771 ft. peak of Langtang Lirung. (Below are some figures for Himalayan gorges.)

River gorge	Height of bed near axis	Width between peaks
Kali Gandak	5000 ft.	12 miles at 24,000 ft.
Trisuli Gandak	6000 ft.	16 miles at 19,000 ft.
Arun	6000 ft.	14 miles at 16,000 ft.

River	Height of bed	Mountain	Distance	Fall per mile peak to river bed
Kali	5000 ft.	Dhaulagiri 26,795 ft.	4 miles	5449 ft.
Hunza	6000 ft.	Rakaposhi 25,550 ft.	9 miles	2172 ft.
Indus	4000 ft.	Nanga Parbat 6,620 ft.	14 miles	1616 ft.
Trisuli	6000 ft.	Langtang Lirung 23,771 ft.	8 miles	2200 ft.

The above comparative tables of heights and widths of the principal Himalayan gorges are taken from *Himalaya Mountains* by Burrard and Hayden.

Our bathe in a clear green pool of the sacred stream fed by the Gosainkund lake afforded so great joy that we willingly renounced the merit, to earn which one must surely suffer pain. On other accounts, too, this was a red-letter day. Polunin began his botanical collection and his activity reminded me that I, too, had a purpose in life. Hitherto I had always contrived to suppress my ardour for science, but on this occasion a friend, an amateur of beetles, had entrusted me with the task of collecting some. They were to be all of one species— 'meligethes'—of which I had been given a rough description—small, black, shiny beggars—but having a poor memory for faces I decided to make sure by sweeping every beetle I met, regardless of age, sex, or species, into what I called my battery of Belsen chambers, small test-tubes impregnated with amyl acetate. This insistence on one species, without limit as to numbers, was a little puzzling to a man who hitherto had not given beetles the thought which, possibly, they deserved. Perhaps they were for swops? On the beetle exchange a man with a few hundred 'meligethese' would have the whip-hand of rival collectors who had dissipated their energies by striving for a little of everything. Still a collection of hundreds of small fellows, all as like as two pins and all clad in sober hues, could hardly delight the eye. Such an assembly, I thought, would be the brighter for the company of some of their more flashy relatives of which happily there was no lack—gorgeously striped, spotted, barred, tricked out in colours more striking than mellow, after the style of an American tie.

Having toiled up from the valley of the little Trisuli we camped in a wheat stubble at the village of Bhragu. This early harvest of wheat, which must have been sown the previous autumn, reassured us about our food supplies. Bhragu village consisted of a few two-storied wooden houses, with some crude carving round the doors and windows, and roofs of rough shingles, roughly put on and held down with stones. The family live on the top floor where a balcony serves as a pleasant day lounge, while the ground floor is used for stables and stores. The people are Tamangs; at least this name, pretty widely and indifferently applied, seemed to satisfy our lieutenant's ethnological

Four miles up from Langtang is this gompa of Kyangin of which the Rev. Nima is also incumbent

The fine fresco is on the inside wall of the verandah of the Kyangin gompa

From the ridge above the first survey station we enjoyed an extensive view eastwards across the hidden Langtang glacier

The view from Langsisa up the East glacier to where the two rock gendarmes, representing the saints Shakya Muni and Guru Rumbruche, stand silhouetted against the cloud

curiosity. They are more Hindu than Buddhist; but since leaving Trisuli bazar we had begun to see 'mani' walls and 'chortens' in the vicinity of villages, and the farther north we went, the more numerous they became. At the next village of Syabrubensi, at the junction of the Langtang Khola and the Trisuli, we saw the first 'gompa'.

Having so little information about the resources of the country, our plan had been to make our headquarters at Thangiet on the west side of the valley which the map showed to be the largest cultivated area of the region. However, our food problem had now been solved by the Sherpa corn chandler who, at the same time, had painted a charming picture of the idyllic life we might lead at Langtang village, two marches up the Langtang Khola, where food, including butter and beer, abounded, and where tough men and strong women would be eager to carry our loads. This welcome and surprising news, the village being over 11,000 ft., decided us to make our base there. Neither the baria naik nor the coolies objected to this change of plan, and meantime the garrison commander at the frontier post of Rasua Garhi, to whom we ought to pay our earliest respects, would have to wait.

On crossing the Langtang Khola by a suspension bridge just above its junction with the Trisuli, we regarded the river with interest. As the melting increased, the glacier-fed rivers were rising fast, and to the raging, brown flood of the Trisuli the Langtang added an impressive volume of equally turbid water. At Syabrubensi near the junction, barely 5000 ft. above sea-level, we stopped to ask about the road. This small village, with scarcely any fields, seemed to live by what it could fleece from travellers—which, I thought, would be very little judging by what they had to offer and the kind of traveller who passed through. It is a dull place, like the other villages on this rather dull trade route where neither mule-trains with jingling bells and scarlet wool-tufted harness, nor tea-houses where the picturesque muleteers forgather, are met. Possibly in winter the road is lively with Tibetans and their mules, but in summer it is thronged only with sweating coolies trudging south with loads of salt. This is obtained, in exchange for rice, from a salt lake at a place called Chang, a day's march beyond Kyerong. At Rasua Garhi they told us some 5000 man-loads pass through yearly. Wool, of course, is the most valuable Tibetan export, most of which passes down the Chumbi valley to Kalimpong. According to Sir Charles Bell the trade of that one route equals that of all the other Tibetan trade routes across the Himalaya from Assam to Kashmir.

The track traverses high above the lower Langtang Khola to the village of Khangjung where we camped alongside a small, poor monastery. In these parts the monasteries are very different from the important, thriving establishments, often very wealthy, of Tibet. The single-roomed building, usually dilapidated and seldom open, is merely a receptacle where, on a kind of altar, are kept two or three Bodhisats of painted or gilded clay and some unlit butter lamps; a few dingy temple banners, masks, and a drum, hang from the roof, and some wood-bound volumes, thick with dust, complete the religious furnishing. So dark is the interior that the wall frescoes can hardly be seen, while those on the verandah walls are partially destroyed by weather. But where they are intact, especially if they are old, the spirited pictures of fierce and terrible deities, saints, demons, or the Wheel of Life, look like the work of pious, vigorous and skilful hands. These are done by no local artists; they have been and still are painted by lamas from Tibet, who thus earn enough money to support them on their pilgrimages to Katmandu or even to the Buddhist shrines of India.

Whether he was a lama or merely a caretaker, the man in charge of these places, with few exceptions, neglected the duties of both. Except at infrequent festivals, the tolling of a bell at dawn and dusk satisfied the demands of religious ceremony, while leaking roofs and peeling wall frescoes testified to their lack of regard for the fabric. The monastery doors remained shut for weeks together so that the villagers, and indeed the lama himself, with less excuse than Falstaff, must have been in danger of forgetting what the inside of a church was made of. Few readers, at some period of their lives, will have escaped hearing the tragic monologue of how Mad Carew, spurred on by his Colonel's daughter, stole a superb emerald from 'the one-eyed yellow idol to the north of Katmandu'. But such being the mournful state of the monasteries to-day north of Katmandu we looked in vain for idols with gleaming emeralds in their eyes.

Syarpagaon, the next village, was the last of the lowland villages, where they have few cattle but lots of goats, and where maize is grown in tiny terraced fields. At Langtang village, 3000 ft. higher, we were to find a different economy. From Syarpagaon the track plunged down to the river bank into gloomy rain forest. Among many strange trees the familiar oaks, maples and firs themselves looked exotic, festooned as they were with lichen, moss, ferns and orchids. The steeper south bank had a dense stand of bamboos. Judging from the vegetation we thought that the lateral valleys received more rain than the north and south trough of the main Trisuli.

From mixed forest we passed to pure pine and then to grassy glades surrounded with roses, pink and white cotoneaster, and orange berberis. The valley opened out but its high and steep sides shut out the snow mountains lying immediately above. Then the low, brown roofs of Langtang came in sight and, having reached the first of the three hamlets, we climbed to the gompa to introduce ourselves to the spiritual and temporal head of the Langtang community. The man who combined the role of lama and headman was about fifty years old with close-cropped iron-grey hair; from his slightly foxy appearance one judged him to be a priest qualified for this world as well as the next. He showed more astonishment than delight at our arrival—which I readily excused on account of the hungry half-hundred trailing behind us whom he rightly feared would require feeding. He brightened up when he heard that the coolies would be here for only one night and conducted us forthwith to a camping ground near the main village.

The barai naik with his flock next morning departed unobtrusively for Katmandu where they would collect the balance of their pay. No farewells were said and no gratuity seemed to be expected. It had certainly been an easy approach march. The track was no worse than any other hill-country track and the coolies had shown themselves docile and willing. They had neither grumbled nor cadged. Cigarettes and baksheesh, if thought of, had not once been mentioned.

CHAPTER IV

THE LANGTANG

THE UPPER LANGTANG IS A FINE, open valley, rich in flowers and grass, and flanked by great mountains. It is a grazier's paradise. At 11,000 ft. one might expect to find a few rough shelters occupied only in the summer, but at Langtang there is a settlement of some thirty families rich in cows, yaks and sheep. These are, besides, like young Osric, spacious in the possession of dirt; for their fields are no mere pocket-handkerchief terraces clinging to the hillside but flat stone-walled fields of an acre or more growing wheat, buckwheat, potatoes, turnips, and a tall, strong-growing beardless barley called 'kuru'.

The grazing extends from the valley bottom to the slopes above and far up the moraines and ablation valleys of both the main and the tributary glaciers; and dotted about are rich alps with stone shelters, called 'kharka', where the herdsmen live and make the butter. Considerable quantities of this are exported to Tibet. In the Langtang gompa I saw twenty-five man-loads of butter sewn up in skins which a lama had bought for his monastery at Kyerong, and which, he told me, represented a year's supply. Besides being drunk in innumerable cups of tea, butter plays an important part in religious ceremony. In well-run monasteries butter lamps burn continually before the images and at certain festivals pounds of butter are moulded into elaborate decorations for the altars. I noticed the Langtang lama placing a dab of it on people's heads as a blessing, while a little is always placed on the edge of the cup or plate offered to a guest.

The valley has religious traditions. Like many out-of-the-way places it was originally the home of the gods, those happy beings, to whom, with their ready means of locomotion, remoteness was of little account. But at a more recent date the beauties of the valley were revealed to mortals in a way reminiscent of that other story—'Saul he went to look for donkeys, and, by God, he found a kingdom'. In this case the missing animal was, of course, a yak which its owner, a very holy man, tracked up the Langtang. The spoor was not difficult to follow, for at Syabrubensi and at Syarpagaon the beast left on a rock the imprint of a foot which is visible to this day. The lama caught his yak at a place called Langsisa, seven or eight miles above Langtang village where, having fulfilled its appointed task, it promptly died. The lama, with less regard for sentiment than for money's worth unfeelingly skinned it and spread the skin on a rock to dry; but the yak had the last laugh; for the skin stuck and remains there to this day, as a big reddish coloured rock at Langsisa plainly testifies.

Near Langsisa there are two other rocks of greater note. A couple of miles up a valley to the east, standing some hundreds of feet above the glacier, are two big rock gendarmes which are said to represent two Buddhist saints, Shakya Muni and Guru Rumbruche. Tibetan lamas come as far as Langsisa to worship them. Since the etymology of many English place-names is still, as it were, anybody's guess, I have little hesitation in offering the following derivations. 'Lang' is Tibetan for cow or yak, 'tang', or more correctly 'dhang', means to follow. Langsisa means the place where the yak died.

A valley with such traditions is, of course, a sanctuary; within it no animal may be slaughtered. According to the lieutenant, the observance of this ban on slaughter, which dated back for hundreds of years, had been neglected and the present headman, Nima Lama, took it upon himself to visit Katmandu to have the matter put right. The original decree, having been looked up and verified, was formally confirmed, and the fine for any breach of the rule was fixed at Rs. 100. Our wish to shoot small birds for specimens had to be met by the issue of a special licence; but apart from two sheep thoughtfully slaughtered for us by a bear of non-Buddhist tendencies, we had no meat while in the valley.

The people of Langtang are very like Tibetans, engagingly cheery, tough and dirty; but they have sufficient regard for appearances to wash their faces occasionally and were scrupulous to remove those lice which strayed to the outside of their garments. They themselves say their ancestry was a mixture of Tibetans from around Kyerong and Tamangs from Helmu—the district to the south of the valley. They now call themselves Lama-Tamang. (It should be noted that 'lama' is the name for a class of Gurungs, one of the Nepal tribes from which many of the so-called Gurkhas are drawn.) They conversed very readily with our Sherpas in what was presumably some sort of Tibetan dialect. According to Tensing their speech is like that of the people of Lachen in north Sikkim.

We had arrived on 5 June, and since the monsoon might be expected to break at any time we immediately began the survey of the middle valley so that we could have fixed points to work from when we reached the frontier ridge at the head of the valley. The triangulated peak of Langtang Lirung, only two miles to the north, could not be seen from the village, and a tiny triangle of white, sometimes visible over the rock wall behind our camp, might or might not have been the tip of a 21,500 ft. peak to the west of it. Accordingly we started next day with six Langtang men carrying three weeks' food, leaving behind Polunin and the escort. With him we also left a Sherpa, a lad called Phutarkay who had been with me on Rakaposhi two years before, who as well as looking after his master had already learnt to press and handle specimens. On the march few strange plants escaped his keen eyes.

Tensing, who combined the roles of sirdar and cook, was widely travelled and an experienced mountaineer whom I had last met on Everest in 1938 when he carried a load to Camp VI. Having spent the war years with an officer of the Chitral Scouts he had further enlarged his mountaineering and ski-ing experience. Since then he had been to Lhasa with an Italian Tibetan scholar, for whom he had purchased whole libraries—he told me they had brought away forty maunds of books. Tensing, who gets on with everyone and handles the local people well, has a charming smile, great steadiness on a mountain, and a deft hand for omelettes which he turns out nicely sloppy but firm. With paragons such as this one can afford to be blind to minor faults. Neither of the others, Da Namgyal and Angtharkay, had had any experience, but the former soon learnt what was expected of him either in camp or on a mountain. Angtharkay, who is not to be confused with his well-known namesake, who is probably the best Sherpa porter ever known, was a little old for the job and a little 'dumb'. In fact I suspected that he had not long come down from his tree. He came to us with a pigtail which I was sorry to see him remove, but it had to make way for the heavy Balaclava helmet which he wore even in the hottest

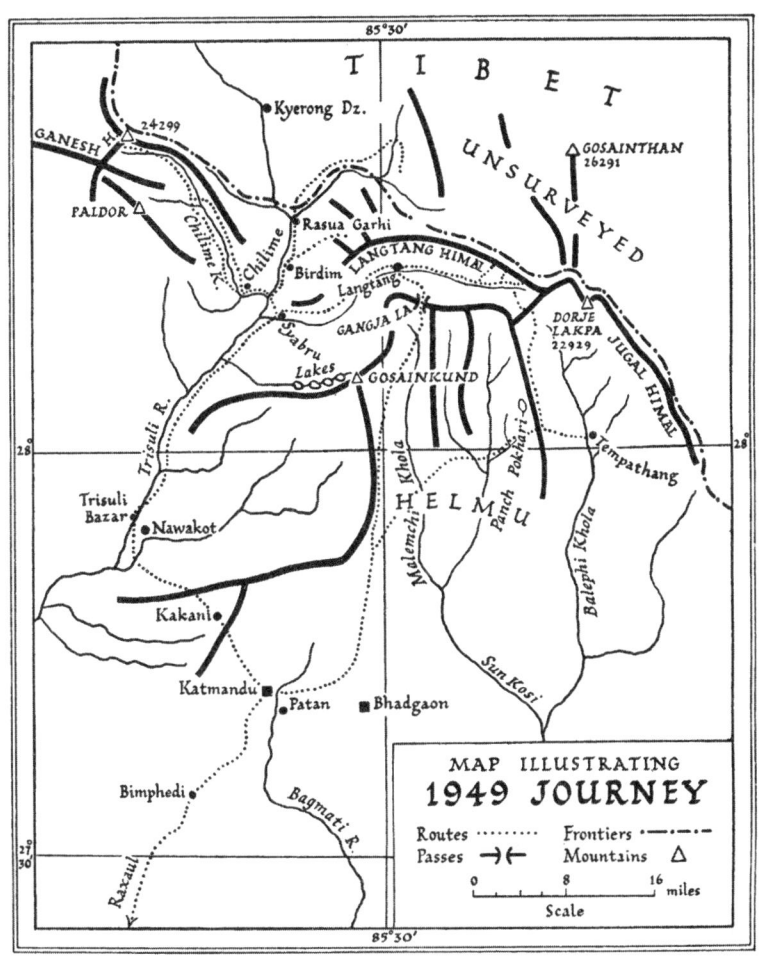

Map 2: Map to illustrate 1949 journey

valleys. I have a liking for men with pigtails because the first three Sherpas with whom I ever travelled all wore their hair long and were all first-rate men. Nowadays, among the Sherpas, long hair and pigtails are outmoded, but not long ago they indicated a good type of unsophisticated man who had not been spoilt by long residence outside Nepal. Angtharkay, unsophisticated enough for anyone, unfortunately lacked mother-wit. He had the air of an earnest buffoon which neither the striped heliotrope pyjama trousers he wore one day, nor the long woollen pants he affected the next, did anything to diminish.

Half a mile above Langtang was another hamlet with large fields of wheat and kuru, still very green, a big chorten, and the longest mani wall I have ever seen—nearly three hundred yards of it. These walls or 'mendongs', which are seven or eight feet high, must be passed on the left. On each side are flat stones with carved Buddhas or religious texts for the benefit of passers-by on either hand; and the equally well-worn paths on both sides of the wall show that the rule is observed. In the main Trisuli valley Buddhism, or at any rate the observance of this particular tenet, seemed to be weakening, for one of the paths round each mani wall tended to fall into disuse. In Timure village, only a day's march from the Tibetan border, some abandoned scoffer had had the hardihood to carry his miserable maize field right up to a mendong, thus abolishing the path on one side.

Having crossed a stream issuing from the snout of the Lirung glacier we camped a short four miles up from Langtang village. The grass flat, white with anemones, where we camped, lay tucked under the juniper-covered moraine of the glacier. Hard by were the gompa of Kyangjin Ghyang, some stone huts and turnip fields, and beyond a wide meadow stretched for a mile or more up the north side of the valley. The Lirung peak, from which the glacier came, and several others, overlooked it, but across the river the south containing wall was comparatively low. It can be crossed by the Gangja La (19,000 ft.) over which lies a direct route to the Helmu district and thence to Katmandu. On that side, the north-facing slope, birch trees and rhododendrons maintained a gallant struggle against the height, which, by altimeter, was 13,500 ft.

Naturally, for two of us the Lirung peak had a powerful appeal. At Katmandu we had admired its graceful lines with longing eyes. It had looked eminently climbable then, as indeed most mountains do when looked at from far off, but now we were forced to admit that its south side, defended by a great cirque, was quite impregnable. However, at the moment, climbing took second place. Neither of us was ready for serious work. Indeed, as the result of some months spent in Australia, Lloyd had become a little gross, a fault which an insufficiently arduous approach march had done nothing to rectify. Moreover, in our cautious eyes, not one of the few Langtang peaks we had seen invited immediate assault, and in new country the urge to explore is hardly to be withstood. Around a corner of the valley a few miles up, the whole Langtang glacier system waited to be unravelled, and at its head lay the untrodden frontier ridge and the unknown country beyond. During the monsoon, we hoped, we might still climb, but the survey work must be done now or never. Our first three weeks, which were moderately fine, proved to be the only fine weeks we were to have.

We spent nearly a week at this gompa camp. Lloyd wished to occupy stations on both sides of the valley before moving up, while I had made the exciting discovery of a way on to what we took to be the frontier ridge to the north. Having walked up the left moraine of the Lirung glacier, Tensing and I turned right-handed up steep grass and gravel slopes until we came to a sort of glacier shelf lying along the foot of the ridge upon which Lirung and its neighbouring 22,000 ft. peak stood. We judged the lowest point to be under 20,000 ft. A little tarn at the foot of the ice offered a convenient and tempting camp site at about 17,000 ft. Going back we made a wide detour over a bleak upland valley of more gravel than grass, where we found a scented cream and mauve primula (*P. macrophylla*) already in flower though old snow still lay about. On the way we took in a great rounded bump of over 17,000 ft., its grass summit incongruously crowned with long bamboo poles and tattered prayer flags.

On the assumption that this ridge would prove to be the frontier ridge upon which we should have a most valuable station, we stocked the tarn camp and occupied it, intending to spend a full week. Early next morning, having gained the glacier shelf, we plodded eastwards on good hard snow to a point below the most accessible part of the ridge. Warned by gathering clouds, Lloyd decided to get busy while he could, so at about 19,000 ft. he put up the machine, as he called

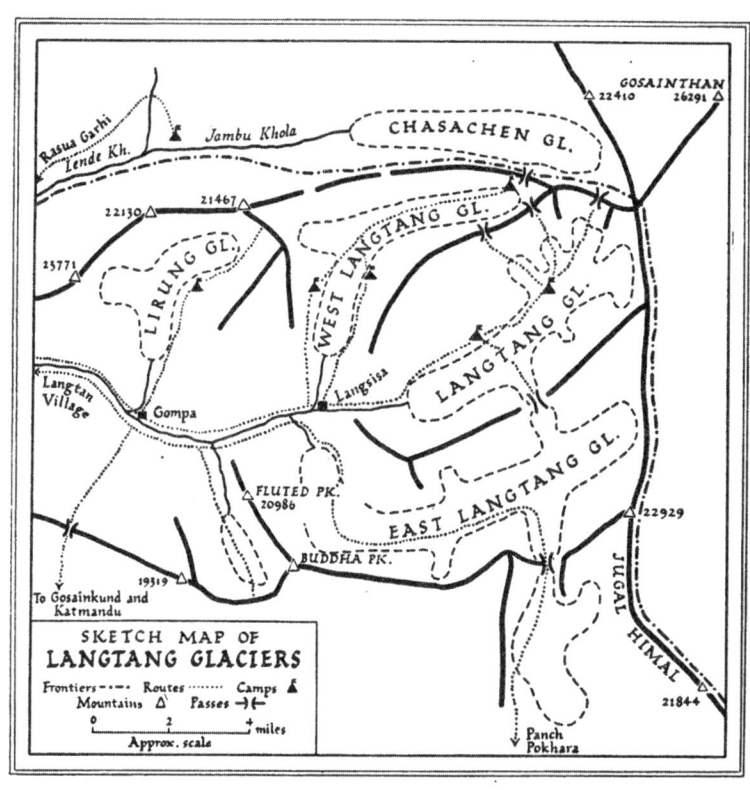

Map 3: Langtang Glaciers

the theodolite, and began taking rounds of angles and photographing the fine confusion of peaks and valleys spreading eastward. Meanwhile Tensing and I pushed on up good snow to the ridge and traversed along it to a small summit. Having expected to see much from here, we were proportionately cast down at seeing so little. Another ridge, the frontier and the watershed, intervened to the north, and between the two lay a high glacier bay from which the ice curled over like a breaking wave before falling abruptly to some hidden arm of the Langtang glacier below. To the north-east, behind a tangle of peaks, rose a lump of a mountain with a long, flattish summit and a western face of more rock than snow. We thought it neither high nor distant enough to be Gosainthan which, according to the map, was over twelve miles away. It so happened that we never saw this mountain again, but Lloyd's survey data show that it was, in fact, Gosainthan.

Under a threatening sky we trudged back to camp through snow which was already soft and wet. A night of rain fulfilled the threat of morning and when we turned out at 4 a.m. it was still falling. Since the frontier ridge could not be reached there was no point in staying, but before going down we wanted to put the theodolite on the small summit reached the day before. What with the drizzle and the waterlogged snow Lloyd soon turned back, leaving Tensing and me to struggle obstinately and rather aimlessly towards a notch in the ridge. Although the snow was too wet for them, a pair of snowshoes I had with me seemed to make for easier progress. Later I wore them a lot and tried to convince myself that those behind, who had no such aids, benefited from the huge steps I made. Having reached the rocks below the notch and found them very loose we contented ourselves with collecting a few inexpensive rock presents for Scott and a couple of hibernating moths for myself. As a lepidopterous insect a moth has something in common with beetles, and I thought that anything that contrived to live at 19,000 ft. deserved an honourable place in any insect museum.

On returning from this damp excursion I went on to Langtang to check the food, where I was astonished by the swift growth resulting from the recent rain—by the many new flowers, the masses of white erica which had suddenly blossomed, and the dwarf rhododendron whose resinous fragrance filled the air. Kyangjin, too, had suddenly come to life. The long bamboo poles of the gompa and the roofs of the now occupied stone huts carried small flags of red and yellow, and the long, grass flat was thick with yaks and horses. Kyangjin is the first stage on the summer grazing itinerary which the yaks graze down before moving successively higher with the advance of summer, the sheep following humbly in their wake eating what is left. The horses roamed at will. They, we were told, were the property of the Government—the reason, perhaps, for their moderate condition.

Our friend Nima Lama had come up, bringing with him an adequate supply of beer, the better to fumigate the gompa and to confront and exorcise any evilly disposed spirits which might have occupied it during the winter months. Tensing had a private chat with Nima Lama, obtaining from him some confidential information which he unhesitatingly passed on to me. Having warned him on no account to let the sahibs know of it, Nima had told him that there was a pass into Tibet at the head of the valley. Neither he nor any living man had seen it, much less used it, for it had been closed at the time of the second Nepal-Tibet war (1854)—whether by man's edict or by some natural cataclysm was not made clear. It is difficult to imagine any shorter or easier way to Tibet than that by the Trisuli valley, but the oldest inhabitant well remembered people coming by the pass, bringing their yaks with them. Now I admire the yak, but his reputation for crossing passes, like that of Himalayan climbers, is apt to be enhanced by time and distance. Still, some weight must be accorded to tradition, and we resumed our journey to the valley head much encouraged by the story of this ancient pass.

We started with a scratch team, two men, three women and a boy, on a fine sunny day. The Langtang has not only the austere beauty of ice mountains accentuated by the friendly smile of flowery meadows alive with cattle—but it has the charm of reticence and the witchery of the unexpected—a quality which Mr Milestone considered more desirable in a garden landscape than the beautiful or the picturesque. A gentle but continuous bend tantalizes its admirers, draws them on impatiently to see beyond the next corner, maintaining for them the thrill of discovery almost to the end. So far we had seen no more than two miles up the valley where the bend began, a place marked by a magnificent peak which we soon acknowledged to be the loveliest gem

Our camp on the roof of the fort at Rasua Garhi; there was no room elsewhere, for the Trisuli washes one side of the fort and on the other a jungle-covered cliff leaves room only for the main track and a few houses

'Sooner rather than later one will be seen off by a stout, affable official in Homburg hat and dark spectacles;' Tensing, on the right, seems to be registering dismay at the idea of taking a photograph at such a serious moment

A flailing fatigue at Langtang village:
'Keeping time, time, time
In a sort of Runic rhyme;'
the rhythm has been broken by the girl on the right who is taking time off to exchange some ribaldry with our Sherpas

In Chilime village; the woman is husking rice in a wooden mortar; in lower Nepal, where rice is the daily bread, they use a pair of wooden hammers worked with the feet for this daily chore

of the valley. On account of the snow fluting traced like the ribs of a fan upon its western face we called it the Fluted Peak. It is a few feet under 21,000 ft., but it stands alone, smiling down upon the valley with a face of glistening purity framed between clean-cut snow ridges of slender symmetry.

As we drew past, fresh vistas of higher but less graceful mountains opened before us. But close at hand, stretching across the floor of the valley—still wide and green—lay a vast moraine, some 500 ft. high, the piled debris of a great glacier descending from the west. The narrowest of gorges, cut by the river draining the main Langtang glacier beyond, alone separated the toe of the moraine from the eastern wall of the valley. Beyond this barrier lay Langsisa, which we should easily have reached the first day. In our haste to see round corners we outran the porters, missed the path which went by the gorge, and charged straight at the giant moraine. While we were scurrying about on top of this eyesore looking vainly for water and a camp site, the porters sat calmly below in a pleasant meadow where presently we were obliged to join them.

Next day Lloyd explored this west glacier, while Tensing and I went to Langsisa and straight on up the main valley. Neither of us got anywhere near the heads of our respective glaciers, both of which seemed to terminate without undue abruptness at the frontier ridge. On returning I found the lieutenant had brought up our Sherpa corn merchant, with whom we did some hard bargaining. In the end I advanced Rs. 100, receiving as security his necklace of large corals. I would not have given sixpence for it, but Tensing assured me it was worth Rs. 200. Anyhow the owner evidently set considerable store by it and not very much on my honesty. He wanted to have it sealed up so that there could be no juggling with the corals.

Three of us, three Sherpas, and two Langtang men, carrying 400 lb. (twelve days' supplies), now moved up the main valley. In an hour we reached Langsisa, a rich meadow on the river bank where there is a stone shelter. Hard by are three inscribed stones set in the ground whence pilgrims make their obeisance to the two saints. The ice of the big east glacier flows down almost to the river on the opposite side, and a couple of miles up the two rock gendarmes or saints stand out prominently. To these our Langtang men at once paid their respects by going down on their knees, along with two Tibetan lamas who had come for the same purpose. Beyond Langsisa the track grew rougher and steeper. We walked for five hours up the right bank, sometimes on moraine and sometimes in the ablation valley below, the tumbled stone and ice of the main Langtang glacier lying on our right. Polunin came part of the way to collect a very lovely primula we had noticed the previous day—a pale blue, scented, bell-shaped flower, five, seven or even nine on the one stem. It was *P. Wollastonii* which Wollaston had first found when, as members of the Everest reconnaissance party of 1921, he and Morshead were travelling in the vicinity of Nyenam. This village lies over the Tibet border about twenty miles east of where we were.

On leaving this camp we were forced on to the glacier up which, in a sort of trough, we made a short but very rough march to a little tarn tucked away behind the moraine of a side glacier. We were still not within striking distance of the frontier ridge but the two local men would go no farther. Up to and a little beyond the last camp we had followed a track which might well be accounted for as a grazing track; but down in the glacier trough I found traces of what might have been its continuation, indicated by stones placed on top of boulders. As there was no grass farther on, this ancient track, if track it was, may have led to a pass. The existence of a pass at the head of the Langtang is thus supported by a track as well as tradition—the keys, or rather the only clues we have, to another Himalayan enigma, the Abominable Snowman.

For the next day we had a full programme. While the Sherpas moved the camp to the head of the glacier, Lloyd and I, carrying the machine, attempted to reach the most westerly of three cols. This precision instrument which, by the way, used plates and had no shutter, made an awkward load. As it was essential to beat the clouds, which usually came over between 9 and 10 a.m., by seven o'clock we had covered the remaining mile or so of level glacier and had begun to climb. From an upper snow shelf which we reached at ten o'clock, the low rock ridge marking the col looked close enough. But it was noon before I got there, while Lloyd, who was still carrying too much weight, sank by the way. Excited though I was, my plodding steps could not be hurried, and when at last I looked over the top to the glacier below, its surface seemed to wrinkle in a derisive smile. The col was not on the frontier ridge and the glacier below was none other than the west Langtang whose high, ugly snout we had rounded on the way to Langsisa. The altimeter registered 20,700 ft, a height which I could easily credit. Unhappily that was the instrument's last coherent message. A knock which it got on the way back, besides shattering the glass, must have affected it internally. Never again did it speak a true word. Instead, with little or no provocation, it would often shoot to heights undreamt of in our philosophy, heights which we could only have attained by means of a balloon.

This was not the only misfortune. When, after a long and fruitless day, we reached the appointed camp—a shelf above the glacier—there were no tents. To save themselves trouble the Sherpas had camped on the glacier, thereby compelling us to lie on devilish knobbly stones with ice underneath instead of on warm, soft gravel. Scott's altimeter, which had not yet met the inevitable fate of all such instruments, made our height 18,000 ft. Rather surprisingly, rice cooked well, and we slept warm in only one sleeping bag.

There were yet two cols to visit. Unless the curling west glacier was longer than the main trunk, which was unlikely, the easternmost col must be on the frontier ridge. In order to ensure reaching it in good time we took a light camp to some rocks at the foot of the snow slope, the height being about 19,000 ft. We spent a poor night and overslept ourselves, for it was warm even in only one sleeping bag and we were both excited. The view from any col, a mountain window opening upon a fresh scene, holds an expectant thrill; how much keener is expectancy if that view promises to reveal unsurveyed country and perhaps a 26,000 ft. mountain.

Aided by this flying start of a thousand feet, on better snow, and with Tensing making light of the thirty-pound theodolite, we reached the col by 7.30 of a fine morning. It proved to be a false col. Nearly a mile away and at the same height lay the true col, and in between was a snow hollow which drained by a sort of backdoor into a tiny branch of the Langtang glacier. On each side of the true col rose high peaks of the order of 22,000 ft. Lloyd remained with the machine on the false col to get a fix from known peaks, while Tensing and I sped on across the still hard snow. Now was our big moment, the moment for which I had been, as Pepys says, in child ever since leaving Katmandu. Our survey plans depended on what we saw and to our disgust we did not see very much. Below us a big glacier flowed westwards, across it lay a knot of mountains, part of a range which stretched north-west into Tibet, effectually blocking our view to the east. We could not even see the junction of this range with the Himalayan crest-line a mile or so to the east of our col, but since there was no hint of the great mountain elsewhere, we surmised that Gosainthan lay just about the point of junction. The key move for the solution of the problem was a descent to the glacier on the Tibetan side, thus violating the frontier. We had no scruples on that score, having persuaded ourselves, with common-sense rather than logic, that no trespass would be committed provided we remained within the uninhabited glacier region.

> He that is robbed, not wanting what is stol'n,
> Let him not know't and he's not robb'd at all.

But it was too steep. Even had we had with us that earlier and better strain of yak, habitual crossers of traditional passes, I do not think we could have taken a camp over that col.

After collecting some spiders and rock fragments we returned to the high camp. We had still to visit the third col which lay between the other two and looked slightly higher. With perhaps as much luck as skill we climbed in dense mist by an intricate corridor, reaching the foot of the final pitch as the mist dissolved. We knew pretty well what to expect this time, and sure enough we looked once more upon the west glacier and beyond it to a mass of undistinguished-looking Tibetan peaks. We had now done our duty. Certainly, for Lloyd, our visits to the three cols held little pleasure, taken up, as they were, with the twiddling of screws, booking of angles, changing plates, all of it having to be done against time. I, on the other hand, once I had recovered from the successive disappointments, had merely to sit munching biscuits while Tensing scrabbled in rock crevices for victims for my Belsen chambers.

Since there was no reaching the unsurveyed territory on the Tibetan side, our survey work had to be confined to the Langtang itself. Nor was this merely painting the lily; for the existing ¼-in. maps published by the Survey of India in 1931 are good only so far as they go. Good enough, that is, to destroy any illusions one might have of being an explorer, all the main peaks having been triangulated and the general run of the main valleys indicated. But the detailed topography of the mountain regions is either not shown or is largely guesswork, thus the glaciers often provided charming surprises and the cols unexpected and puzzling vistas.

The station on this col was the last for some time. Next day, 22 June, when we began moving down, expecting to complete several stations on the way, the weather broke. Monsoon conditions of mist, rain, with rarely any sunshine, established themselves and prevailed almost unbroken for the rest of our stay.

On the way down Tensing and I crossed the main glacier to take a one-night camp up a tributary glacier to the east. The eastern side of the Langtang glacier is a very high wall of mountains unbroken except by this one glacier. Having crossed a high pass at its head, and having gone some way down the other side, we recognized below us the east branch of the Langtang which, after making an abrupt bend close to the two rock images, follows a course almost parallel to the main glacier. Beyond it we noticed yet another col leading southeast, a discovery of which we made good use later when we tried to reach the Jugal Himal. In a sanctuary one would expect to see game, but in this valley alone did we see any—three wary tahr, the rufous, shaggy Himalayan goat. At much lower altitudes we had occasionally seen a small deer which we took to be a musk deer, and on one occasion we had assumed without any strict enquiry the presence of some kindly disposed bears. Apart from that we saw no game, not even a marmot.

Twice, once at sunset and again at dawn, we carried the theodolite to the top of the 500 ft. moraine which in better weather would have made an excellent station, and then in disgust we went straight down to Langtang village. On this stroll, the more pleasant because it was all downhill, we met with a fresh crop of flowers, most of them, like Mr Pyecroft's lilac, 'stinkin' their blossomin' little hearts out'. Besides the tall cream primulas, nearly two feet high, there were little ground orchids of a delicate pink, bronze bell-shaped fritillaries, copper-coloured lilies, and great hairy yellow poppies. Lurking behind a bush of white briar, clutching a catapult, was a dark, hungry-looking figure, wearing, by way of dazzle camouflage, an American shirt. It was bird-skinner Toni who, with more zeal than sense, had left Bombay without waiting for the release of either stick-gun or ammunition.

CHAPTER V

RASUA GARHI

WE HAD NOW TO TRANSFER OURSELVES and our baggage to the frontier post of Rasua Garhi, whence we hoped to reach the north side of Langtang Lirung and possibly to climb it. At this point the Nepalese have pushed their frontier to the north of the Himalaya to the Lende Khola, a river which joins the Trisuli at Rasua. No doubt it flows from the glacier upon which we had looked down from the col. Thus there was a small strip of country between the Langtang Himal and the river which, politically, we were free to explore. In the event, physical difficulties curtailed this freedom.

We were to move with twenty-four coolies on the 29th, but on the appointed morning, apart from the imposing array of loads laid out by the Sherpas, there was little sign of departure. Men, women and children would stroll up, regard the waiting loads with some distaste, hoist one or two tentatively, and then stroll back to the village for breakfast. To keep a dog and bark oneself is foolish. We had a shrill pack—the havildar, the sepoys and the Sherpas—yet I waited fussily until all the loads were safely away and then discovered that no one remained to carry the one upon which I was sitting, my personal kit. That the majority of our porters were women would surprise no one who had studied life in the Langtang. In addition to their household work the women do the digging, the weeding, carry muck to the fields and harvest the crop. Except for a few who are up the hill with the cattle, the men sit about and weave mats. In a more perfect world, no doubt, they will just sit.

These mats are in constant demand, and they could hardly be woven more deftly even by fairer hands. Every household has a number of these big, close-woven mats, easily portable, with which a shelter can be rigged in a matter of minutes. They carry half a dozen up to a kharka and with the aid of a few forked sticks and a ridge pole build a tunnel-like shelter some ten feet wide and five feet high, closing the ends of the tunnel with a rough stone wall. If the mats are laid singly the shelter is almost weatherproof, when placed double it is perfectly so. Whenever we camped at a village, a mat kitchen for ourselves and one for the sepoys was quickly run up.

In spite of a late and long-drawn-out start—a matter of two hours between the head and the tail—all made Syarpagaon that evening. A note in my game-book reminds me that it was such a grand day for beetles that the extremely mournful appearance of a heavy bag of little black beggars had to be offset by the inclusion of a scarlet tick. Instead of descending to Syabrubensi, we continued to contour some 2000 ft. above the river to the village of Birdim. As it was raining hard the headman invited us to use the gompa, which was in comparatively good order and remarkable for its wind-driven prayer wheels and a bell of very lovely tone. The fact that we were sometimes accommodated in gompas or on their verandahs did not wholly account for the regret one felt at their common neglect. On general grounds the neglect of any place where men once worshipped is to be regretted, but the realist, I suppose, before allowing himself to be much perturbed, would want to know what kind of worship went on in these gompas. No doubt it was never a very exalted kind—by no means pure Buddhism, but a superstitious animism mainly concerned with the propitiation of a hierarchy of malign and terrible demons, over which, nevertheless, from wall, altar, and banner, the placid eye of the Master presides. However, a belief in demons and the pains of hell is better than nothing. Just as one beats the saddle so that the ass may ponder, so imaginary terror is a harmless and efficacious preceptor; and the weakening of even such a belief as this (as the neglect of the gompas implies) is to be deplored if there is nothing to take its place.

We were invited to the headman's house where his family lived together in one spacious upper room furnished with shelves, cupboards, chests, and a raised dais for a comprehensive bed. On a stone hearth in the middle was the fire from which the smoke of juniper wood had coloured ceiling and rafters to a highly polished black, so bright and so clean to touch that one first thought it had been coated with black enamel. A traveller came in to borrow the family's stone hand-mill to grind some barley for a meal. In half an hour's hard work he turned out less than two pounds of uncommonly coarse flour; but few villages are without water-mills, so that in one respect they are less backward than the Romans were.

From Birdim the track dropped to join the main road in the valley near the biggish village of Timure. This is the village where some land-hungry heathen has planted and fenced his maize right alongside a row of five noble and ancient chortens, so that the south-bound traveller must pass them, willy-nilly, on the unlucky side. In villages in the-valley bottom, where the climate is warm, maize is the main crop, and even rice can be grown. Timure lies barely 6000 ft. above sea level. Having passed another village at the mouth of the Gatte Khola, a large tributary crossed by a suspension bridge, we reached Rasua Garhi lying in the narrowest and deepest part of the gorge. There was no village to speak of and the alert-looking militiamen who met us led us at once within a substantial stone fort, its wall embrasured for cannon and loopholed for rifles. The fort had been squeezed in between the Trisuli river and one rock wall of the gorge. Fifty yards to the front ran the Lende Khola, little if any less in violence or volume than the Langtang Khola, and nowhere to be crossed except by a bridge.

The fort, they said, was about a hundred years old, built probably about the time of the second Nepal-Tibet war (1854). The ostensible *casus belli* was the maltreatment of Nepalese traders in Lhasa, but the Nepalese, then ruled by the redoubtable Jung Bahadur, were in fact planning to retake the mountainous territory south of Kyerong and Kuti (Nyenam) which the Chinese had annexed to Tibet after the first war in 1792. Acting with his usual vigour, Jung Bahadur sent two forces against these places, both of which were taken. At Kyerong there was no opposition and, after Kuti had been lost and re-captured, negotiations were opened. By a peace treaty made in 1856 the Gurkha troops withdrew to the present boundary.

Having pitched our brightly coloured tents on the greensward inside the walls we were conducted by the stout babu-like commander out through the gate and down to the Lende to admire the wooden cantilever bridge, half of which is maintained by Nepal and half by Tibet. A glance up the Nepal side of the river, where steep rock slabs thickly clad in a curious mixture of pine and bamboo running up for a thousand feet, served to chill our hopes. The Tibetan side, where there is a path, is much more gentle. By the bridge stood a stone slab inscribed with Chinese characters which no one present even pretended to be able to read. Nor do I think we should have learned from it anything useful, the number of 'li', for example, to Kyerong. More probably the industrious mason had bent his talents to imparting to travellers one or more of those sublime and immortal glimpses of the obvious which the Chinese relish so much: 'Every road leads in two directions', perhaps, or 'When struck by a thunderbolt it is superfluous to consult the Book of Dates as to the meaning of the omen.'

Apart from this stone there was nothing, not even an empty sentry-box, to denote that one had crossed a frontier. And this absence of any hint of might, majesty, dominion or power, is in accord with Tibetan genius which up to very recent years has managed to maintain its privacy behind quite imaginary barriers. Of course, should one happen to intrude, sooner rather than later one is seen off, not by an armed guard but by some stout affable official in Homburg hat and dark spectacles. Along the southern frontier of Tibet, from Assam to Kashmir, there are many passes and river gateways but nowhere are there any guards. This passive policy seems to have been clearly implied in one of the articles of the treaty which put an end to the war of 1854, in which, *inter alia*, it lays down that 'Tibet being merely a country of Monasteries of Lamas and a place for recitation of prayers and practice of religious austerities, if any foreign country attacks, Gorkha will afford such assistance and protection as it can'.

It has been amply demonstrated that there is now no part of the earth so wild, remote or unprofitable, that it is unlikely to become the scene of alarms and excursions. Nevertheless, I felt sorry for the commander of these nimble little militiamen in their neat blue uniforms, for it seemed that his prospects of advancing in his profession through some feat of arms were pretty slender. The garrison, in its boredom, must have welcomed the diversion we afforded. Five thousand man-loads of salt spread over the whole year cannot be a very absorbing spectacle, and since there are no customs' exactions, the men of the garrison have not the usual solace of frontier posts of making themselves a nuisance to travellers. Trade is blessedly free. We ourselves imported by the hand of our Sherpa corn merchant some quite drinkable raksi from Kyerong and paid no duty.

Local opinion affirmed that there was no way along the Nepal side of the Lende Khola and our eyes told us that on this occasion local opinion was probably right. There was, however, a path leading to a high grazing alp known as Dudh Khund, which lay vaguely in the required direction. Dudh Khund, or Milk Lake, is a common descriptive name for a lake whose water is opaque or any colour but white. We decided to visit the Milk Lake. Four of the Langtang squad stayed with us, but the majority went on to Kyerong. Owing either to trade or to a common origin there is a close association between Langtang and Kyerong.

By preparing overnight the necessary loads for a fortnight's absence we did a quick turn round. With an additional four local men we left the following morning, having sent on word to a village above Timure that a guide would be wanted. At Timure we quitted the valley to strike in a brutally direct manner up the pine-clad hillside. In the three days to the lake this uncompromising track continued as it had begun, seldom conceding anything to weakness by making a zigzag.

At the hamlet of Kedet at about 8000 ft. we had to wait for our guide who had regarded the message, perhaps not unnaturally, as a rather crude leg-pull. While he accustomed his ideas to unwelcome reality and the knowledge that his hour had struck, we refreshed ourselves with charred potatoes and beer which, from its colour, one concluded had been drawn from the Milk Lake. At length all was ready and, after some more hard going, we camped at an abandoned monastery at about 10,000 ft. The last two days in the main valley had been bright, but from now until our premature return a week later we hardly saw the sun. At Rasua, however, it continued fine, thus confirming our impression that, for some reason, the main valley received less rain than the tributary valleys. Probably it is a question of altitude rather than the lie of the land. At this time we considered the monsoon to be extremely heavy, while at Katmandu they had begun to talk of it failing.

Leeches now began, literally, to intrude upon our attention. They, too, seemed to vary in numbers with the altitude. In the main valley there were none, above Kedet a few stragglers or harbingers of the coming storm, and then ever-increasing numbers which reached their maximum at 11,000 and 12,000 ft. But height is only one factor; later

View of the range in Tibet running north-west seen from the col at the head of the Langtang glacier; the westward flowing glacier with the well-marked moraine is the Chasachen—a name given to it by Peter Aufschneiter and Harrer, two Austrians who escaped from internment at Dehra Dun in 1944, got to Tibet, and in the course of a remarkable journey to Lhasa spent some months at Kyerong exploring the country

'A big snow peak filling the head of the valley;' the photograph hardly does this noble view justice, but the weather of the Ganesh Himal made photography more of a lottery than ever

Looking across the East Langtang glacier on the way to the pass leading to the Jugal Himal; the fine peak (*c.* 22,000 ft.) is only one of several equally high which form the eastern wall of the main glacier

in the year we met them elsewhere at much lower altitudes in yet greater numbers.

An account in the *Journal of the Bombay Natural History Society* by Mr B. E. Smythies of a journey from Katmandu to the Gangja La along a part of the pilgrim track to Gosainkund, which, as a forest officer, he had been allowed to make, had filled me with foreboding. At one place he had had to put up a mosquito net to ward off leeches at night. At Calcutta I had made some enquiries as to whether a war which had seen the invention of atomic bombs and self-heating soups had not also given birth to something of more general benefit such as a leech repellent. My surmise was correct. The back-room boys had taken time off from nuclear fission to scribble the required formula. Dimethylphthalate or DMP the stuff was called. In Calcutta there was none to be had. Either it had not been a success or some War Disposals Board had sold it as toothpaste. I learnt, however, that an anti-mosquito preparation called 'Squitofax' contained a small quantity of the right venom, and sure enough a little smeared round the top of the boots or ankle puttees did discourage leeches from exploring higher. Paraffin, brine, or dry salt rubbed in, are no less effective, and are likely to be on hand in the most casually equipped expedition. With a moderate infestation, the wearing of boots with sewn-in tongues, ankle puttees and trousers, is good protection, as the leeches can be either flicked off individually when they begin climbing one's legs, or left to amuse or choke themselves in the eyelets of one's boots. Sometimes one or two unusually gifted or agile creatures manage to penetrate the defences to enjoy a well-earned drink without the blood donor's knowledge. The local men used to provide us with little bamboo sticks for brushing off leeches; for in picking or flicking them off with the fingers one is apt to be so flurried by their clinging ways as to flick them on to the back of the man in front.

The great majority of leeches get in on the ground floor, that is, by way of the boots. Half of these may be so small or so emaciated, perhaps no bigger than threads, that they are unable to aspire higher. But the robust fellows, one or two inches long, black, brown, or yellow, soon satisfy themselves that there is no nutriment in leather and advance with great rapidity up the trousers, making for the soft under-belly. If they are in strength, thirty, forty, or fifty of them, all climbing at once, then there is nothing for it but to halt, take off one's rucksack, and set to work to get rid of them with both hands or with the stick, a process which may have to be repeated every two or three hundred yards until clear of the badly infested area. Before moving on after these mopping-up operations the wise man has a good look at his rucksack; if any leeches are left lurking there they have a very easy covered approach to the back of one's neck. On the way back in September we passed through one or two really badly infested places, so bad that it might have been worth while soaking one's trousers in paraffin or brine. Whether the smell of the one or the hygroscopic effect of the other would be more insupportable than leeches is questionable. Walking along a leech-infested path one is usually fully occupied with home affairs, but it was interesting to note how the weight of the attack upon different men varied. The Europeans were easily the most acquisitive, and if one of us suffered more leech bites than another, it could be attributed to carelessness or to walking alone with nobody behind to give warning of an impending stab in the back. The Sherpas seemed to have less trouble keeping themselves free, seldom arriving in camp with a tell-tale trickle of blood or blood-soaked socks. As they were usually carrying salt and paraffin they may have made free use of it, but the fact that even their boots seemed to attract fewer leeches than mine annoyed me. In such matters there is much to be said for equality of misery. They, however, were far excelled by the local men who, in some miraculous way, remained more or less unscathed in spite of their bare feet and legs. I hesitate to say whether they possess some inherent immunity or whether they achieved it by extreme deftness in placing their feet and avoiding contact with the hundreds of menacing, weaving heads, stretching out hungrily from every stone, twig, or blade of grass.

From Gompaling the path mounted as abruptly and unswervingly upright as ever, until at last it landed us by a cairn on a sort of promontory. Not far away on the mist-wreathed hillside we saw a stone shelter and some cows. This place they called Nyangsusa, the place of the 'nyang' or tahr, and its height cannot have been much below 13,000 ft. Having got there about midday and having drunk a great deal of milk, pressed on us by the Sherpas as a sort of sedative, we were told that there was no question of going on. In this matter of camping, the regular staff, like the Sherpas, do as they are told.

If there are only two or three local men in the party their views can be safely ignored, but if they outnumber the Sherpas then they will probably decide where the party is to camp. They may be cajoled with extraordinary eloquence or sometimes bribed to go on; but no ordinary bribe will do because it is no use offering an extra day's pay for a double march when they can earn the same by doing it in two easy stages. We had therefore to settle down to eighteen hours upon our backs. A wet fog discouraged sightseeing; it was not good beetling weather; and only Polunin found occupation in a meadow where pink and crimson anemones, orange potentilla, and tall white primulas, all but hid the grass. Thick carpets of moss covering the boulders testified to the wetness of this place, but we had not yet plumbed the profoundest depths of humidity.

We began the final climb to the Dudh lakes (there was an upper and a lower) on a dull morning after a wet night. But soon the sulky clouds slowly drew apart revealing a rain-washed, livid, spacious landscape, and in the distance, above a more solid bank of cloud, rose four high peaks. They were the Ganesh Himal, one of which, a great snowy dome, seemed to invite a closer acquaintance. To the north the Trisuli valley lay clear for several miles beyond Rasua to the neighbourhood of Kyerong, which the guide, without much fear of contradiction, declared he could see. It took time to persuade him that the lower lake which we presently reached, though a lovely place for a picnic, was not our goal, and then the party settled down to heavy collar work up a long scree slope. The faint path landed us, without much obvious purpose, at the foot of a gully which looked too rough and steep even for goats. Encouraged by a diminutive but undeniable cairn the Sherpas led the spreadeagled field up 500 ft. to a sort of pass at about 16,000 ft. In the clammy mist we could see nothing from this vantage point beyond the ill-defined path at our feet. Passing over a desolate but calm sea of flat slabs, the path began descending to a grass shoulder at the foot of which lay the lake, some two acres in extent and of a cloudy green. Its opacity showed that the water came from a glacier which, we judged by the height, could not be far away. Indeed, we soon learnt that it was near from the characteristic sounds, which reminded me of how the discoverers of Jan Mayen island, in similarly thick weather, had found the land by ear rather than by eye.

There were no sheep about, nor had any been there for some time, but under some big boulders were the shelters once used by the shepherds. As to our whereabouts we had no clue, except that the water of the lake drained north-westwards, probably into the Lende Khola. But at sundown, with dramatic suddenness, the clouds vanished. One moment we looked across the forlorn lake to a grey void, the next to a mountain which to our astonished gaze seemed about to topple into the lake. In *Letters from High Latitudes* Lord Dufferin describes an even more startling revelation—that of the summit of Beerenberg on Jan Mayen seen from the deck of the *Foam*; 'the solid roof of grey suddenly split asunder, and I beheld through the gap thousands of feet overhead, as if suspended in the crystal sky—a cone of illuminated snow. There at last was the long sought for mountain actually tumbling down upon our heads.' Our vision gave us more astonishment than delight, for this was undoubtedly the 21,500 ft. peak well to the west of Langtang Lirung. At least we now knew where we were, and it was a long way from the northern slopes of Lirung. Not caring much for the look of this peak we decided to ignore it, flattering ourselves that we were after bigger game. Nevertheless, there was no ignoring a long, spiny ridge which it thrust out to the north and which somehow we must cross.

Scott was not well, Polunin had plenty to occupy him, so Lloyd and I decided to go on with three Sherpas and five Langtang men, the local guides having reached the uttermost bourn of their knowledge. We could carry enough food for an absence of ten days. A wet night delayed our start—the tents having to be dried a little—but the clouds remained high enough for us to see that a crossing of the spiny ridge must be sought for lower down. Though much might be hoped for from time and chance, yet we heartily grudged having to throw away any hard-earned height, well knowing that we could not throw away much before becoming involved in a bush-crawl. The chief incentive for attempting a shot in the dark such as this Dudh Khund trip lay in the fact that at 14,000 ft. vegetation ceases and movement becomes easier.

In the expectation of having not to descend very far, and resolute against doing so, we set off lightheartedly down an old grass-covered moraine by the side of the lake stream, our enemy the ridge on the other. Height, like money, is slowly won and quickly lost; no miser could have viewed with more anguish his dwindling hoard of gold than did we our rapidly diminishing height. After going for half an hour, during which we must have dropped 1500 ft., we called a halt while Lloyd and I crossed the stream to prospect a possible route across the ridge. Apart from finding some lovely blue poppies (*Meconopsis horridula*), we wasted our time. The route proved too 'thin' for laden men, so we returned and continued the descent. From grass to a strong growth of dwarf rhododendron was but a short transition, and soon we began grappling with their full-sized relatives, backed by assorted juniper, bamboo and thorn.

Wingate, of Burma fame, used to tell his chindits never to report jungle as impenetrable without first penetrating it; and for men with cutting weapons and strong arms there should be no such thing as the 'impenetrable jungle' in which travellers frequently find themselves. But before demonstrating practically the truth of this one ought to be clear about the distance to be penetrated and convinced that the effort is worth while. In our case we were sure of neither, and even if our followers agreed to try we had neither time nor energy to spare to hack out a trail for three or four days. While Lloyd and I, sitting on a boulder in a stream—the only space free from jungle—discussed this, one of the local men volunteered the information that the north side of the Langtang might be reached by marching for one day up the Tibetan side of the Lende Khola and crossing back into Nepal by a bridge of whose existence he knew. Lamenting that he had not mentioned it before we had left Rasua Garhi we decided to cut our losses. In three rain-soaked hours, the measure of our rash descent, we climbed back to the lake.

Although this decision was probably wise, our losses proved to be irretrievable. Three days later we found that the bridge in question had been washed away, with the result that we were obliged to spend a second day on the north side of the river on the way to another bridge farther upstream. Delay, as it has often done before, proved fatal to our hopes. The arrival in our camp of a stout, affable official, in Homburg hat and dark spectacles, sent expressly for the purpose, reminded us that we were on the wrong side of the Lende Khola.

CHAPTER VI

THE GANESH HIMAL

◆

THUS FOILED WE TURNED WESTWARDS to the Ganesh Himal; Lloyd and I still in pursuit of a peak we could climb—for none of the Langtang peaks seemed in that category—and the others, who all the time had been busy after their kind, in search of fresh ground. So far the uniformity of the rock and the absence of any fossils had failed to please our geologist. Fossils, of course, are desirable finds which even a layman can recognize. But if every bit of rock held a tell-tale fossil, geology would be little better than stamp-collecting—a pastime at the mercy of any fool with a magnifying glass—instead of a highly speculative science interpreting earth history in its own melodious but difficult language.

After a day's rest to give Scott a chance to recover from a bout of dysentery (for which he was being treated without aggravating effect with pomegranate bark), and to write letters of apology to Kyerong, we set off down the valley. (Happily the incident at the close of the previous chapter, upon which one would hardly wish to dwell, had no political repercussions.) Short of Syabrubensi we crossed the Trisuli by a wooden cantilever bridge, climbed over a spur, and entered the valley of the Chilime. This river, the sole drainage for the eastern side of the Ganesh Himal, was much smaller than either the Langtang or the Lende Khola; while Thangiet, which had loomed so important on the map, comprised three small, dirty, decaying villages inhabited incongruously by Newars. Obviously we would get no porters there, so, late though it was, we pushed on to Chilime. Inhabited by Tamangs, this village seemed more prosperous but no more salubrious. Sitting in a drizzle in a muddy rice stubble I paid off all but three of our local coolies, while the lieutenant harangued the astonished headman on the subject of mat shelters and the necessity for speed in erecting them.

Leaving Scott temporarily in the care of the escort, together with Toni who needed more catapult practice, we started next day (13 July) with ten coolies carrying three weeks' food. We had the usual difficulty in getting clear of the village, the seven Chilime coolies having to fettle themselves up, admonish their wives, and eat their breakfasts. Poor specimens of *homo sapiens* they were, too, as we presently found, weak in the legs and not very strong in their heads. A few miles up the valley we crossed the river to the right bank where, rather to our surprise, the track abandoned the valley altogether. We had little confidence in the Chilime men as guides. They could give us only the vaguest information about camp sites; invariably there was nothing, or nothing better, anywhere beyond where we had halted to make the enquiry. They seemed stunned with the magnitude of their task or with remorse at leaving their families. The camp site at which we finally stopped quite early in the afternoon proved to be the most dismal imaginable; a quagmire in a clearing, tenanted for the most part with giant stinging nettles, horse-flies, and gloomy oaks dripping with moss, and carrying on their branches whole gardens of ferns. That night it rained too hard and too persistently for our tents which before this had begun to drip on less provocation. We found that a gas-cape draped over one end allowed the inmate to focus the drips on one spot. A high altitude single-fly tent cannot be completely rain-proof, but it should withstand a lot of rain provided care is taken not to touch the inside of the fabric. A piece of advice, to a man in a small tent, like advising a man on a tight-rope not to fall off.

The drizzle which continued all day was of little consequence because the forest already ran with water; the path was a stream, the trees dripped, and every bamboo one touched shook down a shower. However, this damp misery expedited the march. Instead of halting every few minutes for a chat and a smoke, the coolies stopped only when forced to by the stress of their loads. The gurgle and splash of water everywhere nearly brought us into collision with two black bears who were fighting or playing in the bed of a stream about twenty yards away and failed to hear us. Considering their terrifying snarls and the hearty clouts they administered to each other, one could not help wishing to remain unnoticed by such rough customers. But suddenly they took alarm and crashed off, evidently more frightened than we were.

At the time we three were well ahead of the porters, who were too far behind even to hear the noise made by the beasts as they cleared off. Nevertheless a circumstantial account was soon current throughout the district of how the old 'gazebo' (me) had beaten off with his ice-axe the attacks of two of the biggest, blackest and most ferocious bears ever seen. Thus easily are reputations acquired among a simple people. Had I become resident in the Langtang, devoting my time to talking about bears I had met and carefully avoiding meeting any others, I should no doubt have become the greatest living authority, the man who killed bears with his naked hands. This black Himalayan bear (*Ursus Tibetanus*, I hope and believe) is our carnivorous, sheep-slaughtering friend of the Langtang. But meat is probably a luxury for him. Like ourselves, he makes do on bamboo shoots, wheat, maize and millet in their season. In standing crops one sees a little 'machan' built for the safety and convenience of the bear-scarer. According to all accounts the black bear's sight and hearing are good, and he is very savage, whereas the two we met were deaf, blind and very timid. But it would never do to presume on the truth of our casual observations.

That afternoon we won clear of the obscene forest and camped at a kharka where there was the usual long mat-roofed shelter like an elongated Nissen hut. We fared very well on milk and the eggs and honey we had brought from below. This honey, dark brown and of a pleasingly original flavour, was so thin that it could be eaten only with a spoon, a fault at which few could cavil.

The next march, which took us into the upper part of the main valley, was long and trying. It rained all the previous night and forbore to let up during the day. But this was customary in the Ganesh Himal which receives more than its fair share of monsoon—or so it seemed to us who lived and moved in a world of mist and drizzle, the sun extinguished apparently for good. Nor did the path improve. One could sympathize with its pioneers whose simple plan had been to climb as quickly as possible until clear of the slime, nettles, bears, horse-flies, leeches, sodden firewood, fern-festooned trees and dripping bamboos, and then to enjoy an easy ridge walk until the opportunity for descending to the grass of the upper Chilime presented itself. The ridge, when attained, was not so easy as all that, for the sharp spines of several lateral ridges had to be crossed like so many miniature passes, and it was so high that even in summer it held beds of old snow.

We began the day with a long and brutal grind up to the ridge, where we waited long in the rain while the suffering coolies reluctantly crawled up in their own good time. The last to arrive, a man of resource, put on such a convincing act of agony and imminent dissolution that he deceived us all and reaped the reward of cunning by being sent back. His loss and the subsequent reorganization left us to carry our own big rucksacks which at any rate served to keep our backs dry. Luckily some of the ghums brought from Katmandu remained serviceable enough to protect the loads of atta and satu which are speedily ruined by wet. These ghums or mats, bent lengthwise and worn over the head like a roof, keep man and load dry.

Late in the afternoon, when the field was strung out over several miles of an arduous course, the leaders came to the last and steepest of climbs to the highest of the miniature passes. We did not know if it was the last, but obviously it was the last the porters would face provided they got so far. On an unknown track, a steep climb coming at the end of a long march will make most coolies cry 'capevi'; if, under such circumstances, one decides to push on one must be prepared to do without some of the loads. Happily, the track now took a decided turn downhill, at first over boulders and scree, then over kindly grass, until out of the mist below came the welcome bleating of sheep. After following a small but turbulent glacier stream for a short way we came at last to a lush meadow alive with sheep and goats, and, in my opinion, vastly improved by the presence of several mat shelters. Warding off the attacks of savage dogs with stones, we made for the nearest shelter, pushed aside the mat door and unceremoniously squeezed our dripping bodies round the fire.

The shepherds plied us with cheese, tasting like dried milk that had somehow got wet, and cheered us with the news that eight days previously they had enjoyed a fine day. When the porters began dribbling in we pitched our wet tents and retired to wet sleeping bags. In Nepal the absence of roomy accommodation such as yorts provide is a great drawback, for the mat shelter is too like a miniature railway tunnel, including the smoke. It is too low to stand upright, there is not much room round the fire, and the outer darkness beyond the fire is taken up with utensils or lambs and young yaks. Two porters who failed to turn up spent their night under a rock on the cold hillside—a misfortune we bore with fortitude since the loads held none of our immediate wants except the dried yeast. If possible we always liked to make bread. When this was not possible I preferred the kind made by the Sherpas—what I called Solu Khumbu bread—to the poor chapatties a hillman usually makes. All that the Sherpas do is to mix flour and water to a dropping consistency and to pour it on to a hot iron plate. Bread so made, light and full of holes, is more digestible than chapatties when made by the average Sherpa who has not the art of turning out the delicious, wafer-thin chapattie of the expert. Another popular bread in India is the 'paratta' which is merely a chapattie thrown into boiling fat, where it immediately blows itself out into a hollow and delightfully crisp biscuit. A Sherpa's heavy-handed version of a chapattie upon being thrown into boiling fat merely sucks up the hot fat and blows itself out when inside the stomach of the man foolish enough to eat it.

Travellers in regions of stubborn mist should not be impatient. To an even greater degree, those shy, reluctant, provoking ways in which a sinuous glacier valley gives up its secrets, will have to be suffered or perhaps enjoyed. In the morning we were permitted to see a little more than our immediate surroundings. Up towards the ridge by which we had come lay a small glacier which we guessed descended from a modest 19,451 ft. mountain named Paldor. Westwards lay a much bigger glacier, and beyond it a wonderful great mountain whose long and spiky summit ridge at once removed it from the category of climbable peaks. In the Himalaya a peak with a name, unless it is a very giant, is not common, so we decided to go in search of Paldor whose name at any rate gave it some significance. Accordingly Lloyd and I with Tensing and Da Namgyal set off with a two-day camp.

A kindly moraine took us directly up until we could step easily on to the dry ice of the lower glacier which we presently forsook for a big cone of hard avalanche snow. Before entering the gully from which this had poured down, we broke out on to the rocks on one side in order to put a camp on a ledge a few hundred feet higher. We reckoned we were about 17,000 ft., high enough to bring Paldor within reach. Rain soon drove us to our tents, but later the weather allowed us to see another thousand feet of our route, though not the mountain itself.

Starting at 6 a.m. on a cloudy morning we traversed back to the glacier, crossed it, and climbed a long snow slope to a plateau from where

The Jugal side of the pass. The descent lay down the rocks in the bottom left-hand corner; the smooth surface of this high glacier basin is marred by the debris of a recent avalanche

Three of the five desolate tarns at Panch Pokhara (Five Lakes)—a little-frequented goal of pilgrims; the smoke rising from the shepherd's mat shelter, with our tent alongside, can just be distinguished

A distant view of the Jugal Himal from a grazing alp on the high Panch Pokhara ridge; on the right is the framework of a shelter used by shepherds when they occupy the kharka; they bring the mats up with them

at last we saw our mountain. Having gained a ridge, steep on both sides but not difficult, we had only to follow it to the summit. As we mounted the snow became worse. Just below the summit my axe went in to the head without finding any hard snow to bite on. By 9.30 we were on top. In better weather we should have had a rewarding view, for Paldor is a southern outlier of the Ganesh group and from it we should have seen down the Trisuli valley to the plains. Its prominence when viewed from the south accounted no doubt for its having a name. On the descent the snow resembled porridge, but we soon sank the long slope by first starting an avalanche and glissading down the hard snow in its wake. Having packed up we went down in mist and drizzle to the sheepfold, well pleased with the success of this modest sortie.

Although there had been no sun all day and although he had worn his glasses most of the time, Tensing had a sharp attack of snow blindness as a result of this excursion. Lloyd and I went up to look at the big glacier to the west in order to assure ourselves it held no surprises like the Langtang. Having crossed the river by a natural rock bridge at another kharka, we walked along the top of a high and very regular moraine until we could see the ice-fall marking the termination of the glacier. Scott joined us that evening bringing with him 150 eggs, a pumpkin, chillies, and a wooden jorum of Tibetan arak. These wooden jorums are thick and hold less than the eye imagines or the rude mountaineer requires. We were relieved therefore to hear that he disliked the stuff.

With nothing more to be done from this camp we moved the whole outfit to another valley. The track crossed the river below the kharka where a great boulder leant over leaving a gap of only a few feet to be bridged. It then turned downstream, obviously heading for the junction of the two valleys. With one accord we four, who were in the van, followed it, but after ambling pleasantly downhill for a mile I became uneasy about the porters. Returning hotfoot to the bridge I learnt from a shepherd that they had gone straight up the hillside, and presently, in a break in the mist, I spotted them. The other three, enjoying too much the novelty of going downhill, had a sterner chase and a sharper lesson.

Having topped the intervening ridge we dropped a couple of thousand feet to the second and bigger valley and camped in some deserted stone huts by the river. Their stone walls and flagged floors lay open to the sky, but the poles and the wood slabs or shingles for the roof were neatly stacked inside. All we needed were the poles, for we had with us two big ground-sheets (eighteen feet by twelve) of very light material which had proved invaluable throughout our journey. With these we made a snug billet, big enough for the whole party, which allowed us to have one fire for cooking and another where we could sit and where Polunin could dry his plants. If it was not ecstasy it was undoubtedly comfort we enjoyed that night sitting round the fire, drinking the last arak in order to subdue or mollify a curious meal of rice and fungi, while outside the rain hissed down and the river roared.

Shortly after our arrival we had a visit from the owners of the huts, who were then living on the other side of the river grazing their yaks. They were Tibetans from Paimanesa, a place a few miles north of Rasua, whence there is a direct path over a pass to the upper Chilime valley. Believing they were in Tibet they regarded us as trespassers. We, however, knew that they were, for the frontier lies north of the main range at this point and coincides with it again a few miles to the west at the big Ganesh peak of 24,299 ft. This peak, which we suspected to be the snowy dome we had seen from near the Dudh Kund lake, had so far eluded us.

At dawn next morning, as if in answer to our prayer, the sight of a great mountain completely filling the head of the valley surprised and delighted us. So perfect were its proportions that at first glance it did not look its full height, but a bearing to it convinced us that it was indeed the highest of the Ganesh group, one which might be called Ganesh mountain. The south-west ridge, if it could be attained, seemed to offer a straightforward way to the summit of this 'snowy pleasure dome'. In spite of the arak Lloyd had stomach trouble, so Polunin and I set off up a valley which bid fair to rival the large richness of the Langtang. Extensive meadows lay on both banks of the river up to the point where it issued from the glacier, and beyond that a wide and grassy ablation valley rose in a series of four long steps.

The abundance of new flowers—a delicate bluebell-shaped codonopsis, purple aconite, crimson and cream louseworts—had persuaded Polunin to stop long before we came to a lake nestling below the moraine at about 16,000 ft. A half mile above the lake the moraine ran out in rock and scree, down which I hurried to the glacier. The mountain, now wreathed in cloud, lay across the glacier which swept out of sight round a buttress at the foot of the south ridge. Making fast going on smooth dry ice I pushed on up the middle until the whole glacier bay came into view—a cirque made up of four monstrously steep and broken ice-falls. Two of these ice cataracts flowed down from the Ganesh peak and two from Pabil (23,361 ft.) which lay to the south-west. There seemed to be no other way on to Ganesh but by the buttress which was separated from the easy south-west ridge by the whole breadth of two ice-falls. Of these only the lower thousand feet of dirty, broken ice could be seen, dropping apparently out of the cloud layer above. On the glacier at the foot of each lay the piled debris of fallen seracs and between them ran a line of black crags. On such a dismal scene, like a dirty, dismantled stage with the curtain only half raised, I was ready to turn my back.

An omelette of six eggs, bread, honey and cake restored the body, but my mind was still haunted by the gloom of that sepulchral cirque, so fearfully savage and black. Yet next day Lloyd and I camped by the Green Lake, as it was called. The name Yang-tso is Tibetan, and as one might expect the water has a bright green hue owing to the quantity of algae growing in it. On our way to the lake the mountain had remained surprisingly clear so that by the time we reached it we had examined and rejected the routes above the buttress, the only weak point in its well-defended lower parts. In the afternoon we discovered that the south-west ridge sprang from a very high col from which one of the tumbled ice torrents descended. The rocks to one side of this seemed a possible route but to reach them we should have to climb some ice-worn slabs immediately under the rotting face of the ice-fall. Back we went down the valley, like that Duke of York who marched his men to the top of a hill and marched them down again.

Meantime Polunin was having a lot of fun with his flowers, being compelled to hang the whole of the billet with drying racks. Scott had turned his attention to a new game, taking rubbings of glacier ice to determine the crystallization at various depths. We must return soon to the Langtang where Lloyd had to tie up the loose ends of the survey, but before leaving I determined to have a final look at the ice-fall which I felt we had not thoroughly examined. For the third time Tensing and

I went up, reaching the cirque, six miles up and several thousands of feet higher by 10.30. Climbing over the debris of ice-blocks to the cliffs of the cirque we sat close under them for safety's sake while we examined the ugly decaying wall of ice a hundred yards away. The ice had either retreated or a chunk had calved off, leaving a narrow passage of ice-worn slabs from which, a few hundred feet up, the rocks to the left of the ice-fall could be gained. The ice-fall itself was far too steep and broken to be climbable. Leaving Tensing, I went up close to the ice to satisfy myself that the slabs could be climbed, or what was equally important, whether they could be climbed in safety. Small fragments of ice whizzing viciously by seemed to hint that they could not. Moreover, a mass of debris showed that seracs had recently broken away from the wall, while the neighbouring cataract, flowing down from Pabil, sent down a frequent discharge of ice blocks.

The greatest drawback to climbing in monsoon conditions, greater even than the bad visibility, is the high temperature. After the monsoon began in June I doubt if it froze on more than one or two nights even at a height of 19,000 ft. The height of this place was about 17,000 ft., but had the nights been really cold one might have climbed under this wall in perfect safety. To weigh the risks attendant upon climbing such a place is a difficult part of the mountaineer's job. Such risks are not easy to assess, especially if there is a very desirable prize to be snatched at the cost of a short exposure to them. If a man refuses to take risks there is nothing to show that he has done right, while if they are taken the proof that he has done wrong may be too conclusive. Had we been able to climb this ticklish place swiftly without loads, or better still without porters, one might not have hesitated, but now prudence or funk prevailed. I regretted the absence of Lloyd who had gone crystal-gazing with Scott, nor was it any use trying to put the onus on Tensing who merely eyed the place lugubriously and said: 'As the Sahib wishes.' Long afterwards I used to lie awake at night tormented by mocking visions of this snowy dome.

We returned by a new route on the long ridge bounding the north side of the main Chilime valley, three of the Tibetans coming with us as carriers and guides. They assured us we should do it in two days, as in fact we did, but had their memories of the route been fresher I feel sure they would have allowed twice that time. No one goes so far or so fast as the man who does not know where he is going. As usual the morning was wet, but it passed pleasantly enough on a gentle ascent where we were refreshed both by many showers and by the sight of new flowers, among them a sort of clover of an intense gentian-like blue. By the time we had crossed two lesser ridges and landed fairly on the main ridge, it was drawing towards three o'clock, high time to ask the guides where they proposed to stop. Whereupon they told us of a pleasant kharka, crawling with yaks, close to a lake to which presently we should begin to descend. The path thought differently. It began to ascend, becoming every moment rougher and more difficult to follow. No one seemed to have used it for many years and when we heard a dog barking in the mist far below I made sure we were wrong.

By now the guides were at the tail of the column a mile back, but the Sherpas assured us we were still on a path and indeed we had now little choice but to follow the woodless and waterless ridge to which we were committed. At six o'clock we came to a deserted kharka where there was not a trace of water, so we pushed on in the gathering gloom of dusk. The mist had gone. Far to the north above the deep indigo of the valleys, already dark in shadow, the pale summits of scores of Tibetan peaks stood out against a leaden sky. Away beyond the black chasm of the Trisuli gorge we saw for the first time the northern slopes of Langtang Lirung. Just before dark we came to another abandoned kharka and again we could find neither wood nor water, essentials which no traveller in Nepal would expect ever to be scarce. Not much relishing the prospect of a thirsty night Lloyd and I, with commendable spirit, launched ourselves down a neighbouring gully, quite determined to go down till we found water and hardly expecting to have to climb back. Having that in mind we descended rapidly with careless abandon. I may have gone down two thousand feet, or perhaps only one, when a faint bellow from above informed me that the coolies refused to follow. Argument was impossible at that range and I remained needlessly puzzled by the recalcitrance of the coolies who, in fact, knew where the water was and had found it. Dragging myself wearily upwards in the dark, full of angry conjecture, I had within me 'a speech of fire that fain would blaze' until at the top the news that water had been found douted it.

Throughout the night it rained cheerfully and we breakfasted in the open in a fine drizzle. Sipping hot tea I regarded with perfect equanimity, almost with satisfaction, the damp, huddled heap of Tibetans who had led us such a long dance along a waterless ridge. Presently the rain stopped, the sun came out. Secure now in the knowledge of where we were going, we enjoyed to the full a long downhill march through all the variegated regions of heath, rhododendron, bamboo, tall silver fir, until we emerged in the yellowing wheat fields of the Chilime valley.

CHAPTER VII

THE LANGTANG AGAIN

◆

Whenever we returned to our base the lieutenant, a most able quartermaster, generally had something good for us to eat. This time he had procured some mangoes from Trisuli bazaar and some locally grown rice, an upland variety of a reddish colour. With the help of twenty-one Chilime coolies of both sexes, many goitrous, and all exceeding poor and beggarly, we moved to Syabrubensi at the junction of the Langtang Khola. From there we sent the havildar and the escort back to Katmandu with some spare loads, and with a dimished party climbed again to Syarpagaon. In spite of their goitres the coolies went well.

We reached Langtang village on 1 August to find it more or less empty, the people having gone to the upper gompa near the snout of the Lirung glacier for a religious festival. With some difficulty we got together a team of five boys and so were able to move on next day. Polunin and his entourage stayed behind to cope with a fresh flush of flowers—notably a delphinium of a right royal blue, a deep purple trumpet-shaped cyananthus, a giant thistle with a head of pink flowers, yellow violets and forget-me-nots. On the way up we met the Langtang people coming down, reeking so abominably of beer that they seemed less like religious celebrants than belated revellers. The weather had momentarily improved. The gloomy permanence of the cloud canopy was broken by a succession of several clear mornings which gave Lloyd a welcome chance to complete the survey. Leaving him thus engaged at Langsisa, Scott and I with two Sherpas and a local man set out to visit the col at the head of the west Langtang glacier which we had already looked down upon from the head of the main glacier.

In order to take advantage of the bend we followed the left bank of the glacier, but when the moraine petered out we were forced away from the glacier up steep scree. What with fatigue and falling rain we were in no mood to be nice about a choice of camp site; so we stopped in a gully at the first available water, a horrible place, with one tent pitched perforce fifty feet above the other and both on cramped platforms. Angtharkay, who was no fairy on his feet, brought our food down from the upper tent where they had a fire and with it a young avalanche of stones—a contingency we had provided for by placing our tent under the lee of a boulder.

From a distant glimpse I had of the col on a reconnaissance made that evening I decided to reach it without making another camp. We therefore started before daylight, crossed the dry glacier, and climbed a huge avalanche cone on the other side. By sun-up we had begun the long, almost level snow trudge to the col, passing on our right the two cols from which we had looked down to this glacier two months before. Then it had been all dry ice, whereas now there were two or three feet of snow of that trying kind with a hard crust which sometimes supported the feet and sometimes didn't. Whether it is better to try to remain on top of snow like this by treading delicately, or to break the crust purposefully at each step to secure a solid foundation, depends upon whether one is in front or behind. Those behind naturally prefer the leader to stamp manfully at each step. On this occasion, having snowshoes on, I trod like a cat, hopefully ignoring such preferences until a series of violent tugs on the rope indicated that one or both of my followers had sunk waist-deep. Having climbed the low rock ridge upon which the col lay we looked once more into Tibet, to the broad, grey band of the Chasuchen glacier 2000 ft. below. The height of this col was 19,500 ft. Tensing agreed that a camp could not be carried down. We might have got down without loads, but our plan was to spend a week there with the machine in order to fix the position of Gosainthan. Since that questionable glimpse of a big mountain from the first station we had seen neither it nor any likely rival. When we came to return, no problems in technique suggested themselves. Whether one stamped or not the snow offered no resistance; snowshoes were worse than useless, for at each step a great fid of wet snow remained on the shoe to be lifted. We spent another night at the same camp, too tired to mind its vertical lay-out or its noisiness. As a sort of second to the thunderous bass occasioned by Angtharkay's earth-shaking footsteps, there was a continuous roar, swelling and diminishing, caused by the cataracts of mingled rock and snow pouring down the gullies of the mountain across the glacier.

In the course of our walk back to Langsisa, from a new and more hopeful angle I tried to assess the chances of grasping a long-coveted prize, the Fluted Peak. The moraine down which we strode was worth studying too. Besides great numbers of blue and yellow poppies, gorgeous cyananthus, and the blue codonopsis we had met in the Ganesh Himal, there was a very beautiful dusty blue flower with a ravishing scent; it was a dwarf, hairy delphinium (*D. brunonianum*). According to Tensing its dried flowers are a preventative or at any rate a discourager of lice. The Langtang people used it for this purpose, but obviously did not use enough.

Two days later the whole party met again at the upper gompa, Kyangjin Ghyang. Only ten days remained before Lloyd and Scott had to start for home, time enough perhaps to snatch victory from defeat. For while it was a comfort to reflect that our mountaineering activities would be veiled under the more respectable cloak of science, there was no concealing from ourselves that as a climbing holiday it had been a failure. That is to say climbing of a more advanced kind than the snow plodding, boulder hopping, and scree scrambling which the Himalaya impose on their votaries as a daily task. For most expeditions this sort of hard labour, along with bouts of load carrying, becomes the accustomed background. A background sombre enough at times, in all conscience, so that if when in camp one is obliged to read Dostoievski (as I was) one begins to think that only a writer of the Russian school of resignation and pity could successfully limn its darkest shadows. But it is not as bad as that. I would not wish anyone to believe that because such arduous day-to-day exertions are passed over more or less in silence the Himalayan climber is therefore a man of ape-like strength and agility, with an immense capacity for breathing rarefied air, drinking melted snow or raw spirit, and eating fungi and bamboo shoots. True, on occasions he must live hard or exert himself to the point of exhaustion, necessarily when at grips with a big peak; but for the most part his condition is one of ease bordering upon comfort; he suffers from heat rather than from cold, from muscular atrophy rather than nervous exhaustion; and for a variety of reasons—the weather, the worsening snow, the porters' fatigue—his days are usually short. Thus he spends more time on his back than on his feet. His occupational disease is bedsores, and a box of books his most cherished load.

The weather's brief respite had ended. It was as unpropitious as it could be, with whole days of mist and drizzle, when Lloyd and I decided to have a go at the Fluted Peak. Nothing else offered. Our project for spending a week on the Chasuchen glacier on the Tibetan side had fallen through, and there was no other peak more desirable or so apparently climbable as the Fluted Peak. Accordingly, on 10 August, with three Sherpas and two Langtang men, we crossed the river by a bridge and turned up the left bank. The grazing on this side, which is almost as good as the other, is apparently reserved for sheep and goats brought from outside the valley. One large flock, we were told, belonged to a member of the Rana family, and another to the villages near Chilime. Having reached a point opposite the big moraine of the west Langtang glacier we turned eastwards up a side nallah and camped at a kharka not far below the snout of a fair-sized glacier.

In the wretched prevailing weather the shelter of a mat hut was not to be lightly forsaken. Moreover, he who knows not whither to go is in no hurry to move, and we were uncertain of the whereabouts of our peak, having seen nothing of it for several days. We spent the morning on the high terminal moraine peering into the misty void across the glacier. There was less mist up the glacier where we could see the col at its head nearly two miles away; and where I was sure there must be a biggish peak—probably the Fluted Peak—to account for the glacier. Lloyd did not agree. Nevertheless, on my confident advice we decided to put a camp on a rock island below the col. In the extravagant hope of 'doing a station' Lloyd left early with the machine to climb a hill behind the kharka, and later the rest of us struck camp and began moving up the glacier. About a mile up, happening at one of our too numerous halts to look back, I saw behind us, almost opposite the kharka, the top of the Fluted Peak glimmering high and white. The clearing lasted but a minute. Before even the critical 'step' on our chosen ridge, which

A quiet corner in Patan; the open-fronted shop with its carved woodwork is typical of the Valley; the crouching grotesque on the temple steps looks like a cross between a guinea-pig and a hare

At Baleji water garden—the recumbent Narayan with head pillowed on cobras; normally the tank is fuller so that only the face, by exposing itself above the water, invites criticism

Coolies resting at a chautara; the banyan, with its aerial roots lopped, is on the left of the pipal

A village on the route to the Marsyandi valley; the fine pipal tree with the stone surround seems to be without its usual banyan mate

we were anxious to see, had emerged, the clouds rolled down. Feeling a little foolish I sent the men across the glacier, in a direction almost opposite to our original line of march, to find a camp, while I loitered behind to pick up Lloyd to whom this welcome vision might not have been revealed. However, he had noted both the peak and our sudden right about turn, upon which he generously refrained from comment.

The Sherpas had found a pleasant oasis for the camp in the ablation valley, where against a convenient boulder they had rigged up a penthouse roof with the big groundsheet. Under this they slept and we ate, for it was very much drier than our tent. Next day the Langtang men went down while the three Sherpas came with us to carry a light camp up the mountain. After a couple of thousand feet of easy going we reached the first snow. The lower part of this south-west ridge is like a wedge with a base, some 400 yards wide, represented by a hanging glacier which converges to a point a thousand feet higher up. From the point the slender ice ridge lies back in a level step before springing up to the summit cone. On the extreme left-hand edge of the wedge where we first attacked it the ice had disappeared, exposing a narrow ledge of steep, loose rock with ice on one side and a precipitous drop on the other. As we climbed it grew steeper, and to avoid a particularly steep or loose bit of rock we had sometimes to move out on to the ice which was covered with a layer of wet unstable snow. We roped up and climbed very close together, for the slightest false step threatened to bring half the ridge in ruins about our ears. None of us liked it, least of all the Sherpas, especially when Lloyd, who was climbing ahead unroped, sent a large rock slithering down the ice just to one side of them. While Lloyd went on a little we called a halt, and when he reported no improvement and no place for a tent we retreated a short way, put up the tent, and sent the Sherpas down with instruction to return in a couple of days.

Climbing on a shattered ridge like this, which is a fair sample of most Himalayan ridges, one finds it difficult to resist the conclusion that were it not for the snow and ice the Himalaya would long ago have assumed the low rounded forms of British hills. When the snow goes there is nothing to stop the loose fragmented rocks of these high narrow ridges finding a more stable resting place in the valley below.

Surely the geologist who climbs such a ridge, pondering the age of the mountains the while, and who feels it disintegrating so alarmingly under his possibly clumsy feet, will be inclined to lop a few millions of years from the aeons of his sublime guesses.

At midday snow began falling. Since we were camped at about 19,000 ft. this phenomenon would not have surprised us had it not been the first snowstorm we had experienced throughout the summer. The storm continued during the night, causing the tent roof to sag and leak, the temperature being above freezing-point. But even in a high camp, joy, of a strictly moderate kind, cometh with the morning. We turned out to find six inches of snow covering the rocks and a few trial steps taken on the nearby ice showed its snow covering to be as wet and unstable as it had been at midday. Any hope we may have still entertained of climbing the ridge—we had not yet seen the ice-step—was thus extinguished for the moment, so we packed up and departed, leaving the tent standing. We were surprised to find snow lying down to 17,000 ft., but at our oasis the rain, which fell steadily, was merely a trifle colder. Tensing, who had heard our jocund shouts upon the misty mountain, was pathetically trying to bake bread on a fire of green dwarf rhododendron leaves, so we sent the Sherpas back to the kharka for wood and milk and settled down to another twenty hours on our backs. We had spent a like time in a horizontal position the previous day. Apart from the danger of contracting bed sores, and chilblains, too, which are encouraged by a sedentary life, I was heinously ill-provided for such long stretches upon the rack of idleness. The fact that I had already read *The Brothers Karamazov* and *The Last Chronicles of Barset* three times each is some measure of the wealth of our leisure and the poverty of our combined library.

Having decided to leave the mountain alone for a couple of days while the rocks freed themselves of snow we spent a morning walking up the glacier to the col at its head, more for the sake of something to do than for anything we were likely to see. Except for a short piece of soggy snow at the top we walked on dry ice, and in three hours were on the ridge at about 19,000 ft., peering into the familiar sea of cloud. We, had, however, the satisfaction of standing on an important watershed, for the valley to the east drains into the Sun Kosi and not the Trisuli. The Kosi is the third most important of Himalayan rivers with a catchment area of 24,000 sq. miles—exceeded only by the Indus and the Brahmaputra, each of which has a catchment area of somewhere in the neighbourhood of 100,000 sq. miles.

Next day I lay at earth while Lloyd went up very early to the vicinity of our high camp to do a station. He had now more energy and went better than I who, after three not over strenuous months, suffered more and more from what one of the earliest climbers of Mont Blanc described as a 'lassitude which could not be conquered without the aid of liquor'—no less than forty-seven bottles of wine and brandy being required to overcome the lassitude of a party of eleven. When we returned to the attack we moved the high camp across to the other side of the wedge by traversing the rocks under the snout of the hanging glacier—on the face of it an unwise manoeuvre, but we moved quickly and kept well clear.

Some snow which fell in the night did not deter us from beginning the climb soon after 5 a.m. On this edge of the hanging glacier a wider band of rock gave us more freedom of choice and the rocks were more stable; only when we had climbed about 500 ft. did the band narrow and finally disappear under the encroaching ice. Here and there rocks still protruded. By using these and by cutting across the intervening ice we reached a steep snow slope below the point where the two sides of the wedge converged. This route, which avoided the ice-step, would, we think, have gone easily in better conditions, but the slope consisted of wet snow lying on ice in which steps would have to be cut, the thick layer of snow having first been cleared away. If similar conditions prevailed for another thousand feet, which was a fair assumption, then the task was too great. We gave up.

The whole party met for the last time at Kyangjin gompa preparatory to the departure of Lloyd and Scott the next day, 20 August. With the assistance of the British High Commissioner's office in Bombay and Delhi the assassin's stick-gun had at last reached us. Bird-skinner Toni (whom on account of his voracity I christened Wolfe Tone) could now begin making amends for his two months' idleness. After some wrangling over porters, for no one from Langtang seemed eager to visit his capital city, Lloyd and Scott started for the Gangja La and the direct route to Katmandu. Polunin with Toni went down the valley to spend a few days fossicking in the forest; while with two Sherpas I went to make a second and more thorough inspection of the col at the head of the West glacier.

Instead of going to Langsisa we stopped at a kharka short of the big moraine with the intention this time of going up the west glacier by the true right bank. The kharka was occupied by herdsmen who were already beginning to move the cattle down from the higher pastures against the approach of the autumn. They told us that in winter two or three feet of snow lie in the valley but that the people remain, most of the men occupying themselves with trade to Kyirong, using sheep for transport. Curiously enough they never seemed to use yaks for carrying. Even when moving up to the higher kharkas the men themselves carried their mats, flour, milking and cooking utensils. In the course of conversation these herdsmen confirmed the existence, or rather the recent presence, of the Abominable Snowman in the Langtang, pointing out to us a cave which had been his favourite haunt. Six years previously these beasts (whose existence is surely no longer a matter for conjecture) had been constant visitors but had apparently migrated elsewhere. The small kind, the size of a child, they called 'chumi', while the big fellow went by the name of 'yilmu'. Since sceptics like to affirm that the tracks made by these creatures are in reality bear tracks, it is worth mentioning that the herdsmen were able to show us some fresh bear tracks. It is noteworthy, too, that although bears were fairly common in the Langtang we saw no tracks on snow, which confirms the natural supposition that it is a rare occurrence for a bear to go above the snow-line. In the absence of rigid proof to the contrary, it is, therefore, safe to assume that if tracks are seen in snow they are not those of a bear.

We came to curse our unlucky choice of route. Though the moraine on the right bank of the glacier was bold and continuous, the long grass and boulders upon its crest constantly invited us to descend either to the glacier or to the ablation valley in search of better going; and having sampled both to return resignedly to the moraine. For most of the day it rained, so that having at last rounded the big bend we were glad enough to creep under a low rock overhang instead of pitching tents. This time, with more confidence than our earlier visit warranted, we took the camp right up to the col. Heavy work it was, too, for the leading man whose thirty-pound load ensured his feet sinking deep into the wet snow whether he trod with the utmost delicacy or stamped hard. We had all had enough by the time we made camp in a snow hollow at the foot of the rocks below the col.

After an unusually cold night, in which snow fell and froze on the tents, we spent a cold half-hour digging out the frozen guys and scraping off the snow preparatory to packing up. Having climbed to the col and dumped the loads, we had soon to acknowledge that our previous impression of the descent on the Tibet side was correct. It had looked difficult then and a closer examination confirmed it. A rib of snow, which early in the season might have taken us down, had turned to ice, and the rocks on either side, which I probed at the end of 120 ft. of rope, were as shifting as the sand. Nor could we see clear to the Chasuchen glacier, for before reaching it the slope heeled over out of sight. Altogether it was a place which we reluctantly decided a laden party had best leave alone.

Wet and defeated we trudged back to our dripping lair. Next day in heavy rain we retreated to the kharka and its store of dry firewood, and thence back to Langtang village. After an absence of nearly a month this appeared quite strange. The waving fields of wheat and kuru had become short stubble, and the remaining fields of ripening buckwheat had turned a bright sorrel. We had long since become acquainted with buckwheat flour which, in my opinion, when merely mixed with water and dropped on to a hot griddle, makes a delicious bread. The bitter tang of the upland variety should appeal to the masculine taste of a mountaineer brought up on glacier sludge and wild rhubarb; while the kind grown at lower altitudes, although free from bitterness, is not insipid. Altogether, it is a wholesome flour, so much lighter than wheat flour that great quantities can be swallowed without the consequences attendant upon cramming the stomach with distressful bread.

Threshing was in full swing, a task laboriously accomplished by hand instead of by the more usual way of driving teams of oxen or asses round a pole fixed in the middle of the threshing floor. Hard and monotonous though the work was, it did not seem to irk the half-dozen men and women standing in two rows each side of a heap of grain swinging their long-bladed flails to a rhythmic chant. Having taken a photograph of the threshing party I had to pay a forfeit, which I did by making a few experimental swipes with the flail. Much practice is needed to bring the blade down, as one must, parallel to the floor without stunning either oneself or one's neighbours.

Only the lieutenant was at Langtang, Polunin having not yet returned from his forest foray. My plan was to find a pass over to the Jugal Himal, the next group of peaks to the east, returning thence to Katmandu where I would meet Polunin about mid-September. Thus, on the point of quitting the Langtang for good, I got the lieutenant to accompany me to inspect the monastery, to say good-bye to the lama, and to make a suitable offering in return for the assistance we had received while in the valley.

It was, in fact, a dry sunny day, but our visit to the lama developed into a very wet morning. First we were shown over the monastery which, as befitted the sanctity of the Langtang, was in excellent preservation and contained some interesting things—among them a library of over two hundred books, long, wood-bound volumes each kept in its own curtained pigeon-hole. An even more treasured possession was a small brass model of a stupa studded with cat's-eyes and turquoises which had been brought from Nyenam (Kuti) by the founder of the monastery. Alongside the usual image of the Buddha reposed another of the first lama, the holy man who had discovered the valley by following his straying yak. Close by were the images of some terrific demoniacal gods who had to be propitiated with models of leaves and cornucopias covered with butter. These offerings were kept in an alcove below the image and changed annually. A drum, a few tattered and dirty 'thang-kas', twenty-five loads of butter over which our friend Nima Lama and the Tibetan lama from Kyirong were still bargaining, and a stuffed red pheasant, made up the furnishings. Perhaps in the interests of natural science I should have made a bid for the bird which, I thought, looked too bedraggled to be a welcome offering to the pundits of Cromwell Road.

Having done the honours of the gompa Nima Lama asked us to his house where his wife made us welcome with fresh buckwheat cakes and a relish of pounded chillies and salt. Tea, of course, was provided for all, but Nima and I devoted our attention to a wooden bottle of undeniable five-star arak conveniently placed between us. The tea, made in Tibetan fashion with butter, came fresh from the churn, a three-foot-long piece of bamboo of nine-inch bore which the operator held upright on the floor by means of a thong attached at the base in which she put her foot. The salty relish provoked a thirst which, thanks to Providence and Nima's foresight, we had the means of assuaging. Presently a second bottle replaced the first and the flood of miscellaneous information offered by Nima Lama and interpreted by the lieutenant, who wisely drank tea, seemed to be getting a little turbid; or perhaps the lama was lucid enough but my attention, distracted by the buckwheat cakes, did not strictly correlate the miscellaneous facts—the butter, saints, salt, red pheasants, straying yaks, ancient passes, Abominable Snowmen, bears, and the price of umbrellas in Katmandu. I managed to grasp his fairly lucid exposition of the trade cycle which began by sending butter to Kyirong where it was exchanged pound for pound with salt; the salt then being carried over the Gangja La to Helmu to be exchanged for rice, which rice was taken to Kyirong during the winter, when butter was scarce. But then, I recall, Nima began to relate an anecdote of how he had been the last man to cross the traditional pass in 1854 just before it was closed, accompanied by the now canonized Guru Rumbruche, then a very old man, carrying a load of salted rice done up in butter which they were going to exchange for twenty-five umbrellas at Kyirong. On the pass they met an Abominable Snowman riding the missing yak, which thereupon turned into a red pheasant which Guru Rumbruche shot with a catapult, thus incurring a fine of Rs.100—and if I cared to pay the fine I could have the pheasant, the very bird I had just been admiring in the gompa.

At this point Mrs Nima Lama removed the arak bottle and reminded her husband that he was due to start for a minor celebration in honour of one Gombu at a sacred rock a day's march up the valley. Preparations for this had been in active progress for a little time; that is to say six long baskets, built for back-packing, were being loaded with a few pitiful parcels of atta and some immense wooden jorums of beer—one halfpennyworth of bread, in fact, to an intolerable deal of sack. In turn the bearers of this precious freight bowed low to present a plateful of grain and a pat of butter to the Rev. Nima Lama, who sat with immense but slightly swaying dignity, and gave each a perfunctory blessing by clapping on their bowed heads three small pieces of butter. Greatly affected by this solemn scene the lieutenant and I bowed too, and withdrew swiftly with unbuttered heads.

CHAPTER VIII

THE JUGAL HIMAL

Thoughts of reaching the Jugal Himal had been in my mind since June, when the col we had glimpsed had dropped a hint of there being a way out to the east. Not only of reaching them but of climbing to a col on the frontier ridge, as we had in the Langtang, whence we might look into Tibet and perhaps pin down the elusive Gosainthan. I took Tensing and DaNamgyal, and two Langtang men volunteered to accompany us as far as Katmandu. These two provided themselves with Tibetan boots and the essential repair kit—needle and thread and spare bits of leather without which the life of such boots on rough going is a matter of days.

Having crossed the river by a bridge near the village we marched up the left bank bound for the east Langtang glacier. A boulder the size of a house afforded our first night's lodging, one side of it sheltering our party and the other a cheery party of men and women who were gathering and drying a bitter root called 'kuchi'. This is used as a febrifuge and fetches Rs. 19 a maund in Katmandu. A glorious evening succeeded by a clear night, and the impression that the river was falling, made me think that the monsoon was over and that we were about to enjoy some lovely autumn weather. An idea which had to be adjusted, for it hardly stopped raining until we reached Katmandu on 16 September.

We had hoped that by now the flowers would be beginning to seed, but there seemed to be a fresh flush. Dark blue and heliotrope carpets of delphiniums and asters covered the grass, and some of the rocks glowed warmly with a coat of bright pink vaccinium. Having traversed round the snout of the east glacier (the Brangbing) opposite Langsisa, we camped at the last grass short of the corner where the rock images of Shakya Muni and Guru Rumbruche stand guard. Upon rounding the corner we were obliged to quit the moraine to launch out on to a wild, tumbled sea of stones until at last we found smoother going on the far side. Late in the afternoon we camped on stones below the smooth ice tongue of a tributary glacier at whose head we hoped to find our pass.

After a coolish night in which a little snow fell we roused out early, but the Langtang men remained huddled under their blankets on a stone shelf they had built for themselves. Since their reluctance to rise was not attributable to the luxury of their couch, it could probably be accounted for by their realization that the Rubicon was at hand. Crossing this pass would bring us a day's march nearer home, but for them it meant a step into the unknown and a long severance from home. With great deliberation they made up their loads, but whether they intended to advance or retreat hung in the balance until a cheering gleam of light thrown by the rising sun upon the mountains opposite turned the scale in our favour. The sprinkling of snow helped us to climb the bare ice of the glacier tongue with a minimum of step-cutting, and the next half-mile of hard snow, sparkling in the early sun, led us easily to the col. From earlier disappointments we knew well that there are two sides to every col, so we pressed eagerly to the top to learn our fate. This time there was no doubt; a hundred feet or so of negotiable rock led to another glacier which, so far as one could tell, for the mist had begun boiling up, held no concealed ice-falls. The footgear of one of the men having already given out, his feet had to be swathed in strips of blanket for the walk down the glacier. After about a mile our glacier joined a bigger glacier near the cirque at its head, and we climbed on to the ancient moraine between the two to survey the scene. In a grass hollow, at a height of about 17,000 ft., lay two small lakes. Overlooking them stood a ruined cairn and close by, stuck upright in the grass, several rusty iron tridents. The Langtang men at once assumed we had reached the Panch Pokhari (Five Lakes), a noted place of pilgrimage of which they had heard; for in their eagerness to believe we were on known ground they readily overlooked the absence of three lakes. The 'trisuli', a name applied to both mountains and rivers of the Himalaya, is the symbol of the Hindu triad. Rarely does one find so high and yet so pleasing a place to camp as upon the banks of these lonely tarns, their still waters reflecting impartially the moods of the sky, and the air fragrant with the superb scent of the blue delphinium. But we did not stay, the aspect of the surrounding mountains discouraging any such plan.

If the roughness of the road they tread counts for righteousness, the pilgrims who once made these lakes their goal acquired much merit. Between them and the distant point where the moraine of the main glacier had to be quitted, lay a long stretch of rough, penitential surface, huge craters and hillocks of stone-covered ice, which, for men from the soft plains, must have been the equivalent of several weeks of hair-shirt wear. In and out of these stony craters we toiled for a long time before the moraine looked tempting enough to induce us to climb it. In the ablation valley beyond, cut off from the desolation of the glacier, we rejoiced in a new and better world of flowers and grass through which we sped in high spirits in a downpour of rain. In a short time we came upon a track and then a kharka with the frame of a shelter still standing. Covering this with the big ground sheet we soon had a fire going.

Early in the morning, before the clouds rolled up, Tensing and I climbed on to the moraine to see where we were. Not far away the glacier terminated and its waters drained south-east into a deep gorge. Beyond we could make out the dark cleft of the main valley, to all appearances an even deeper gorge, where, the rivers still running high, we could count upon meeting all sorts of trouble. Southwards from the kharka a well-defined path apparently followed the ridge lying parallel to the main valley to the Panch Pokhari. We were not long in making up our minds which way to go. Apart from our wish to see the sacred lakes, the path was a temptation which we did not try to resist. If the main valley could not be reached from above, why should we not enter it from below from the nearest village? According to the map there was a village called Tempathang on the east side of the valley close to a bridge; whence, from our experience of the Langtang and the Ganesh, we might expect to find a track to some high alp in the heart of the Jugal Himal.

Accordingly we packed up and began a march which was to last until nightfall. On we went, crossing a succession of small streams and sharp ridges, past many deserted kharkas, until at midday in thick mist we emerged upon a wide down. In the distance we could hear dogs barking. Just as a soldier cannot do wrong by marching towards the sound of the guns, so the traveller in unknown country cannot do better than march towards the sound of dogs, sheep, cattle, or any other

The track to Bimtakhoti leads through magnificent forest of black fir; this permits only occasional glimpses of Manaslu and its satellites; one of the more startling of these is seen here

The north ridge of Manaslu leading to the summit 'plateau' with the summit itself showing just to the right of the cloud pillar; the only recommendation for this long and difficult ridge is that one can at least get on to it by means of a col which lies hidden in the cloud on the left

token of human habitation. Unfortunately we neglected this rule and in our eagerness to reach the valley took a well-marked path leading downhill through straight-growing juniper trees and bamboo. After dropping very steeply for about a thousand feet, the path, evidently one used by shepherds cutting wood, petered out; and having wasted an hour over this, the first of several attempts to reach the valley, we resumed the march along the proper path in heavy rain.

About two o'clock we came to an occupied kharka where two loud-voiced Tamangs received us with less warmth than we thought our due. Having parted grudgingly with some curds they informed us in a hearty bawl that Panch Pokhari was 'not far away'—ominous words of encouragement, I thought, from men obviously anxious to see our backs. A little later we accosted a half-naked shrimp of a man who surprised us less by giving the same answer than by the extraordinary energy with which he gave it. I have often admired (for a short time at any rate) the loud, virile way in which Frenchmen and other Continentals converse, but these goatherds of the Panch Pokhari ridge seemed to be all descendants of Stentor who, I am told, had the voice of fifty men. At the next kharka, where there was a sodden, fireless hovel, I myself thought to galvanize the listless inmates with a hearty roar. Nobody took any notice except Tensing who was so startled that he hastily offered me a cold potato he had brought from Langtang. Indeed it was time for us to be settling down somewhere for a meal and to pass the night, and had not these men assured us in a powerful bellow that the lakes were now 'quite near' we should have stopped there, miserable though it was.

At dusk my drooping spirits were cheered by the sight of an old moss-grown chorten, and very faintly out of the mist and gathering dark came the bleating of sheep. When Tensing, who was far behind, had caught up I got him to try what he could do in the bellowing line; and upon getting a reply we headed into the mist away from the path, trusting that those behind would hear and act upon this long-range exchange. At last we came to a lake and by it a long matting shelter. Wading through a sea of sheep we went inside. No one got up to offer us a place by the meagre fire and no one offered to mend it until Tensing took the matter into his own hands and threw on an armful of logs. Even the uninvited guest is sometimes critical of his welcome; the shepherds of these parts, I reflected, are merely loud-spoken, churlish skinflints, all cry and little wool. But it has since occurred to me that if a couple of dripping strangers burst in about supper time to claim the best seats by the fire, at the same time heaving on a bucket of coal, my welcome to them might be cool. Yet the fact that both Tensing and I were disappointed by our welcome is a measure of the hospitality expected and nearly always received at the rough, kindly hands of Himalayan peasants and shepherds. Happy the countries where the people are so uncivilized that hospitality is not a virtue but second nature; the better for being accorded spontaneously, without the careful preparations we are often obliged to make when entertaining; the screwing of the host's mind to the requisite sticking point of geniality—and in due season the long premeditated revenge. Tensing's liberality with their firewood and the number of socks I peeled off made an impression. Perhaps it occurred to them that they might be entertaining angels unawares, so they presently got out their milk and butter and offered it at fully commensurate prices. But after such a long, wet day, seated in front of a blazing fire of which we had now pretty well taken possession, drinking hot tea, we could afford to ignore these little rubs as easily as we could ignore the rain hissing down pitilessly upon the wretched sheep outside.

Unlike the pilgrimage to the Gosainkund lake which is an annual affair, no pilgrims besides ourselves had visited Panch Pokhari that year. There are five shallow lakes and some shelters for the accommodation of pilgrims. These were unroofed, the roofing poles and planks being stacked inside like those of the huts of the Chilime valley. We resumed our walk along the ridge, having over our left shoulders the high tops of the Jugal Himal—from which we were drawing steadily away—rising grandly above the clouds. Presently we came to an open glade where another path crossed the ridge at right angles. We were now about level with Tempathang which lay immediately below us on our left, so we took this cross track and began plunging down through a thick forest of bamboo and fir. When we had gone too far to think of climbing back, the track divided. Having taken the steepest we were not long in coming to a rough bamboo shelter used by men engaged in cutting and stripping bamboo for weaving mats. It was deserted so we climbed back and tried the other path which, after luring us irretrievably deep into the jungle, ended at a similar hut. However, some embers still smouldered inside and in response to our shouts two men climbed up carrying long bundles, of thin, pliant bamboos. They laughed at our notion of finding a path through the forest to Tempathang—the proper path followed the ridge—but at the mention of money they pricked up their ears and thought there might be something in my proposal that they should carve a way down for us with their kukris. We were too far from Tempathang for that, they said, but for Rs. 3 they would put us on a path on the way to a kharka where we could spend the night. Girding up their loins—that is with their legs bared to the buttock—they shot off through the forest, slashing away bamboos and branches to ease our progress, though in fact it was so steep that we fell or slithered down through any obstructions. In half an hour we emerged on to a muddy track where cattle had recently passed. In a short time, they said, we should reach a kharka. Whereupon, feeling as grateful to them as if we were already there I handed them Rs.3. Justice should be tempered with doubt. We soon regretted this premature bestowal of their due. We had but to suggest withholding the reward until they had shown us something more reassuring than a miry and infrequently used path, and the clamour that would no doubt have ensued would have taught us how matters stood. Two hours later, having descended a thousand feet to a stream and having climbed a like amount out of it, we were still crawling up an apparently unending slope in heavy rain and gathering darkness. At last we came to the derelict moss-covered remains of a bamboo-cutter's shelter. After a long search we found a spring so we settled there for the night as best we could with soaking loads and bedding. There is no want like the want of a fire, and in a dripping forest, where rain has been falling for several weeks, the chances of satisfying it might seem to be slight. Every dead or fallen branch was, of course, sodden, but where there are bamboos one may always have a fire; for dead bamboo, even though the hollow inside is full of water, will burn. Very soon we had a cheerful blaze, the bamboos popping like pistols as the water inside boiled and the steam burst out.

In the morning, with rain still falling, we resumed the track which went up and up, until in two hour's time we came out on the ridge and the same well-defined track which we had quitted twenty-four hours earlier. At a kharka a mile on, perhaps that which we were to have reached the previous night, the track at last left the ridge for the valley; and after a steep descent of four or five thousand feet we came to the bridge and the maize fields of Tempathang, a small village inhabited by Sherpas. Tensing and Da Namgyal were, of course, at home and had there been anything worth eating in the village we might have had it. They could give us nothing but green mealie cobs and, what was worse, the information that there was no path up the valley; for their grazing alps had long since been abandoned, the track to them, through long disuse and fallen bridges, being no longer passable.

Having no time to test the truth of this statement, we started back next day with the intention of meeting Polunin who was coming out by the direct route to Katmandu over the Gangja La. Moving westwards across the grain of the country meant our having to cross four deep drainage troughs and their correspondingly high ridges. One night we would be sleeping among fir trees and rhododendrons and the next in a sub-tropical valley where rice, mangoes and even bananas grew. Before reaching the ridge along which lay the path to the Gangja La, we had to part company with one of the Langtang men whose feet had given out. We left him at a Sherpa village where the headman was connected by marriage with our old friend Nima Lama of Langtang with whom he, the headman, had one taste in common—a liking for arak. At the gompa a festival was in progress, indeed judging by the uproar it had been going on for some time. The headman did his best to make up for the unsocial behaviour of a rather strait-laced lama, a man more like a fakir wearing a bun of what looked like tow coiled on top of his head. In his very capable hands we soon absorbed a little of the festival spirit. With the necessary allowance for local conditions the people of these parts act upon the principle:

> There's nought so much the spirit calms
> As rum and true religion.

We waited for the main body at the village of Tharke Ghyang in the Helmu district. It is a big village of some five hundred inhabitants, few of whom can have refrained from putting their heads inside my tent very soon after our arrival. They had, I think, less admiration for its internal arrangements than for my stoicism in supporting the conditions inside. Indeed, after two days of continuous rain, I was compelled to pitch the tent afresh under a roof. This arrangement gave more privacy, but short of posting sentries the headman had no power to restrain their curiosity. He made amends by inviting me to his house where we drank Tibetan tea unwatched by intruders. Like most Helmu women his wife was good-looking and kept house admirably. All her brass or copper pots, pans and utensils—and there were many— gleamed brightly in their allotted places.

I was housed close by the monastery, a building half corrugated iron and half picturesque decay. Under the sound roof reposed the show piece, a prayer wheel of crudely ornamented brass about ten feet high and eight in diameter. The walls of the room where this monster revolved were being redecorated under the direction of a Tibetan lama who drew the designs and supervised their painting by six local artists. Besides the conventional portraits of the Buddha, his disciples, the Wheel of Life, and some domestic scenes which were 'resolutely and offensively coarse', the lama's rampant imagination delighted in hairy monkeys, sea serpents and leopards He depicted one leopard balancing head downwards on an eight-leaved lotus. The lama thus earned money to help him on his pilgrimage to the Buddhist shrines of India; a devout purpose which I, too, was expected to forward. And I was ready enough to help a man who so well understood the art of travel that he had already passed two years in accomplishing a journey which normally takes ten days.

Having joined forces with Polunin's party, we continued down the ridge between the Malemchi and Indrawati rivers until near their junction, where we crossed the former by a chain bridge. Such 'ridgeways' are common in these parts where the valley routes, especially in summer, are liable to interruption either from landslides or from the numerous side-streams, few of which are bridged. Immediately after crossing the Malemchi we were confronted by one of these insignificant side-streams in spate. It would have brought us to a full stop but for the timely help of four local men who carried the whole party, even the Langtang men, across on their backs. The next day we crossed the Sheopuri Lekh to enter the Katmandu valley at the north-eastern end by a track which crosses the dam of the Sundari power-station. Silt brought down by the recent flood had put this temporarily out of action. And so on 16 September, strolling through the yellowing rice fields of the valley, we brought our journey to an end.

From the feast of mountains spread before us, Lloyd and I had come more or less empty away—a well-merited rebuke, perhaps, for attempting to prostitute art to science. But there were other reasons, one being that handy scapegoat the weather which can be invoked to conceal our weakness or to prove our indomitable spirit. Although weather conditions during the monsoon are seldom good, up to the present most Himalayan climbing has been undertaken during the summer months. The pre-monsoon period is too short, a month to six weeks at the most. April, or even early May, are too soon to start because the remaining winter snow hinders the approach and increases the avalanche danger, and on big mountains it is too cold. In theory the post-monsoon period is longer, say at a maximum from mid-September to mid-November, but climbing is liable to be brought prematurely to an end by an early fall of winter snow, such as the three-day storm in mid-October 1929 which rendered so hazardous the retreat of the Bavarians from the north-east spur of Kangchenjunga. On three occasions only have big or fairly big mountains been climbed in the autumn. On 20 October 1907 the Norwegians Rubenson and Monrad Aas failed by only 100 ft. to climb Kabru (24,263 ft.); in 1935 the same mountain was climbed by C. R. Cooke and a Sherpa on as late a date as 18 November; and on 5 November 1937 Brig. John Hunt climbed the south-west summit of Nepal Peak (23,500 ft.). Both mountains are in Sikkim where the monsoon is as heavy as it is in Nepal. In recording his climb Brig. Hunt remarked: 'The factors of deep snow (the result of a heavy fall in early October) and high winds affected considerably our efforts at the time, and loom large in my general impressions of our winter visit to the Zemu glacier. Should this heavy precipitation be a regular feature of the late monsoon in this part, and assuming that high winds are normal, then there are serious objections to high ascents at this time of year.' What it amounts to is that seasonal weather is rather less predictable than weather day by day. It is a lottery, and it is better so. If climbing could be done always under a blazing sun, on windless days, on hard snow and warm rock, it would have little merit, and many aspiring spirits would find, like Othello, their occupation gone.

There is much to be said for and against climbing during the monsoon months. Snow precipitation is not as great as might be expected; at high altitudes a heavy fall in October or November may exceed that which falls during the whole monsoon period. At least my own limited experience points that way; had I climbed on Nanga Parbat, which seems to receive some overwhelming summer snowfalls, I might think otherwise. The unreasonable warmth such as we met with certainly precludes the danger of frostbite; on the other hand, it may so increase the danger of falling stones and ice as to deny even the making of an attempt upon certain routes. The extremely poor visibility which hampered us is mostly peculiar to the eastern half of the Himalaya where the monsoon is heaviest. It is a depressing feature. After a succession of blind days one begins to fear that reconnaissance, let alone climbing, is impossible. But all things, including a break in the monsoon, come to him who knows how to wait, thus in attempting to climb unknown mountains time is an important factor. In summer a party should have ample time, whereas before the monsoon it is in a desperate hurry to finish the climb before it breaks. Perfunctory methods are seldom advisable when dealing with mountains, yet—to revert to our attempts—I felt that we were trying to take peaks, so to speak, in our stride. Rather than court it in proper form we preferred to pass on, hoping that some other peak would surrender at sight. When this did not happen and when our time was nearly up, we were obliged to make a more serious, yet a too hasty bid for the Fluted Peak in the worst conditions.

Singleness of purpose is a sound principle. The killing of two birds with one stone, however desirable, is seldom achieved intentionally and never by aiming consciously at both. I am not implying that the presence of the collectors or the strong whiff of science which pervaded the party impaired our aim, but that a lot of luck will be needed if the climbing of a good peak is to be included in the exploration of a large, mountainous area.

Although the mountaineers had thus come hungry away, the bellies of the scientists had been filled with good things. Not that this really applies to field collectors like Polunin and Scott, for with the field collector, as with the honey-bee, it is a case of *sic vos non vobis*. Perhaps the irreverent or the uninstructed will ask, like little Peterkin: 'But what good came of it at last?' And personally, in the role of old Kaspar, I should have to answer: 'Why that I cannot tell.' A similar reply might be made by the field collector himself who, unless he has the time and ability to attend to it himself, may not live to see his collection neatly arranged and ticketed. When specimens are swallowed in the maw of that vast repository of the dead in Cromwell Road, their digestion, for various good reasons, is a properly deliberate affair. Along with thousands of others of their kind from many outlandish parts of the world, Polunin's hardly-won harvest of plants, his butterflies and toads, his slightly ruffled birdskins, must there await their resurrection; their sorting and classifying by expert and critical hands, quick to reject the unworthy or to consign the uncouth specimen to a fiery doom. Severe is the scrutiny of the high priests of science and unblemished must be the offerings laid upon her altars by the neophyte.

As for Scott's rocks, specimens less subject to the vicissitudes of time and chance, a few, after being sawn, polished, and scrutinized under microscopes, may perhaps find an honourable tomb at St Andrews in a glass case, to be looked at, one hopes, by earnest disciples of William Smith on days when it is too wet for golf.

PART TWO

Annapurna Himal

1950

CHAPTER IX

THE START

———◆———

THE DOOR TO THE NEPAL HIMALAYA having been opened I felt it should, if possible, be kept open. So upon paying my farewell respects to H.H. the Maharajah I asked tentatively for permission to go next year (1950) to the Annapurna Himal. Napoleon, on the eve of a campaign, used to place his finger on the map and remark quietly to his awestruck staff that there on such and such a date he would fight a victorious and decisive battle. An intelligent appreciation enabled him to forecast events, to select time and place, and to lay his plans accordingly. Although they are in constant practice, our honourable mandarins seldom plan so precisely as this; and all that I could achieve after the Master's model was to put a finger on the map and suggest hesitatingly to myself that there in 1950—weather and world situation permitting—a campaign of some sort, probably indecisive, ought to take place. 'There' happened to be the Annapurna Himal, because on the map that region seemed to be the most mountainous of a singularly mountainous country.

The Himalayan Committee followed this private approach with a formal application. The favourable reply came so late that little more than a month remained to collect a party and stores and to arrange the necessary passages for April. My intention had been to take a small party such as had previously wandered unobtrusively in the Langtang Himal, collecting plants and birds, battering rocks, amending the existing maps, but attempting no great mountains. Such aims may be thought paltry for a rude and hardy mountaineer but they are aims which, as I have pointed out, facilitate the raising of funds; and are, perhaps, proper enough for a man (like the sage in *Rasselas*) 'whose years have tamed his passions without clouding his reason'.

However, the Himalayan Committee, having in mind the necessity of building up a nucleus of experienced Himalayan climbers such as had existed between the wars, preferred to send a larger party. In the thirties several British parties visited the Himalaya every year, but since the war there have been few. Unsettled conditions and greatly increased costs have been a deterrent. Indeed in recent years too few British climbers have gone even to the Alps, for it is there and not in the Himalaya where technique is learnt and where climbing experience can be quickly gained.

Since 1947 the Swiss have sent four successful parties to the Himalaya, and this year (1950) the French and the Norwegians have re-entered the field and scored great achievements. There is no harm in applying the spur of national rivalry to Himalayan climbing so long as the principles of sound mountaineering are kept steadily in mind. Though it may be desirable, it is exceptional for successful climbing parties to be of mixed nationality, for a party composed of friends who have climbed together before or men who have been brought up in the same climbing traditions is inherently stronger.

In these post-war years life is so real and so earnest, especially for the inmates of a Welfare State, that one hesitates a long time before asking a man to squander money and time on a Himalayan trip. A hollow laugh or a shocked hoist of the eyebrows is the reply one expects and usually gets, according to the man's circumstances and moral outlook. Nevertheless, in a short time I had found five who were free to come and who were reckless or depraved enough to brush aside all impediments. Col. D. G. Lowndes, who had spent most of his life in India with the Garwhal Rifles and had travelled widely in the hills, came as botanist. Major J. O. M. Roberts, M.C., of the 1/2nd Gurkhas managed to obtain leave, and since he spoke Gurkhali and had been on several Himalayan trips, including the attempt on Masherbrum (25,660 ft.) in 1938, he was a sound choice. Dr C. H. Evans, as well as being an experienced climber, gave to the party the comforting insurance of medical aid. Honour a physician according to thy need of him, saith the Preacher, but it was not Evans's fault that we needed him most after he had left us. J. H. Emlyn Jones, M.B.E., an experienced Alpine climber, launched a spirited and successful blow at the chains which bound him to a surveyor's office; and to complete the party we had a young New Zealand Rhodes Scholar, W. P. Packard, who had climbed much in New Zealand before becoming a student of geography at University College, Oxford. He, too, was tied by economic and

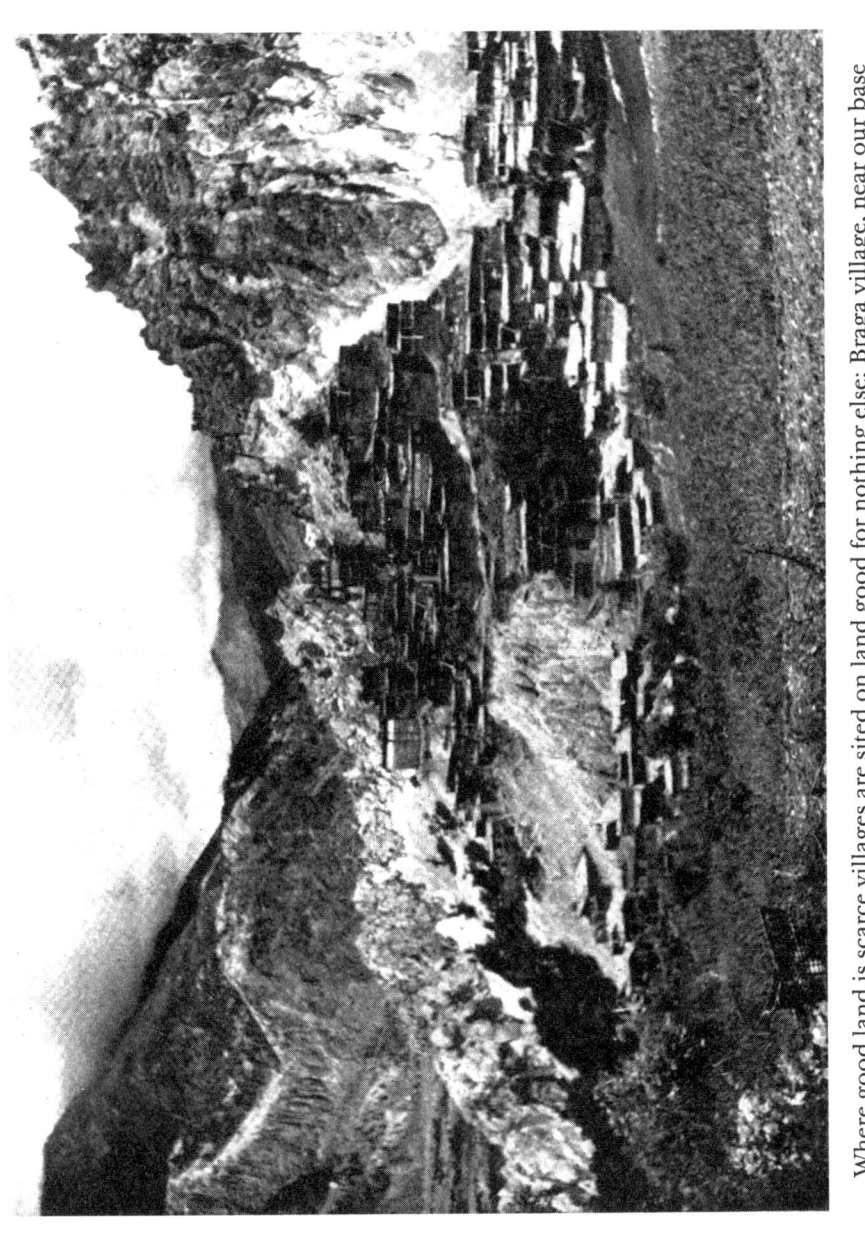

Where good land is scarce villages are sited on land good for nothing else; Braga village, near our base camp, is a good example of this rule; the building with the broad white band below the roof is the gompa

From our base camp in this glade we looked across the valley to Annapurna IV, the snow peak in the middle of the ridge; prominent to the right is the 'snow dome', and our route lay along the ridge leading up to it from left to right; the ice step, which took two days to climb, is two-thirds of the way to the 'dome' and looks merely like a steeper bit of the ridge

academic chains which were not easily broken. That three of the six names have a Welsh flavour was merely coincidence and not a retort to an all-Scottish party which was then being organized. Lowndes, reasonably enough, disliked being considered a handmaid of science so that, in effect, her sole servant was Packard. Even his allegiance was not complete, for we had a private agreement that he should set foot on at least one mountain. Originally I had hoped that he would undertake some survey work, such work having the merit of producing results which can be understood and which may be of value. But the only light photo-theodolite in England, one which could be carried up a mountain, was earmarked for another expedition, so instead Packard undertook the study of land utilization and soil erosion which were his special subjects. Himalayan villages are so remote that they are not likely to reap any practical benefit from such enquiry; but, perhaps, on that account it will be no less gratifying to our world planners. Even had the theodolite been available our late arrival in the field, coupled with Packard's early departure, would have prevented our using it to much effect in the short time available before the onset of the monsoon; for although the cloud canopy in the Annapurna during the monsoon is neither so dense nor so consistent as in the Langtang, it is bad enough to preclude survey work. There is nothing more baffling for the surveyor than

> Mountains on whose barren breast
> The labouring clouds do often rest.

Apart from snowshoes, which we never used, and pack-boards, our equipment contained nothing new. In the Annapurna range flattish, névé-covered glaciers, where snowshoes can be used with advantage, proved to be conspicuously absent. The pack-boards were massive structures of the Yukon type, built evidently for professional packers, old timers, 'forty-niners', and such like, men who could 'take it' in every sense. The boards themselves weighed nine pounds. Nevertheless the Sherpas and in time even the local coolies grew fond of them. Provided the canvas back is kept really taut they make a very comfortable load; a lighter type made of plywood should be excellent. Most of us took nailed boots as well as the moulded rubber 'Vibram' type, suggesting that while we wished to move with the times we had not enough confidence in the new to discard the old. For rough walking the 'Vibram' soled boot is more comfortable than the nailed. It is supreme for that everyday Himalayan pastime of boulder-hopping (provided the boulders are dry), and is generally suitable for climbing except on wet rock, wet ice, or fresh snow on rock. It is a matter of taste. Provided one is aware of their limitations and uses care—which, whatever his footgear, a climber must always do, placing his feet circumspectly though not meticulously—they are as good as nailed boots and sometimes better.

The French moralist Vauvenargues remarked that great thoughts come from the stomach. An eighteenth-century French writer is not every man's fireside study—till this minute I had not heard of him—and while we can afford to disregard a Frenchman writing about morals, we cannot when he writes about the stomach. A remark so profound evidently comes from a man of deep insight and robust appetite; and whether true or not there is no doubt about the converse—that great thought should be bestowed on the stomach—especially with a large party, that is a party of more than one, when it becomes necessary to take thought as to what the others shall eat. Of mountaineers in general it cannot be said that:

> Life is with such all beer and skittles,
> They are not difficult to please
> About their victuals.

Or, as the Chinese sage puts it more succinctly, 'a full belly is the great thing; all else is luxury'. Some are prepared to swallow large quantities of the fundamentals, such as bread and rice, provided there is a little something sweet or spicy to assist the swallowing. Others say, give us the luxuries and we will dispense with the necessities, or in other words they like a little bread with their butter and/or jam. Having no great love for austerity I sympathized with them, and since the Annapurna are not so difficult to reach that every extra pound taken becomes a matter of concern, we took luxuries enough and lived uncommonly well.

Perhaps this bald statement, at which some might marvel, should be supported by a few figures. It is a little distasteful to mingle food with figures. I hold strongly with the Albanian proverb, 'When travelling

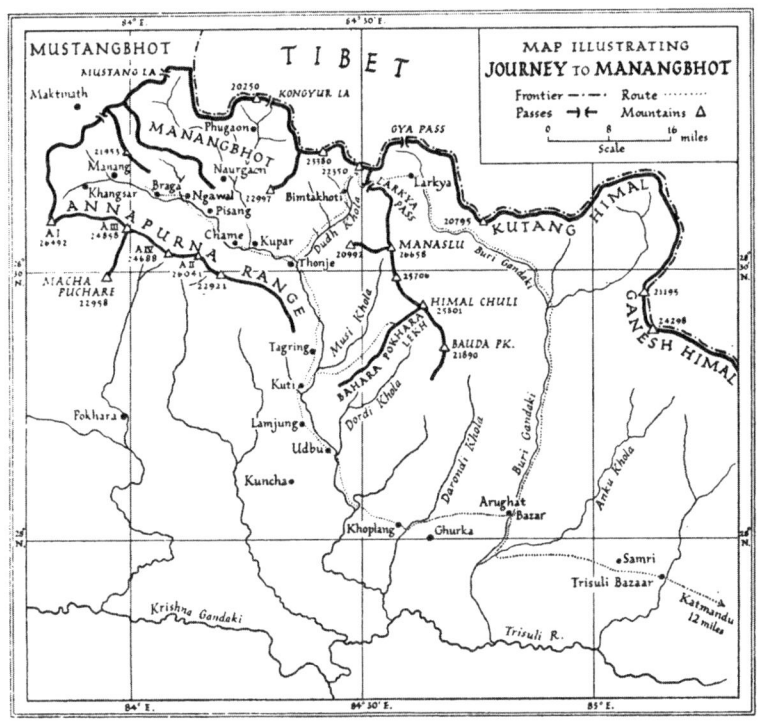

Map 4: Journey to Manangbhot

don't reckon the distance and when eating never reckon the amount.' Unhappily such generous advice cannot be followed on an expedition, or, for that matter, under present conditions at home. Apart from solids we took a total of 190 lb. of trimmings—cheese, butter, jams, peanut butter, raisins, chocolate, and dried egg—which for the time spent in the field, 700 man-days, worked out at three ounces a day of one or the other. We were fortunate in having genuine Cheddar cheese which I had not smelt since 1939—in glorious and happy contrast with the cheese we took to the Langtang, red plastic bricks, thoughtfully wrapped in cellophane as a warning that they should not be touched. For hard living above the snowline we had biscuit and pemmican, and enough sugar to allow each man five ounces a day throughout the trip. We even brought some sugar back, an event rather to be wondered at than acclaimed. The solid setting for these gastronomic pearls was rice, more or less *ad lib.*, bread, limited by the size of loaf one could bake, and whatever could be picked up locally such as potatoes, lentils, buckwheat, milk, more butter, occasionally meat, very occasional game and beer, which many consider a food. On the whole it strikes me as the conception of a liberal mind, a diet adapted to meet the needs of the fastidious glutton and the voracious epicure. How different from that of the Antarctic traveller who, on his sledge journeys at any rate, lives on biscuit, pemmican, chocolate, butter, cocoa, un-alleviated by bread or even rice. Of all who face discomfort for fun or in pursuit of knowledge the Himalayan traveller enjoys the least deprivation and deserves the least sympathy.

 Three of the party and all the baggage went to Bombay by sea. Of necessity the sea is much used by an island race, but Mr Woodhouse with whom, except in the matter of gruel, I often agree, once observed that he had long been convinced that the sea was very rarely of use to anybody. It would be unjust perhaps to blame the sea for what was the fault of the ship, for she started late and lost us a week which we could ill afford. As she had originally been billed to sail on Good Friday, I thought this mishap might be only the first of a series of disasters ending with her final disappearance in mid-ocean. But nothing more happened. I went direct to Calcutta by air, ostensibly to pick up the Sherpas and the accursed stick-gun, in reality to avoid the task of seeing rather more than a ton of baggage across India. Lowndes, the seasoned Indian traveller, undertook that and had reason to regret it. Crossing India by train in the month of April is hot work, and our party of four found it hotter than usual owing to their compartment going up in flames somewhere the wrong side of Lucknow. This caused more delay, and the loss of some kit which was borne with equanimity since most of it belonged to Roberts. He met me at Calcutta and together we awaited the others at Raxaul. When they eventually did arrive, they looked like men who had gone through fire and water, as indeed they had. Those of us who were meeting for the first time struggled to conceal their dismay and to put a bright face on the matter.

The party was now complete, our four Sherpas having wisely elected to come direct from Darjeeling to Raxaul without going through the mild hell of a journey to Calcutta. Since partition this journey, formerly a simple one-night affair, involves two crossings of the India-Pakistan frontier with all that that implies. Recently, by linking up various almost unexplored branch lines and arranging a ferry service over the Ganges, the Indian railway authorities have contrived a way round which goes to Siliguri (for Darjeeling) and thence to Assam. This is known as the 'Assam Link', but it is a pretty frail link. It is the sort of journey undertaken only by those in their first youth when the years stretch unendingly ahead; the rest, if they can afford it, save much time and more vexation by going by air.

On 5 May we reached Katmandu where Lady Falconer assumed the burden of looking after four of us at the Embassy, Col. Proud taking the other two to his house. The intervention of the week-end and some trouble in pinning down the coolie contractor prevented our leaving before the 10th, ten days later than I had planned. Even so there was enough to do and much hospitality to be enjoyed in the four days allowed. With the help of Col. Proud we contracted for fifty coolies at Rs. 2.25 (about 3s. 6d.) a day, half-rate for their return unladen, and they to find their own food. Lieut. S. B. Malla, at my request, was again detailed to accompany us, so with his sepoys and our coolies we were about sixty strong.

At the beginning of such a journey one should, of course, be on fire to start, the feet tingling to tread the trail, the back itching for its unaccustomed load, a fierce contempt for motorcars uppermost in one's mind. Nevertheless we gladly accepted a lift as far as Baleji water garden. Here we sorrowfully took to our feet, remarking with ill-disguised apprehension the length, the height, and the shadelessness of the Sheopuri Lekh over which we must that day go. The coolies whom we had seen out of the compound much earlier in the day, and who should have half finished their task, apparently felt much the same, for they sat smoking under a giant pipal tree whose shade they were loath to quit. Having admonished them without effect we retired to the water garden where we envied the giant carp floating idly in the still pool, and photographed once again the recumbent Narayan on his stone bed of cobras. Two live snakes flickered about his feet, for the statue which should have been mostly submerged was now mostly exposed. Few statues can stand this; the majority, and this one was no exception, are better submerged.

Having thus wasted much time and the best part of the day, we at last straggled off across the flat valley and began the long ascent. After suffering fully as much as we had anticipated we stopped at our old camp site under Kaulia hill where the Sherpas put up our brave array of bright green tents. There was one for each of us—small Meades, big Meades, and a gigantic Whymper tent for the botanist. Scientists, even mere collectors, must have room to work and think, and space for their appliances. Lowndes with his museum boxes neatly arranged as bedside table, dressing table, work table, and party wall, thus occupied a sort of mansion. Around this was a suburb of humbler dwellings, some of which, by reason of their occupant's habits, ranked almost as slums. In contrast with that of Emlyn Jones, who in spite of having a great deal had a place for everything and everything in its place, was my own abode, which resembled a hurrah's nest—everything on top and nothing at hand—the whole generously sprinkled with spent matches and tobacco ash.

Our route diverged from that of 1949 at Trisuli Bazaar where we arrived next day to be welcomed by Trisuli Trixie and the usual crowd. This year we were eighteen days earlier, a difference in time reflected in the state of the river which was now lower and almost blue, the melting snow having not yet had time to discolour it. The altitude here is under 2000 ft.

The sultry weather, and the muck-sweat in which we arrived enhanced the delights of leaping into this cool, bright river. Some of the party, however, were already feeling the heat, for they arrived late along with the coolies. These men have their own pace which neither threats nor cajolery can alter. So long as the day's destination is agreed upon before starting—a point upon which opinions will need to be reconciled—it is foolish to worry about the coolies who nine times out of ten will in time cast up. On the other hand the experienced traveller never feels at ease far from his baggage; he wants it in early, especially if there is rain about; and so the prudent man frequently loiters along with the coolies though he well knows that his presence will not hinder them from sitting down any less frequently. Like the Egyptians, their strength is to sit still.

The man who elects to march with Nepalese coolies will find their behaviour unusually exasperating, because in central Nepal the opportunities for sitting down in comfort are too numerous. The proverb that 'he who sits upon a stone is twice glad' is not applicable in warm countries such as Nepal where much time is spent resting upon what are known as 'chautaras'—the coolies' joy and the traveller's bane. In this pleasant land where all loads are carried upon men's backs, where the tracks are rough and steep and the days hot, various pious and public-spirited men—of whom in my opinion there have been too many—perpetuate their names by planting two fast-growing shady trees and building round them a rectangular or sometimes a circular stone dais with a lower parapet as a seat.

These trees, which are believed by natives to be the male and female of the same species, are usually a pipal (*Ficus religiosa*) and a banyan (*Ficus bengalensis*). The pipal, which has a round leaf terminating in a spike, is sacred to both Hindu and Buddhist. It was under a pipal tree at Bodh Gaya, one of the holiest places in the Buddhist world, that Prince Gautama obtained enlightenment and became the Buddha. Hindus hold that Brahma lives at the root, Vishnu in its stem, and Siva at the top. The banyan, which is also sacred to Hindus, has a similar leaf except for the spike and sends down aerial roots. The roots of the chautara banyan are lopped, but Hooker records a banyan tree in the Botanical Gardens, Calcutta, which shaded an area 300 ft. in diameter.

Both banyan and pipal grow quickly into wide-branching giants under whose grateful shade some dozens of coolies can take their ease, their loads off their backs and their weight off their feet. For in a well-built chautara the parapet is so nicely adjusted that as a man comes to rest against it, like a ship to a quayside, the parapet receives his bottom and the dais his load. Much thought is bestowed upon the site; an open space commanding a view, the top of any steep ascent, or the vicinity of a spring is sure to have its chautara. The name of the pious benefactor is often carved on one of the stones. There is never any lack of them on a much-used track. On long ascents they occur frequently and sometimes they are spaced at such regular intervals that the distance to a place may be reckoned in so many halts of chautaras, for no laden coolie would be so impetuous as to pass one by. This interval is about half-a-mile—a distance which a laden man would cover in perhaps a quarter of an hour, by which time his back is thought to be in need of straightening. There is a Nepali proverb—or if there isn't there should be—that the sight of a chautara makes the coolie's back ache. (Derived, of course, from the Bengali proverb that the sight of a horse makes the traveller lame.)

Such an abundance of wayside impediments added to the normal retarding effect of a sixty-pound load reduce the average speed of a Nepali coolie to one and a half miles per hour, so that few Europeans have the patience to stay with them to keep an eye on their baggage. Until one reaches a mature age, say ninety or more, it is difficult to conform to this pace. Should one insist on being a patient ass and marching (save the mark) with the baggage, the only way to obtain peace of mind is to assume the ass's burden. And then even a modest forty-pound load makes the coolies' pace too brisk and the distance between chautaras seem almost interminable.

There is a modified chautara, without any banyan tree, to be seen nearer home—on the Green Park side of Piccadilly. In 1861, at the suggestion of R. A. Slaney, Esq., M.P. for Shrewsbury, the Vestry of St George's, Hanover Square, put up a stone rest 'for the benefit of porters and others carrying burdens'. I have never had the luck to see it being used either by porters or by anyone else; not even by members of the Alpine Club, although their headquarters are not far away and although this same stone is on the direct route across the Green Park to Victoria and the Alps. Such men may be seen carrying a heavy rucksack, but doubtless they are too proud to be seen resting it.

CHAPTER X

THE MARSYANDI

A TRAVELLER CROSSING NEPAL from east to west cuts across the grain of the country, for nearly all the rivers flow southwards from the Himalaya to the plains of India. Before dropping into the valley of the Marsyandi which would lead us to the Annapurna Himal, we had to cross two other great drainage troughs, both part of the Sapt Gandaki system, the Trisuli and the Buri Gandaki. The Trisuli now lay behind us but we had several lesser tributary valleys as well as the Buri Gandaki ahead, so that in the first ten days we had a lot of up-and-down work in which we lost rather than gained height. We enjoyed a daily change of climate, camping sometimes in a warm valley below 2000 ft. and sometimes on cool ridges at 5000 ft. On the map each day's march looked pitifully short. But in such country there is no monotony. Up to the ridge ahead or down to the next river there is always something to go for and something fresh to see. Let the saddle-sore cyclist caper joyfully across the flat, but for the man on foot, the more broken the country the better. He sees not whither he must go nor whence he has come; neither far enough ahead, nor behind, to modify his cheerful estimate of the distance run or to be done. When on foot

... I do not want to see
The distant scene; one step enough for me.

But man is a creature of his environment. However reasonable and true such ideas are to a man seated in a chair, they take on a different hue when the same man is 'bummelling' along the tracks of Nepal. Witness the notes made of one march—'up a steep narrow track, like walking in a sewer, 500 stone steps up to Samri—no view—2000 ft. down—hellish steep and rough track—porters slow—no view—no bananas—no raksi'. The broken nature of the country seems to have struck the writer as an offence and the absence of food and drink as a stumbling-block.

In Nepal one can live off the country in a sombre fashion, but it is no place in which to make a gastronomic tour. There are no wayside shops as in Sikkim where one can drink sweet tea or sip maize beer through bamboo tubes; no hospitable villagers who in Tibet dispense buttered tea and blood and buckwheat cakes as a matter of course; no yorts overflowing with cream, yoghourt, and hot barley bread as in Sinkiang; and no apples, pears, peaches, apricots, fresh or dried, such as one stuffs oneself with in Hunza. May, of course, is a bad month for fruit, but outside the valley there is little to be had except bananas and small oranges. Coming back in September we ate a great many of these. Even on a main route such as we were on—to Gurkha, Kuncha and Pokhara—there were no wayside stalls where tea and chapatties might beguile the tedium of the way. Occasionally at some favourite chautara where coolies gathered in great numbers there might be a few women from a nearby village selling rice beer from large wooden jorums. At every likely place we raised the cry of 'dai'* but rarely did we obtain this incipient yoghourt, thin and watery but refreshing. Roberts, too, would appeal eloquently, frequently, and often successfully for raksi, a spirit made indifferently from rice, maize, millet, potatoes or pretty well anything that grows. When it was good, which was seldom, we concluded that the ingenuity of man and the bounty of nature had rarely been put to better use.

What with casting about like questing hounds for these finer products of the country, or waiting by chautaras for one of the sepoys to return, usually empty-handed, from a like quest, the day passed quickly. Roberts had long chats with the many Gurkha soldiers either going on leave or returning; the astonishment of a man who came from the same battalion, as one or two of them did, meeting one of his officers so far inside Nepal was extreme. (Hitherto visiting British officers of Gurkha regiments have been confined to the terai or Katmandu itself.) We enjoyed two odd encounters; one with the Sherpa and his wife who had acted for us as corn and rice merchants in the Langtang the previous year; and another with a man who claimed to be Nain

---

* Dai mixed with gur and water is a good drink. 'Gur' is the unrefined sugar, like fudge, made locally. 'With a lump of gur in one hand and a stone in the other' is a proverbial Pathan expression, descriptive of a diplomatic approach.

Looking north across the Marsyandi valley from Camp II; the Naurgaon peak (22,997 ft.) can be seen on the left, and Manaslu, with a cloud girdle, on the right; the scaly looking ridge in front of it leads up to Annapurna II

A similar view from below Camp III; the snow slopes coming into view on the right are the north face of Annapurna II; they are relentless and continuous

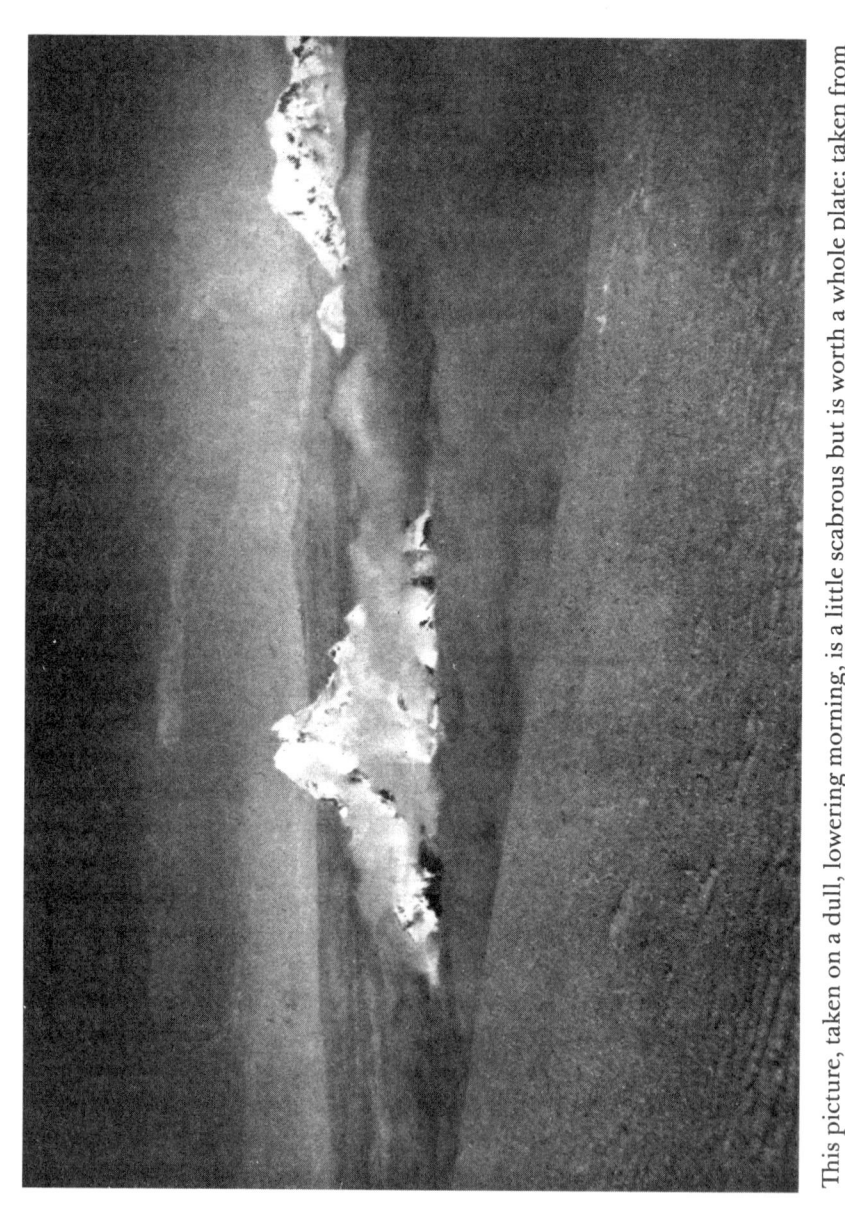

This picture, taken on a dull, lowering morning, is a little scabrous but is worth a whole plate; taken from the main ridge above Camp IV it shows the remarkable 'Fishtail' (Macha Puchare) floating on a sea of cloud

Singh, one of the Gurkha N.C.O.s who had been to Everest with either the 1922 or 1924 party. If he was then he had certainly worn very well.

What cannot be mended must be enjoyed. We accommodated ourselves to the dignified pace of the porters and spent much time standing and staring, foregoing any expectation of seeing them arrive before 3 p.m., more often 5 p.m. Occasionally we saw a few of them before that. During a long midday halt word would go round that the leading coolies had reached the last chautara, whereupon we would hastily organize a sweepstake, the winning ticket bearing the name of the coolie who first hove in sight. Only some six out of the fifty odd were well enough known or considered likely to be in the running. Indeed it was only by coming in very early or damnably late that a man stood out from the ruck. Whoever drew the man known as 'Cheese' was thought to have a winning chance; for 'Cheese' carried a load which, owing to the warm weather, was an incubus which any man would wish to shed as quickly as possible. Any one of the 'Sugars' was a strong favourite, a sugar bag of ½ cwt. making a very compact load.

As well as our own small escort commanded by Lieut. Sher Bahadur Malla we had a local escort for our passage through each district. With one notable exception the men did no service for us personally, but they formed an inexpensive ornament to our train and no doubt assisted our harassed headman of coolies to buy food for his hungry half hundred. The exception was the escort from District No. 2 West which included a 'shikari'. This man, with the aid of an ancient muzzle loader and a caged 'call' bird, supplied us with a brace of black partridges every day he was with us. Having shot a partridge, he opened its head and gave the brains to the Judas bird as a reward for its betrayal.

The boundary of District No. 2 West is the Buri Gandaki river which we reached on the fifth day, to camp in a mango tope by the river at a place called Arughat Bazar. Except for what we could learn from the map we knew nothing of the Marsyandi route or of the Annapurna Himal, and having no agreed plan to which we must adhere we were tempted to strike up the Buri Gandaki where mountains seemed plentiful and were more quickly reached. We began to feel troubled by the length of the approach march and its persistently low level. Here we were, already five days out, still under 2000 ft., and in five more marches we should be no higher. Whereas by turning up the Buri

Gandaki we might gain height at once and finish the march in a week. However, we stuck to our course, which was perhaps as well. Three of the party who later returned down the Buri Gandaki found the going bad, and food and transport scarce.

Next day from a camp (Khanchok) on a ridge at 4000 ft. we had a clear view of Himal Chuli (25,801 ft.) nearly thirty miles to the north. This mountain did not exactly lie in our path, but with a few limitations we were prepared, like Hamlet's French falconers, to fly at anything we saw. Binoculars and monoculars were trained on its glistening spire, but even at thirty miles, a distance at which most mountains are easily climbable, we had doubts about Himal Chuli. Just to its south lay a beautiful snow peak called Baudha (21,890 ft.) presenting to us an apparently easy ridge; but such was the loftiness of our thoughts at that time that we gave it only a passing glance. Four months later when we were looking for a peak we could climb, Roberts and I regretted this oversight. Neither of us could remember whether Baudha had looked climbable or not.

Upon Baudha's snow slopes and glaciers rises the Darondi Khola in which we enjoyed some of the best bathing of the march. The river flowed through a grassy vale overlooked by a wooded ridge, several thousand feet above, upon the top of which stands the town and temple of Gurkha. It is from rajputs who originally settled at Gurkha that the present reigning family descends; and it was the king of Gurkha and his followers who, in the eighteenth century, overcame all the neighbouring small states, including Katmandu and the valley, and established Gurkha rule over a kingdom a great deal larger than the present Nepal.

Having bathed in and crossed the Chepe Khola, which is another of Baudha's clear and kindly streams, we camped by an aged and stricken pipal tree on a grass plateau high above the Marsyandi. The villages on this plateau were the homes of Brahmans who looked upon us and our horde as little better than outcasts, as of course we were. Roberts knew better than to ask for raksi here; one might as well expect to find fish on trees as alcohol amongst these stern Rechabites, addicted to very plain living and correspondingly high thinking. They grudgingly sold us a small piece of honeycomb containing a little honey and many bees and grubs.

The grubs and the gloomy unsmiling Brahmans reminded me that it was time to begin collecting beetles. Meligethes was still the cry, as well it might be, since out of the 800 beetles which had passed through my Belsen battery the previous summer only three were of that family. One of these, however, had proved to be a new kind, so that instead of my commission as collector being revoked, I had been provided with a bigger battery of tubes and a number of Meligethes specimens. Thus equipped I had no excuse for indiscriminate slaughter, confounding the innocent, such as ladybirds and ticks, with the guilty.

Two days later, after crossing the Marsyandi by a suspension bridge, we parted company with the main Kuncha-Pokhara track and headed north up the west bank of the river. It is smaller than the Trisuli but it was already dark and discoloured owing, we found, to a crumbling hillside higher up and also to the tributary Dudh Khola or Milk river which always ran a dirty white. From Tarpu (2523 ft.) at the junction of the clear-watered Khudi Khola, which drains the eastern extremity of the Annapurna range, we at last began to gain height with the comforting assurance that on subsequent marches it would not be thrown away.

No sooner had we cleared Tarpu village than Himal Chuli again thrust itself upon our notice, at what seemed fairly close range. It was still some twenty miles distant, but even at that the critical eye of a mountaineer could detect some unmistakable blemishes on its glistening western face. Later in the year Roberts and I were able to confirm by a closer inspection that these unfavourable impressions were justified.

Himal Chuli is not the only great peak on the twenty-five-mile-long ridge of which Baudha is the southern extremity; besides these two there are also an unnamed peak of 25,700 ft., Manaslu (26,668 ft.), and another unnamed peak of 24,150 ft. This huge southerly spur is part of the Great Himalaya range, but is isolated from the Annapurna Himal by the Marsyandi gorge, and from the Ganesh Himal to the east by the Buri Gandaki. In central and western Nepal there are two distinct high crest zones; the Great Himalaya which carries the highest peaks, and farther north, the so-called Ladakh range which, in general, marks the Nepal-Tibet frontier. North of Manaslu and the unnamed 24,150 ft. peak the two crest-zones are in contact, linked by a high ridge over which there is a much-used pass of 17,000 ft. To find a 'Ladakh' range cropping up in Nepal is confusing. Prof. Mason calls the name 'mainly a speculative invention', for the continuity of the Ladakh range so far east has never been proved either geographically or geologically.

When from our camp at Khanchok we first saw Himal Chuli we had also identified the forbidding looking summits of the unnamed 25,700 ft. peak and Manaslu. The precipitous appearance of their eastern faces fronting upon the Buri Gandaki valley had had not a little to do with our rejection of that valley as a field of operations. We felt, however, that we had been a little off-hand in writing off a twenty-five-mile-long range on such flimsy grounds; we therefore kept an open mind and were prepared to make a dart in that direction if the opportunity arose.

Beyond Tarpu we entered *terra incognita*; few if any of our coolies and certainly none of the escort had ever been up the Marsyandi. Nevertheless it is a fairly important route where coolies pass constantly, carrying rice up and salt down. Although there was a marked diminution in the number of chautaras our pace did not improve, the roughness of the way obliging the coolies to rest more frequently though less conveniently. Perhaps their absence did not mean that pious and public-spirited men were becoming rare but that they were less rich; beyond Tarpu the country becomes too rugged for any man to wish to add field to field. Tarpu itself seemed to be the home of the last and by no means the least wealthy and public-spirited landowner, a man who has at his own cost built a steel suspension bridge over the Khudi Khola. He it was who sent us a lavish gift of rice, ghi, dal, pepper, turmeric and a plump fowl. We did not see our benefactor, who lived some way off and was ill, but Charles Evans made some return by prescribing for him intuitively and, as we heard later, successfully.

Although the rich rice land ceases at 5000 ft. cultivation goes on up to 12,000 ft., becoming ever less rewarding and demanding harder labour. As the slopes steepen the need for terraces and the labour of making them become greater, and as the height increases the growing season becomes shorter. A chief trouble of those who cultivate the higher, steeper valleys came vividly to our notice on the way to Tagring, the first halt beyond Tarpu. After a long march, when the sight of the village close at hand lent encouragement to the weary, we found we were cut off from it by a great, ugly gash in the hillside scored by a landslide. To cross in safety, while boulders and debris were still slithering down, we had to climb high, thus prolonging an already long march. As is generally the way the camp site was on the far side of the village, and when at last we reached it we sat for an hour in a steady drizzle awaiting the coolies.

Under the stress of these small trials we were feeling a little peevish when a group of village elders came to pay their respects and to ask us, in our wisdom, what they could do to check the landslide. Our troubles seemed shamefully trivial in the face of this major disaster of theirs. Many of their hard-won terraced fields had already been carried away by the landslip which was now threatening to engulf some houses and might in time destroy both fields and village. Could nothing be done to check it, they asked, with complete faith in the scientific resource of the Paleface. Packard, the student of land erosion, had to admit that there was nothing within their means. Only concrete, or vast quantities of fascines and labour beyond their resources, could stop the gradual deepening and widening of the newly formed ravine which would whittle away the hillside until it met solid rock. Many of these big slips quickly stabilize themselves but the Tagring slip proved to be a running sore. Returning along the opposite side of the valley four months later, Roberts and I had our attention again drawn to it by a persistent rumble increasing often to a roar as the constant trickle of mud and boulders suddenly gathered weight and momentum.

Whether it takes place little by little or in one swift calamity soil erosion is generally attributed to man's careless greed, his idleness or neglect. It would not, I think, be fair to blame the people of these valleys on the Himalayan fringe for the frequent landslips which occur there. In turning the steep slopes into fruitful fields they have been neither lazy nor neglectful. Such slopes, of 30° or 40° or more, are laboriously built up in terraces from ten to thirty feet wide, whose retaining walls may be from five to fifteen feet high, according to the angle of the slope. I have not counted them, but I can well believe there might be a couple of hundred of such hard-won fields on a hillside particularly favoured in soil and aspect whose every foot is put to use. The task of building must be spread over years and their maintenance calls for constant labour over and above that of routine cropping.

One might say that on such hillsides the forest never should have been cleared, in which case the country must be left uninhabited; or that belts of trees should have been planted which would imply first the giving up of their goats by the villagers. It has been pointed out before that but for erosion in the foothills of the Himalaya there would be no fertile Gangetic plain, and similarly no rich Nile delta and no fat Mississippi flood-plain. Yet whatever may be done by man to check erosion in the hills, dwellers in the plains need have little fear that the slow process of erosion so beneficial to them will not go on. Unless perhaps, in the case of interference with the river system on so huge a scale as that of the projected Kosi dam, when all the silt might become imprisoned in the lake above the dam.

Beyond Tagring the valley rapidly becomes a gorge. On the right bank, except for a small pocket of flattish land where there are a few fields and the hovels of their indigent owners, there is neither village nor even camp site. Although the occupants of this place were in the convalescent stages of smallpox we were obliged to camp there. The track, having crossed the river by a bamboo bridge which the rapidly rising river would soon demolish, embarked upon the passage of a series of cliffs. To overcome these the builders of the road had exercised boldness and ingenuity, stringing wooden galleries across the face. Such structures, known as 'parri', are common in the Gilgit region where they are usually stout enough; in the Marsyandi they were pretty frail, particularly the handrails which were better left alone or at the most touched rather than grasped. They were seldom wider than a single plank and were reached by a stone staircase or up-ended logs with footholds cut in them. When the river was low many of these catwalks could be avoided by a little boulder-hopping in the river bed. In the rains the traveller has no choice. He must then mind his step, for the planks are greasy with rain or with spray from the surging river.

Having passed the gorge the track recrossed the river, just below its junction with the Dudh Khola, where there is a village called Thonje. We were now north of the main Himalayan crest-line, and although the altitude was little higher than Tagring the people, the villages and the vegetation had all changed. As a hint of the sterner country above them, severe forests of pine and fir had taken possession of the slopes. Instead of the high-pitched thatch roofs and brick walls of white and terra-cotta, the long, low houses were built of stone with smoke-stained shingle roofs, the lopped tip of a conifer tree tied on one gable end as a charm against leopards, ghosts, bears, Snowmen or tax collectors. At our appearance a number of Tibetan-like men and boys in a variety of queer hats burst into astonished laughter, and we instinctively took refuge in the first house which, sure enough, was a beer shop. I felt we had practically arrived. Such houses and such men, ragged, tough and cheerful, both alike reeking of juniper smoke, speak of high valleys upon the threshold of great mountains.

CHAPTER XI

MANANGBHOT

———◆———

HAVING SQUANDERED A FEW ANNAS on beer, as full of thick sediment as the Dudh Khola, we crossed over to Thonje and camped close to the river. Standing as it does at the junction of two valleys and two well-used routes, Thonje is a key place to which we held what we hoped was a master key. This was a letter of introduction from our rich landowner friend to his son who lived and reigned there. There are a number of smaller villages near enough to Thonje for them to pay some attention to the requests of its headman, so that we were advantageously placed for transport and food. Thus we were able to dispense with the Katmandu men, now out of their element climatically and culturally, and engage local men who could take us up to Manangbhot at the head of the Marsyandi.

We still had an alternative to Manangbhot, and as it would take time to recruit fifty widely scattered volunteers, or to overcome their reluctance to being pressed, we decided to halt four days while a reconnaissance party made a dart up the Dudh Khola valley. Here was a chance to see Manaslu and the neighbouring peaks at close range which no mountaineer could resist. Four of us undertook the reconnaissance while Lowndes and Packard remained with the baggage. As Lowndes's main interest lay in the collecting of palaeo-arctic plants, butterflies and birds, the time had not yet come for him to unfold his blotting-paper or unfurl his butterfly net, for Thonje is only 6000 ft. above sea-level. It was, however, a fair sample of a lower Himalayan village, so that Packard could open his enquiry into land utilization.

We started after lunch on 23 May, having spent the morning writing letters and arguing with the Katmandu men. Although they begged hard I refused to hand over any cash, they having agreed to receive the balance due to them in Katmandu. If we were to pay our way for the next four months it was necessary to conserve the money we had brought, amounting to Rs. 6000. All of this was in silver, weighing about 100 lb., for the people of these remote parts have old-fashioned ideas about paper money. Thus, whenever I paid out cash, the pangs which a miser suffers in diminishing his irreplaceable hoard were balanced by the satisfaction a traveller has in reducing the weight of his loads.

The track up the Dudh Khola is a well-used salt route. Taking advantage of the dry weather a number of coolies were carrying up rice to exchange for salt at Bimtakhoti at the head of the valley. During the monsoon, when travel becomes unpleasant, the traffic declines, to revive again in September when 'zos' as well as coolies begin bringing salt down to Thonje. The only village in the valley is Tilje, a couple of miles up, where the main track crosses the river by a wooden cantilever bridge. In order to isolate themselves against the prevalent smallpox, the enlightened people of Tilje had closed the bridge with a thorn barrier. Coolie traffic had to use a worse alternative route, but we were armed with a note from the Thonje headman which we presented across the barrier on the point of an ice-axe in the fashion appropriate to 'compromised' persons. This talisman opened the barrier. We passed through the village—one of the dirtiest I have seen—and camped beyond it.

The place of the scattered oaks and maple through which the track wound was soon usurped by silver fir whose dark, stately ranks marched up the ever-steepening valley walls in grave contrast with the merry, foaming river. A bright morning tantalized us with exciting but imperfect glimpses of great mountains until the clouds thickened and made an end. Having camped in a glade at about 9500 ft. we defied the ensuing drizzle with a noble fire. Leaving the men to follow we set off early next day for Bimtakhoti, passing several cheery parties of coolies still cooking their breakfasts by the rock overhangs under which they had slept. After climbing steeply for 1000 ft. the track levelled off. From this belvedere we looked over the dark forest to the debris of a glacier below and beyond to the cirque at the foot of Manaslu from which it flowed. On the right two sky-piercing towers of rock and ice struck us with amazement, almost eclipsing by their savage splendour the calm, monumental mass of Manaslu. From a low snow col the long north ridge of the mountain climbed airily over a bump of the order of 25,000 ft., dropped 1000 ft., and then rose sharply to a snow plateau. On this remote pedestal, lying well back, stood the summit pyramid.

I imagine that a party of mountaineers confronted by a mountain which they think of climbing is not unlike a committee of distinguished Academicians confronted by a picture which they think of hanging. First they have to decide which is the right way up, then, perhaps, what, if anything, it means; whether it is a landscape or a portrait, a mountain or a nightmare; the texture of the paint and whether it is fixed or likely to flake off in avalanches; and finally the danger which they will incur of being thought too bold or too timid. The younger members may possibly see more sense in it than the elder, will interpret it more favourably, and will above all shrink from the suspicion of having old-fashioned ideas. There is thus such wide scope for argument and disagreement that it is remarkable that pictures are ever hung or mountains climbed.

A man looking at a big mountain from a valley has naturally only a worm's-eye view. Thus we had first an acrimonious discussion as to the whereabouts of the actual summit; which was not settled, and would never have been, until by moving on a bit we brought it into view. But so distant, and so foreshortened was our view of the upper part, that we gave this major consideration the benefit of the doubt, and concentrated our attention on the north ridge whereby lay the only possibility of approach. That the foot of this ridge could be reached by means of a low snow col was about the only point that I could see in its favour; but the dazzling beauty of its immaculate curve spanning the sky, its length, and perhaps its difficulties, together formed a powerful attraction for Emlyn Jones. He must have had an Alpine scale in mind. The ridge might have attracted me, too, had the mountain been only half as high; but to take porters and camps over a long, high, difficult ridge, to descend a thousand feet, to climb again to the plateau (which was probably less of a plateau than it looked), to toil across it for a mile or more and then be confronted by the unknown problems of the final pyramid were, in my opinion, tasks beyond our powers.

Anyhow I was loath to pit an untried party against so great a mountain. I still cherished hopes of finding one high enough to test our powers of acclimatization, and yet easy enough to give us a good chance of climbing it. We therefore decided to leave Manaslu and the

Lieut. S. B. Malla skins a bird, watched by a small audience; of these the biggest with the long hair is undoubtedly a boy, and the urchin in the middle with curly hair is probably a girl

Three generations at Tange—mother, daughter, and small granddaughter who is hiding in the shadow of the bowl; a broken conch shell is favourite wrist wear; the man with the sinister moustache is a Tibetan trader

Phugaon; the clay, gravel, and boulders of the nearly vertical cliffs of old river terraces are more firmly knit together than seems likely; otherwise the houses seen here, with a desirable view over the river, would not stand very long

Tange; behind is the wide bed of the Tange Khola and the curiously eroded cliffs of river detritus; the big chorten is coloured brick-red and white; to the right of it is a 'battery' of smaller chortens in two lines of five all under one roof

other peaks of this long southerly spur to better men and to seek our objective in the Annapurna Himal which offered several great and glittering prizes.

Having sent word back to our porters to make camp we pushed on, climbing steadily through forest until the trees ended abruptly halfway up a very large moraine of white granite boulders. The track led up the moraine and then through the mounds and hollows of a wide debris-covered glacier. Here the white ramparts of the Ladakh range, several miles to the north, came into sight, and we halted to examine two of its named peaks, Himlung Himal (23,380 ft.) and Cheo Himal (22,350 ft.), and to try to identify the unnamed peak of 24,150 ft. lying on the ridge connecting the Ladakh range with Manaslu. We failed to do this to our satisfaction, nor did we think either of the two Ladakh peaks were intended for climbing. Beyond the glacier we found ourselves in a pleasant grass flat with a birch-covered slope on one side and the high embankment of the moraine on the other. A clear stream rippled at the foot of the birch slope, while below the moraine nestled the few stone houses of Bimtakhoti. Later in the year, as a cripple, I spent ten days at Bimtakhoti; a longer time than its interest really warranted but not long enough for its loveliness to pall. On this first flying visit we were delighted by the bright stream and the purple primulas along its banks, by the pale green of the young birch framing white and crimson rhododendrons, by the mani wall and the browsing sheep, with the shapely Ladakh peaks in front and the mighty Manaslu behind.

After inspecting a store where rice was being weighed and stored against the expected flow of salt—for the passes had been open only a week—we went back to camp in the forest on the far side of the glacier. Thence we did a double march back to Thonje where we found everything in train for the final stage of our journey to Manangbhot. The forty-six coolies necessary for this move assembled and started by instalments. At 11.30 a.m. nine loads—the heaviest, of course—still lay forlornly on the ground; but at last all were claimed and after marching for a short half-hour we overtook the rest of the party having its morning draught at the euphoniously named village of Bagarchap. Evidently the latecomers knew more about the marching habits of their friends than we did.

Beyond Thonje signs of Tibetan culture became common. There the sole manifestation was a big mani wall round which the old women marched morning and evening sprinkling the stones with water. At Bagarchap they had an entrance gateway crowned by three miniature chortens painted black, white and yellow. The houses, though neither huddled together nor built on a cliff like a Tibetan village, had similar flat roofs of rammed earth. A log with steps cut in the shape of a half-moon gave access to the roof, the favoured resort for gossip and for watching the passing scene.

Thence our procession moved off more or less together, three of us remaining behind to urge on stragglers. One whom we presently came upon lying by the path was insensible to urging, breathing stertorously, bubbling at the mouth, apparently in the fatal stage of a fit; but one did not have to be qualified to diagnose the fit as alcoholic. Gyalgen, the Sherpa headman and cook, administered a few strong, unavailing kicks and hurried on, anxious, so he said, to get in early to make bread. We three, who did not think as quickly as Gyalgen, had to divide the man's load between us. Thus burdened we went on leaving the body lying by the path, hoping that if a man-eating leopard came along the smell of beer would not put him off his meal. This lad was slightly the less objectionable of two whom Lowndes had unluckily picked out of the Katmandu cohort to remain with him as personal attendants against the time when the Sherpas would be leaping upon the mountains. He did not repeat this offence, but he did worse by wrecking, through curiosity and clumsiness, his master's camera. The other, known as 'Squeaker' on account of a high raucous voice, was a good monkey spoilt. He was idle, cheeky and unreliable, chattered incessantly, pilfered, and behaved generally like one of his tailed relatives at Shimbunath. These two stuck to us like burrs. They received less pay than the Sherpas and were equipped only with a warm blanket; but apart from the fact that quietness is worth buying they cost Lowndes the use of his camera and the party a lot of stolen food.

We were now beyond the main Himalayan axis and heading slightly north of west through a forest of oak and sycamore. The little lichen or moss on the trees suggested that in this valley, north of the Annapurna ridge, we would be in the rain shadow and that conditions might be less moist than in the Langtang. The coolies ended better than they had begun, going on until late evening, when we camped by a side stream just short of Thangja, a pleasant village surrounded by fields of young wheat. The next village we came to, in spite of its name of Chāme, vied for filthiness with Tilje. The small gompa was in keeping, neglected outside, dark and dirty inside, furnished with nothing but a tattered temple banner and a thigh-bone horn. At a height of 9000 ft. the track, carpeted with pine needles, lay through a forest of scattered pines with neither undergrowth nor bamboos. Everything pointed to a tolerably dry climate.

This suspicion, or rather hope, strengthened after the third day's march. Within a mile we crossed the Marsyandi three times by well-built suspension bridges, finishing on the south bank on a broad path running through more pines. Where the forest had been burnt, either purposely or by chance, a strong growth of young trees showed that it was self-regenerating. Looking over to the opposite bank the climbers were astonished by the sight of a clean, unbroken slab of rock, a mile wide and more than a thousand feet high, a landslip having stripped off the shallow overburden. Incautiously we expressed a wish to know what kind of rock this was and were promptly told by our expert. We had no option but humbly to acquiesce in the name supplied which was, I think, argillaceous schist. It seemed as likely as any, and the rock, lying at too easy an angle to offer good climbing, deserved no better. At times one felt like comparing our geologist with the Master of Balliol College, for what he didn't know wasn't knowledge; but such feelings were prompted by envy and envy is a kind of praise.

At last we emerged from the pines and descended to a shallow mere on a wide flat where a few ponies grazed. Grass grew by the shore and by the springs which fed the lake, but beyond, up the valley, the eye met only yellow gravel slopes grudgingly supporting straggling pines and stunted junipers. The landscape had the bare, brown aspect of the North-west Frontier. Wherever water flowed grass and trees flourished, yet it was clear that the rainfall alone was not enough to support vegetation. Lowndes looked glum. Mindful of our dark experiences in the Langtang I rejoiced at these welcome signs, but the appearance of this semi-desert did not please our botanist who had come prepared to be wet but happy amid a wealth of flowers. It was now the end of May and we had seen only a few bronze and white ground orchids, some big white anemones, a small crimson primula, some saxifrage and spiraea, and little else. Meantime we had six large boxes to fill and the farther we went the drier the country appeared. However, Lowndes had plenty to do later. The flower growth proved to be nowhere so abundant as in the Langtang, but above 14,000 ft., where during the monsoon constant cloud lay, he found an ample variety.

While the eyes and thoughts of our botanist dwelt despondently on the barren floor of the valley, the rest of us raised our eyes to the hills. We had already seen the 22,921 ft. peak and something of the north ridge of Annapurna II beyond—enough in fact to strike it off our diminishing list of possible mountain routes. In the hope of seeing more we camped a little early at a small hamlet where a nallah ran up towards the north face of the mountain. Across the river was Pisang, looking like a Ladakh village with its cream-washed stone walls and flat roofs. Notwithstanding the satisfactory evidence of a dry climate, a steady drizzle continued all afternoon.

Meantime we had begun to make the acquaintance of a few of the denizens of this strange valley. Sher Bahadur, prompted, no doubt, by wishful thinking, had long since aroused expectant curiosity by asserting that we should find it as rich and as well cultivated as the valley of Katmandu. He also told us the people were gypsies and highly sophisticated. We had already had some proof of this in an encounter with three women who addressed us in Hindustani, and a man who demanded 'baksheesh' for allowing himself to be photographed. In the remoter Himalaya it is rare to find a man who speaks this linguafranca of the plains; rarer still a woman, who, if she stays at home and works as hard as hill-women must, has neither time nor opportunity for languages. In fact one would suspect a woman who did speak Hindustani of having made a business of entertaining travellers, and of being for business purposes not a very sturdy moralist. However, the people of this Pisang suburb seemed so dirty and ignorant that the women might at once be acquitted of either improvement or impropriety.

30 May, we hoped, would be the last day's march. We sent the men off early so that they would reach Manang or a village near it, while we climbed a few hundred feet above the bed of the nallah in order to see round a corner. By starting first, Roberts reached a viewpoint just

before an obstinate cloud sat down on the particular part of the north face which interested us. Belatedly we gazed at a fragment of snow with a mass of cloud lying above it which Roberts assured us concealed the main ridge itself and an easy way on to it. Having sent on the coolies we could not take a camp up the nallah to verify this, and luckily the necessity for so doing never arose. By next day we had discovered that Roberts must have been deceived by extreme foreshortening of the view. Upon this viewpoint stood a chorten crowned by a carved wood symbol, perhaps the perfect eight-leaf lotus, and the problem of the moment was to take a picture of this against a mountain background. Some of us almost stood on our heads to achieve it. In the early days of an expedition everyone suffers from snap-happiness just as a novice with a rifle aches with buck-fever. Regardless of the lighting, the first views of rock, river and hill—'base, common, and popular, such as you may see anywhere in wild, mountainous districts'—are eagerly taken as though the like never would again be seen. Later on, the remaining film is jealously hoarded and one becomes so fastidious about subject and lighting that many good pictures are missed.

On this, their last day, the coolies went with a will. We found them waiting for us at a small hamlet on the north bank of the river where they thought we ought to camp. The fields, the young wheat in them springing green, were irrigated with water from a source in the pines above; and we learnt later that nearly all the crops grown at Manangbhot are irrigated. Before siting our base camp on this apparently suitable spot, we went on a mile to look at the village of Braga. Passing under a massive gateway crowned with a full-size chorten and shaded by a fine old poplar of immense girth, we entered upon a meadow of short grass. This otherwise attractive site was wet in places and completely overlooked by the village set halfway up fantastically eroded cliffs of yellow conglomerate. These strange cliffs, and the houses precariously clinging to them tier by tier, had a truly Tibetan air; which was much enhanced when a horde of barefooted ragamuffins poured down and surrounded us. In a country where flat, arable land is rare not a foot of it can be spared for house sites; villages therefore are built on the nearest waste land, no matter how rocky or how steep; and since labour and material are scarce, the houses are built wall to wall and almost floor to floor, the finished article resembling a picturesque, insanitary medieval castle with the serfs' huts clustered round the walls.

After considering the matter we decided that all the advantages of living at Braga—labour, eggs, beer, and raksi, at hand—were not worth the loss of privacy. We therefore went back and after a little search found a shelf on the hillside among the pines a few hundred feet above the hamlet. A trickle of water ran through it, and some ten miles of the north face of the Annapurna Himal confronted us across the valley. Happy in having wood, water, seclusion, and a noble view, we settled down for the summer at Manangbhot.

CHAPTER XII

TO THE MOUNTAIN

MANANGBHOT IS THE NAME of the district which roughly covers the region between the Annapurna Himal and the Tibet border less than twenty miles to the north. The settled part comprises some dozen small villages in the upper Marsyandi valley, and of these Manangbhot (shortened by us to Manang) is the biggest; there are also two villages high up on the tributary Naur Khola which rises in the Ladakh range and joins the Marsyandi below Chāme. In Nepali 'bhotiya' means Tibetan, and 'bhot' is the name for Tibet; Tibetans call their country Bod which in colloquial use is aspirated into Bhot. Two other districts of Nepal, Mustangbhot at the head of the Kali valley and Chharkabhot still farther west, have the suffix 'bhot'.

The inhabitants of these places, and indeed most of those who dwell along the Nepal-Tibet border, have more affinities with Tibet than with Nepal. They speak a Tibetan dialect, practise a similar corrupt form of Buddhism, and have the same manners, customs and dress. They trade both to the north and to the south. The easiest and shortest routes lie to the south, and food, particularly rice for which they have a great liking, can be got only from Nepal, so that the strongest link lies in that direction. But though they belong to Nepal it is doubtful if the ordinary man at Katmandu would recognise them as fellow subjects or be much flattered by the knowledge that they were. They receive, I imagine, but little attention from the Nepalese authorities and pay them little either in the way of taxes, services or respect. Certainly none of the officials from the nearest administrative centre of Kuncha, who occasionally and reluctantly visited us, had ever been to Manangbhot or knew anything about it. As we now saw, Sher Bahadur's notions of a valley rivalling that of Katmandu were wide of the mark; we had not yet visited Manang itself but we could see that it was only a larger village with rather more cultivation; and since it is about 11,500 ft. up, little more could be expected. Yet we found the people a peculiar Himalayan community.

The headmen of these villages, particularly of Manang, were a law unto themselves. In fact the men as a whole had that free and independent air, traditionally ascribed to any hardy mountain race, which we rejoice to find and like to encourage until it begins to conflict with our own needs. The reason, I think, for their strikingly independent ways and for their manners, which were always offhand and sometimes impudent, was that many of them were great traders, spending the winter months in cities like Delhi and Calcutta or as far afield as Rangoon and Singapore. Hence Sher Bahadur's story of their being gypsies and of their wealth, which was in part true. Thus they were familiar with train, boat and even air travel, and with the Paleface and some of his less commendable ways. In these cities, where their strange features, stranger dress, and cheerful smiles are a welcome change from the usual run of mournful hawkers, gloomy fakirs, and whining beggars, they blarney the ignorant, learn how to spoil the Egyptians and to speak Hindustani garnished with American 'cinemese', and return wearing wrist-watches and Army boots without laces. We found no wireless sets in Manangbhot, but a man whom we attempted to photograph retorted by whipping out a camera himself.

On the whole they were not pleased to see us and I was not delighted with them. The traveller to remote parts wishes, indeed expects, to find the natives unsophisticated enough to regard him with the respect which he seldom gets at home. At Manangbhot he will be disappointed. As well as their lack of regard for us they were not at all eager either to sell us food or to provide transport; nor was it surprising that our money held little inducement, for their winter trading ventures seemed lucrative enough for them to devote the summer months to drinking beer and raksi. Thrice happy mortals; or to mangle Goldsmith

> How happy he who crowns in Manangbhot
> A month of labour with a drinking bout.

On these forays into civilization their stock-in-trade consists of musk pods, silajit*, medicinal herbs, semi-precious stones, skins and, I suspect, a great deal of impudence.

These impressions were not all gathered the first day, but we had a quick hint that in Manangbhot we were neither so welcome nor of such consequence as we thought, in the dilatoriness with which the headmen responded to Sher Bahadur's summons and their intimation that no coolies would be available for three days. Each village had several headmen and we had always to deal with representatives from each of several neighbouring villages. The principles of democracy, of one man one vote, and of fair shares for all, were well understood; and no Whitehall mandarin could teach these worthies anything about the technique of dealing with requests from outsiders. If we wanted to buy food or hire labour, each representative had to be consulted and each village had the privilege or the penalty of supplying its quota.

---

*   Silajit or 'pathar ka passeo' (meaning 'rock-sweat'). I heard of this mysterious substance from Sher Bahadur who described it as a brown or black treacly fluid which oozes from rock faces; it is collected and sold in Katmandu and India where it is highly prized as a sovereign remedy, and is used, too, in dyeing, printing, and tanning. I never found or saw any, but a fact so strange as a rock exuding a soft substance led me to pursue the enquiry and I ran my quarry to earth in the old India Office Library.

Hamilton in his *Account of the Kingdom of Nepal* (1819) mentions it as a product of Nepal and refers to some he saw in a bat-haunted cave at Hanria Hill in Behar. 'I saw the silajit besmearing the face of the rock where it issued from a crevice in the quartz; the consistency of thin honey, of a dirty earth colour, with a strong disagreeable smell like cow's urine. The whole appearance is disgusting.'

In the *J.B.O.R.S.* 1917, vol. 3, there is a chemical analysis of this Hanria silajit: 'Semi-liquid, dark brown, smell reminiscent of guano, 65 p.c. organic, perhaps the result of water trickling through deposits of bats, also dissolving out some silica and other constituents of the rock.'

This explains the 'black' silajit but there is also a 'white' silajit which is a mineral substance. In *J.A.S.B.* vol. 2, I found an analysis of this but no explanation. It merely described it as '95 p.c. sulphate of alumina, an exudation from the surface of soft rocks'.

Thus, if we wanted six coolies, Manangbhot, after debate, would send two old crones, Braga and Khangsar one man each, Ngawal a boy and the village idiot, each of whom would arrive at different times or even on different days. Sher Bahadur, native and to the manner born, coped with them patiently, seldom losing his temper. Lowndes, on the other hand, who saw more of them than the rest of us and had more need for the casual employment of coolies and ponies, found them trying, and frequently came to the boil; for discipline and that cheerful, willing obedience to which he had been accustomed are not in the tradition of Manangbhot.

On the whole we got on well enough, and so long as we gave several days' notice of an intended move, or several weeks if we wanted food, we were never thwarted. In fact it occurred to me later that they had treated us very well, since they had good reason for regarding us with an indifference closely bordering on aversion; for Packard, in the name of science, had an insatiable curiosity about their private affairs which marked him down at once as either an official or a tax-collector—both unfamiliar species at Manangbhot and, on that account, all the more suspect. Through Sher Bahadur, who shared the odium, he plied these innocent citizens with questions just as though they were the guilty inmates of some Welfare State—questions about their crops, stock, farming methods, their trade, their wives and children, their health, morals and religion.

A secure base and a sound plan are essential for any striking force. We had found our base and had celebrated our arrival there in a suitable way; liquor, by the way, being the one thing instantly procurable without the approval of a committee of elders. (If Roberts's outsize water-bottle was sent to Braga it came back filled with the right stuff pretty smartly.) In theory we were well placed for striking at any peak on the twenty-five-mile-long Annapurna ridge in front of us, at any one of the scattered peaks behind us, or at those which closed the head of the valley on the west, on the Muktinath range.

At this time we were favoured by clear mornings, and on our second day without moving far from camp, we saw an objective and a possible route to it. The Annapurna Himal* consists of a long unbroken

---

* 'Anna', we were told, means a 'measure'. 'Purna' means 'heaped-up'.

Looking north up the wide basin of the Kali river towards Tibet, the expected wall of snow mountains is missing; missing, too, is any clothing in the way of forest or grass for the bare bones of this chaotic landscape

A good example of 'organ-pipe' erosion on the cliffs of an old river terrace 2000 ft. above the Kali; the sheep and goats which carry loads between Mustang and Muktinath must find it hungry travelling on this route

The Naur Khola bridge; it might collapse of its own weight, but since it is 500 ft. above the river it is not likely to be washed away; there is a door at the archway, but a better way of preventing spirits from crossing is to kindle a small fire of juniper twigs on the lintel

Muktinath temple; for ages past Muktinath has been a goal for pilgrims, but the present temple is not an old building; the water from the sacred spring, which rises close by, can be seen falling over the wall behind the temple

ridge. The eastern end marked by a summit of 22,921 ft. and the western end by one of 26,492 ft. known as Annapurna I. (A high ridge, the Muktinath range, links Annapurna I to the Ladakh range and forms the watershed between the upper Kali and the Marsyandi.) Between these two peaks the Annapurna range nowhere falls below 20,000 ft. and on it (from east to west) are Annapurna II (26,041 ft.); Annapurna IV (24,688 ft.); Annapurna III (24,858 ft.); two peaks of 23,000 ft. in close attendance upon A-I, and an outlier to the south called Macha Puchare or the Fishtail (22,958 ft.). Three of the major peaks were in full view from our base, but Annapurna I lies well back and so could not be seen from the Marsyandi valley. This is the great peak which the dash and determination of the French party led by Maurice Herzog overcame on 3 June, three days after our arrival at Manangbhot. We knew, of course, like the rest of the world, that a French party was in the Kali valley bent on climbing Dhaulagiri (26,795 ft.); and we had heard that two of them had been at Manangbhot three weeks before, having crossed a high pass, the Tilicho, to the north of Annapurna I. From this we had concluded correctly that Dhaulagiri had proved too tough a nut and that they were looking for a mountain to climb, probably Annapurna I. Their visit to Manangbhot had also served to reassure them about us; for being needlessly disturbed by rumours amongst their Sherpas that a British party was in the vicinity, they assumed that we should immediately make for the highest peak and possibly race them to the summit. This was flattering but, of course, quite untrue. We had no time to reconnoitre Annapurna I which, according to their account, cannot be climbed from the Manangbhot side.

One of the fascinations of looking at mountains is their knack of changing their appearance when viewed from different places or even in different weather.

> The hills are shadows and they flow
> From form to form and nothing stands,
> They melt like mists; the solid lands
> Like clouds they shape themselves and go.

From this vantage point, what we saw through binoculars and telescopes of the ridge in the neighbourhood of A-II could not easily be reconciled with what we had seen from near Pisang. But in time the pieces fell into place. The first conclusion we drew from the completed puzzle was that Roberts's route to the ridge was a myth, born of mist, foreshortening, and a heated imagination; and the second that there seemed to be no other way. Only from the broad back of the main ridge west of A-II or of A-IV could either of these peaks be reached, while A-III, bristling with gendarmes and cornices, could not be reached at all. At least that was my first impression.

But after prolonged scrutiny I thought there was a way. Starting from the head of a nallah across the main valley a snow-rib seemed to lead at a moderate angle to a big snow-dome on the ridge almost midway between A-III and A-IV. At about 19,000 ft. there was an unmistakably abrupt ice-step which could not be avoided and higher up a similar obstacle. But it was that or nothing. There was no other way on to the main ridge which promised to be a safe highway along whose airy crest a camp might be carried to the foot of A-IV or perhaps even A-II. From the dome to the first peak is nearly two miles at an average height of 22,000 ft., and from there to A-II, at an average height of 24,000 ft., is a like distance. The ridge was therefore no cakewalk, but I was optimistic enough to think that the party could climb A-IV and that, depending on circumstances, a strong bid might be made for A-II.

At midday Charles Evans and I ascended the dry, barren hillside above the camp in the hope that from higher up the difficult ice step would look less uncompromising. On returning we learnt that Emlyn Jones and Roberts, on second thoughts, had withdrawn their courageously direct alternative route, so we decided to have a go at A-IV (with a mental reservation about A-II) by my route without any further ado.

The next day, l June, was spent in sorting loads for a three weeks' sojourn on the mountain and the making of five camps. This meant that a total of 700 lb. must be taken up the mountain at the start, that the Europeans must carry their own kits, and that no more than two standing camps could be left. These hard facts modified my hopes. In fact with only four Sherpas, two of whom had not been on a mountain before, and five climbers of unknown strength, a peak so high and so distant as A-II was scarcely an attainable prize. One of the most formidable features of a climb on any mountain is its length. This obvious point is of most consequence in the Himalaya where a long traverse without gaining much height, or worse still a temporary loss of height, reduces the chances of success and increases the risks. The ideal is a steadily rising face or ridge, the steeper the better within reason, where every step is a positive gain and where the time spent on the mountain is at a minimum.

It might be thought that the necessity of carrying one's own load would be a rigid guide in making it up. Most of us managed to finish the job with a load slightly on the wrong side of thirty pounds, but Emlyn Jones's remained obstinately at forty pounds. Twenty coolies had been promised for an early start on 2 June; finally, with fifteen, we left just before midday. A few were men but the majority were women and children, one of them not yet weaned. However, the weanling did not have to carry but was carried on top of its mother's load where it was within easy reach of its food. Fortunately the Sabzi Chu nallah was so short that we reckoned two easy marches would bring us to a site for a base near the foot of the rib. We could hardly expect our loads to be carried any higher by what might be called an over-sexed team of coolies.

We followed an easy path through pine forest, crossed the small river by a single-plank bridge over which the women had their loads carried, and camped at about 12,500 ft. by the last firewood—birch, rhododendron and dwarf willow scrub. At Emlyn's suggestion we added to our loads a few bundles of willow wands for marking the route on the mountain.

It may be true that no home is complete without a woman, but it is possible to dispense with them in camp. No doubt our she-coolies were a comfort to the men, but for us they performed no womanly offices. On the march they gave more trouble than the men and they were much slower. Yet anyone who had the courage to comment on their pace was immediately overwhelmed by a flood of complaint and abuse from the whole troupe. That evening a steady drizzle set in, against which the improvised shelters of the coolies were of little avail. To us, lying snug in our tents, it was satisfactory to reflect that 'by observing the miseries of others fortitude is strengthened and the mind brought to a more extensive knowledge of our powers'.

In the morning rain still fell and it was cheering to see that the women were as indifferent to it as the men. Indifference to discomfort is a very essential virtue in one's servants when no comfort can be provided for them. Like the squire of a knight-errant who, according to Sancho, must be sound of body, strong of limb, a silent sufferer of heat and cold, hunger and thirst. They all ate heartily of a breakfast such as only the condemned man, whom one reads of shudderingly, could eat with impunity. A large 'degchi' of meal having been boiled to a semi-stiff state, was parcelled out on flat stones according to the number in the mess. Each man scooped a hole in the top of his young mountain, dropped in a little dried yoghourt to impart a cheesy flavour, added a handful of red pepper, and filled it with hot water. After that I always expected the volcano to erupt, but the man merely took a lump of dough from the base of his mountain, dipped it in the crater of red hot lava, and swallowed it.

The approach to Himalayan mountains is usually by way of a long glacier which may provide either a pleasant promenade or a penitential way. In either event it is an obvious route and sometimes affords a party a flying start for the climb itself from the glacier head at 17,000 or 18,000 ft. A classic example is the head of the East Rongbuk at 21,500 ft. to which height one merely walks. But on the north side of the Annapurna range there are no real glaciers. By this I mean glaciers with big lateral moraines filling several miles of flattish valley; here we found mere ice-falls which petered out on the mountain side at about 15,000 ft. before ever reaching a valley. True, opposite Manang village there is one whose snout touches the Marsyandi, but there the river is adjacent to the mountain and except for the last hundred feet or so this glacier is an ice cataract. From beyond our first camp in the Sabzi Chu valley, which is only about four miles long, we climbed the vast moraine of a glacier of a bygone age. All that remained of it now was a short stretch of living ice which we had to cross at about 16,000 ft. to reach the foot of the rib.

The plod up this moraine took us all the morning. It was pleasant work, however, the sun having come out, as we trod upon short turf, the dwarf rhododendron, now in flower, filling the air with its aromatic scent. The women made heavy weather of it. The day had started badly for one of them who had fallen flat on her back when crossing a small stream. I laughed happily at this (although, I suppose, no gentleman would have done so) until I discovered the clumsy creature was carrying a fifty-six pound bag of sugar. Both Gyalgen and I then greeted her on the near shore with some suitable observations, receiving a volley of abuse from the sisterhood in return; but when we opened the bag we found that the packers in Liverpool had done their job so well that no harm had been done.

In a sort of hanging valley, where the slope eased off and where the grass gave way to gravel, we began searching for a camp site. As a dog describes small circles before bedding himself down, so the Sherpas circled round looking for places flat enough for our half-dozen tents without too much digging. At a height of close on 15,000 ft. the last wood was far below, but we had carried enough up to cook with for a few days. Roberts and I, the experienced Himalayan climbers, both had headaches, or at least we were the two who confessed to having them.

Having paid off the coolies and beaten Emlyn Jones for the first and only time at chess, I roused out a carrying party. Four of us and three Sherpas, carrying about 220 lb., set off to make a dump at the foot of the mountain. For about half a mile we followed the bed of a small stream which ran down our shallow valley, then turned right-handed over a moraine and dropped down on to the dry ice of a small glacier on the other side. It was barely half a mile wide, and having crossed it we climbed some scree for a couple of hundred feet and dumped our loads under a boulder. Fatigue, perhaps, prompted our choice, for it was not a sound place for a dump. Higher up were some slabs, the plinth of the mountain, and above them a wide, shallow, snow-filled depression which narrowed gradually to a funnel. Some of the ammunition which a mountain normally throws at one—rocks, ice or snow— would likely be directed by this funnel to the depression and so on to our dump or on to ourselves if we happened to be there. Later a large avalanche did come down, sweeping the depression clear of snow, but by then the dump had been cleared and we were high above it.

We woke to find it snowing gently but firmly and by breakfast time several inches had fallen. At 15,000 ft. we could regard this with equanimity or even welcome it for imposing a day of idleness, but for the French who were that day (4 June) descending from their high camp at Annapurna I the storm had grave consequences. Pa Norbu was sent down to Base to bring up more 'satu' (parched flour), and in the afternoon, the weather brightening, we made another carry. This time we moved the dump to an overhanging ledge at the foot of the slabs.

A sparkling day succeeded the storm, but we decided to give the sun a chance to clear the fresh snow before we moved higher. I went down to Base to have a word with Lowndes, who happened to be out, and to bring back more books and tobacco, neither of which can ever be in too great plenty on a mountain. Sher Bahadur reported that he and Lowndes had had a little *brusquerie* with the Manang notables who, besides wanting to know the reason for our presence, attributed to it the shortage of rain. This complaint may have been laid before the recent copious fall, but in any case, having with us an official escort, we were minions of Authority to whom all ills are rightly attributable:

> Who makes the quartern loaf and Luddites rise?
> Who fills the butcher's shop with large blue flies?

The snow speeded my passage down, for I glissaded about a thousand feet, and did not hinder my return, since by late afternoon most of it had gone. Having bathed on the way up I was preparing to dry off in the sun when the sight of five vultures, eyeing my naked body with hopeful interest, caused me to dress hurriedly.

A frosty night presaged unfailingly a lovely day. Starting early with another load for the dump we left there at 7.30 to make a carry to Camp I, which we vainly hoped might be somewhere in the vicinity of the ice-step. Nine of us climbed on two long ropes, keeping on the left of the depression to avoid the threat of the funnel. High above glistened a wall of ice, from which fragments might well fall. On this the Sherpas kept their eyes glued, for having nothing whatever of fatalism in their make-up they seem to be even more sensitive than we are to such threats. Out of deference to their views (which are often sound) we made for a gully as far as possible from the funnel, taking the step-kicking in half-hourly spells. A steepening of the gully forced us on to loose rocks, but the Sherpas, carrying fifty pounds against our twenty-five, climbed very steadily and not a stone was disturbed. After more snow plugging we reached by midday a bit of bare scree well below the step. Complete and decisive unanimity of opinion concurred in making this Camp I. We put up a tent, stowed 300 lb. of junk inside and, in order to avoid the rocks, went down another gully rather close to the funnel. If, during a climb, nothing falls from where it is expected, there is a tendency to assume that nothing ever will fall; but when descending, of course, less time is spent in the threatened area.

On the following day we five took up residence at Camp I. The Sherpas, who should have joined us the day after with the rest of the loads, were not able to come, one of them having to go down to Base to fetch all the remaining spare axes. In the gully on the way up we had encountered some ice upon which, at almost the first blow, I broke my axe (a new one) at the head. Two days later I broke another on the ice-step. Snapping axes thus, like carrots, does not necessarily imply great vigour in the wielder. A misdirected blow or a faulty shaft is much more likely. Like much else nowadays axes are not what they used to be. The pick bends, the blade chips, or the shaft, as we have seen, comes away in one's hand. A good axe should remain serviceable until it goes into honourable retirement with its owner, provided it comes to no untimely end by being dropped on a mountain or drowned in some fierce river which its owner is attempting to ford.

CHAPTER XIII

ON THE MOUNTAIN

At our first camp on the mountain we were rudely greeted by a squall with thunder and some snow. Although the height was only about 18,000 ft. it was very cold, a welcome sign that the warm monsoon current had not yet invaded the Marsyandi valley. Despite the cold, diligent search disclosed a trickle of water which saved us the trouble of melting snow; nevertheless, a supper of biscuit and pemmican reminded us that we were in for a short spell of hard living.

As the biscuits were my choice I had no right to complain, but being now without any teeth to speak of I found them singularly unappetizing. The teeth had been carelessly dropped in the Trisuli river when bathing there the second morning out, and no doubt they were now entering the Bay of Bengal. Such a blow so early in the campaign, by making eating, smoking a pipe, and talking, a little awkward, struck at my morale. Taciturnity can be borne and so far I had managed to smoke and eat, but chewing biscuits was another matter, particularly the brutally hard kind I had foolishly provided. One cannot, of course, foresee every calamity. The biscuits, packed and hermetically sealed in neat one-pound tins, were those carried in ship's lifeboats. They were officially approved, as one might easily suppose, by the Board of Trade, for they provide a sufficiency of calories and defy the ravages of weevils and time. And since shipwrecked mariners are either drowned before they have a chance to complain about their rations or so happy at being rescued that they forget, such biscuits are still in use and no official of the Board of Trade has yet been stoned to death with them.

A happy feature of Camp I, and of all our camps except the last, was the early hour at which the sun struck it. So, enjoying that too rare combination of bright sun and hard snow, we began climbing towards the ice-step upon which so much depended. Climbing on two ropes we accomplished 500 ft. in the first forty minutes, which could not be described as storming along but was good enough. Approaching the step our rib narrowed and steepened, and soon we were gazing up anxiously at the wall of ice.

Regard for truth prevents my calling this a vertical wall of ice, but it was near enough and a good eighty feet high. As we had foreseen it could not be turned, for there were great chasms on either side, so there was nothing for it but to cut bucket steps and fix ropes—a job, we thought, which would take two days. We were relieved to find it no worse and were cheered by the level snow plateau above and by the ease with which the second step of steep ice beyond could be avoided. Before going down we gazed long and earnestly at the final pyramid of Annapurna II which, now that we were closer, looked more difficult. Apart from this and the weak condition of Emlyn Jones, our morning was satisfactory.

Evans, the doctor, was worried about Emlyn Jones, who had come very near to collapse. We tried to persuade him to go down to Base but he thought a day's rest would put him right, for he attributed his weakness to lack of acclimatization, as it might well be. The rest of us went up again to attack the wall. Carving out my third step with some nonchalance, for I was then only three feet from the floor, I broke the second axe, a spare one belonging to Roberts. We found that our ice pitons, which were about a foot long, could not be driven in, so we were forced to use short rock pitons. These held firm only if the pull on them came from directly beneath, a pull from any other direction bringing them out faster than corks. However, one driven in directly above the man cutting steps, gave him some moral support, and crampons added to his confidence.

That afternoon we were joined in Camp I by the Sherpas who reported, with the complacency of a successful prophet of woe, that a large piece of ice-cliff above the funnel had broken off in the night and had poured down over the dump. Besides the remaining loads they brought spare ice-axes and a loaf of bread, thus enabling me to have at least one square meal. As Don Quixote observed, his teeth having been knocked out in an encounter, a mouth without molars is worse than a mill without stones. The others with fully equipped mouths had no complaints, indeed rather liked the biscuits. 'With bread and iron we can get to China', as the French commissar of revolutionary days remarked for the comfort and consideration of an extremely ill-fed, hard-used army. If the bread, as one suspects, was hard bread, a technical term for biscuit, he spoke with more rhetoric than truth.

Thus fortified we returned to the attack on the wall. Taking the Sherpas up we sent them back for a second load while we worked on the steps. A mild cheer greeted Packard as he finished the job with a long and trying lead, his ice training in the New Zealand Alps standing him in good stead. Using a spare axe as an anchor he fixed a 200 ft. rope. With its help I went up and fixed another rope by anchoring it to the shaft of my broken axe. It did not occur to me at the time, but one sees now that this was an act of faith little less than sublime.

All was set for a move to Camp II, and the time had come to make a hard decision about Emlyn Jones whom I thought ought to go down from Camp I so that his escort could get back the same day. However, we finally decided that he should start with us the next day, but that if he went no better on the way to the step he must quit.

At a point half-way to the step he himself solved our perplexity by deciding to go down forthwith. Roberts and Charles Evans, who confided to me that his pulse was almost nil, went with him. Only those who have had to turn back on a big mountain in similar circumstances can understand his bitter disappointment. On reaching the step Packard went up with three Sherpas while Gyalgen and I remained below to handle and tie on the loads. Hauling them on so long a rope, which bit deep into the snow on the lip of the wall, was hard work. It took three hours. When I went up I so disliked the proximity of the proposed camp site to the edge of the cliff that we moved everything a hundred yards further back. Before we had settled in, Evans and Roberts were back at the foot of the steps waiting to be helped up; after which we lifted the fixed ropes and stowed them. There was something of solemn finality about this act of severing our link with earth-bound things; a Caesarian touch of 'iacta alea est'; but we could comfort ourselves with the thought that with bread, rope and an ice-axe we could at least get down.

Useful though it might be to have a fit spare man, the fifth man is like the fifth wheel of a coach. Most convenient is the party of four, as we now were. Two tents are enough; and if these are pitched close together door-to-door it is almost as good as having the party under one roof. (An American climber has designed a tent which is 'zipped' to another one at the door, so making one tent of two.) Thus we could

Some of the 108 spouts from which the pilgrims to Muktinath successively drink; the water is delicious, but obviously none of the pilgrims have heard of Brillat Savarin and his dictum that 'since water is the only beverage that quenches thirst it can be drunk only in small quantities'

Off-loading bags of salt from zos at Bimtakhoti; like yaks they are handled and tethered by means of a wooden ring in the nostrils; the one with a collar of small bells and tassels is the leader; the big, deep-toned bell slung under his neck is worn by all the zos

Our camp by the sacred lake on the Bahara Pokhara Lekh where pilgrims bathe and where monal pheasants commit suicide

lie at ease and throw biscuits, the jam tin, butter and jokes at each other. As a reward for having overcome the step, we foreswore pemmican and regaled ourselves with a tin of self-heating soup which Emlyn Jones had brought out to try. Such tins are too heavy to hump about on a long journey, but for a night's bivouac they do well.

To avoid the second ice-step we traversed to the left for half a mile and then diagonally upwards towards the dome. On the traverse, passing under a lurching serac of horrible frailty, the combined prayers of the party for a temporary suspension of the laws of gravity were offered to whatever mountain deity attends to such matters. The second leg of our course led up a crevassed snow-field backed by cliffs of rock and ice which, as we drew near the dome, merged into a steep unbroken slope. The quality of the snow varied; first good, then deep and soft, and finally thin with ice underneath. In the soft snow, where movement was laborious, we graciously handed the lead to Gyalgen who, in time, landed us triumphantly on a broad snow slope to the west of and below the dome. Gyalgen was an experienced climber (in 1938 he had been on Everest), but except for this flash there seemed little fire left in him. He did no more than was necessary and on one occasion less. The other three, who were steady, reliable lads, took their cue from him, their sirdar, and thus showed less enthusiasm than I had expected for the high places of the Universe. Gyalgen was at his best in the kitchen, and much can be forgiven a man who can be depended upon to produce something eatable very quickly under any conditions. But his manner was not ingratiating, and he had started badly as far as I was concerned by ripping up half-a-dozen canvas food bags and turning them into a cover for his own sleeping-bag; an act which, under other circumstances, might have earned him a decoration for cool daring and initiative.

After plodding up this gentle slope for a short half-mile we arrived under the lee of the main Annapurna ridge. The first instinct of a mountaineer upon reaching a ridge is to look over the other side, but on this occasion none of us had the energy to do so. We pitched a tent, dumped the loads, and went down. Next day we occupied this camp. Some snow which had fallen during a warm night had obliterated our tracks, and as we all carried loads we found the going very heavy. On this part of the route, particularly on the broad slopes of the ridge, we planted our willow wands, for in descending it was essential to hit off the right line on the steep part below the dome. After drinking pint mugs of sweet tea we mustered energy to crawl to the ridge where we looked out over a sea of cloud pierced by the fang-like summit of Macha Puchare. Away to our left the final pyramid of Annapurna II looked remote as ever and no more attractive. However, one more lift of 2000 ft. should put us within striking distance of A-IV, to attain which became more and more a desirable first prize instead of merely a consolation for defeat by A-II. My two R.A.F. altimeters showed the height of Camp III to be 20,800 ft.; which, as is usually the way, was much lower than we reckoned.

Upon turning out early next morning for photography we found that the sea of cloud to the south had spread northwards and submerged the Marsyandi valley. Only a few white and distant tops remained in sight to remind us of the existence of solid land. This dense and widespread canopy assured us that monsoon conditions were established, but whether the weather would become worse or better, or in what way, was anybody's guess. Of our seven days on the mountain so far three had been fine which, I suppose, is as much as one can expect from mountain weather.

From the camp the broad back of the ridge extended eastwards almost horizontally for some way until it narrowed and mounted steadily to articulate with a shoulder of Annapurna IV at close on 24,000 ft. Its subsequent behaviour had now become of less concern to us, but it appeared to drop a little before rising to the foot of the rocky pyramid of Annapurna II, two miles beyond. Halfway up the rise to the shoulder of Annapurna IV, where a break in the slope intervened, seemed the obvious site for the next camp. In examining the route from below, we had paid only slight attention to this section which we had regarded as little more than a snow trudge. We had done it less than justice. Now the angle seemed high, the ridge narrow, and in its lower part so broken by terraces and crevasses that there might be no through way.

Opinion seemed to be in favour of avoiding this broken section by a descending traverse, regaining the ridge higher up by a steep snow slope. I thought I could see a way through. Not relishing the climb back to the ridge I was bent on clinging to it and insisted on trying, and for once my judgement proved correct. By sticking firmly to the crest of the ridge we worked our way up by an interesting and enjoyable route, skirting crevasses and linking terrace to terrace until the angle lessened and the ridge broadened. On the south side parts of the route were a little exposed for laden men, but in the excellent snow a well-driven axe held like a bower anchor. That day we went no further than a snow boss about 1000 ft. above Camp III. Charles Evans and Packard were going very well. Roberts was labouring a little, while I suffered increasingly from mountaineer's foot—reluctance to put one in front of the other. No sooner had we got down to the level ridge than a blizzard swept over it so furiously that, in the short time required to reach the tents, our outgoing tracks were obliterated. On this part of the route, where they seemed least necessary, our few remaining willow wands had been planted too far apart to be seen in a storm.

By now the amount of food consumed, together with tent, rope and other gear left at Camp II, had reduced our total weight to within the compass of two lifts by the Sherpas alone, each carrying less than thirty pounds. On the first carry to Camp IV we arranged the loads so that the three Europeans could stay there until the others moved up next day. In this way one of us could look after the descending Sherpas, a task which I undertook; not because I felt more fitted for it than the others, but less fitted for Camp IV. Indeed, on the climb up I felt so feeble that I plodded disconsolately at the tail-end of a rope, kicking never a step. After a long rest at the boss we struggled on until we came to a snug snow hollow in the lee of an ice-cliff just below the flat bit of ridge which we had marked down for a camp site. The altimeters recorded a height of 22,400 ft. Thus we were camped only 2200 ft. below the summit of Annapurna IV which, I thought, two at least of the party were fit enough to reach.

In wishing the others good luck I hoped that when we came up the next day they would be coming down from the summit of Annapurna IV. In that happy event we might think of pushing a camp forward along the ridge for at least a reconnaissance of Annapurna II, having now become reconciled to the fact that the party was not equal to doing more. The Sherpas and I started down in thickening mist, the precursor of a blizzard like that of the previous day. Even on a ridge it is fatally easy in thick weather and driving snow to miss the way, to quit the ridge too soon, or to stay on it too long. The broken nature of the lower part of ours made this perhaps even easier; on the other hand the familiar shapes of terraces and crevasses, when they did appear, played the reassuring part of signposts.

Although the wide back of the flat ridge below gave ample scope for erratic wandering, the leading man unerringly picked up the occasional faint irregularities—the only traces which the wind-driven snow had left of our tracks. When the tents came in sight I sent the Sherpas on and took a long rest, before creeping home at the best pace a piece of ruined nature could contrive.

When dawn of the 16th broke murky, misty and snowy, inaction seemed the inevitable and most sensible course. For the Camp IV party, straining, one hoped, at the leash, it would be provoking enough, but so far as I was concerned nothing could be better. Musing thus contentedly without wondering overmuch what the Sherpas, who seemed restless, were up to, I was shocked when they began striking my tent. The precept 'not too much zeal' may be very well for disillusioned old men, but zeal in others, however inconvenient, is not lightly to be discouraged. It is too often a transient state of mind, shortlived and possibly non-recurrent. Dissembling any surprise, I rose reluctantly and packed. The wind had dropped and in spite of some desultory snowfall visibility seemed fair. Zeal was indeed transient; by the time we had reached the foot of the climb little remained. All steps had to be kicked afresh, and Da Namgyal, the best of a mediocre quartette, led through the difficult part. Pa Norbu, having kicked a few steps, cried enough; and Gyalgen, who had to be ordered, led for only a short time with numerous halts. I was incapable of kicking steps, but by ringing the changes on Da Namgyal and Pa Norbu, we crawled slowly up. Snow was still falling gently when we surprised the inmates of Camp IV who were wisely lying at earth.

Morning dawned fine but gusty. Having a bad headache, and having breakfasted like a worn-out libertine on tea and aspirin, I had no intention of moving. Roberts seemed to be feeling much the same, so Evans and Packard set off alone to see what they could do. Just as it is:

> ... Pleasant to gaze at the sailors,
> To gaze without having to sail...

so Roberts and I watched the progress of the climbers with the complacency of gods watching the struggles of good men against adversity. They soon crossed the short, flat piece of ridge above the camp and came into sight moving slowly but steadily up the foot of the 1500 ft. slope towards the shoulder. Meantime the sky began to assume a threatening aspect, and we were disappointed but not surprised to see them turn back after about two and a half hours, when they were still a long way below the shoulder. Soon after 10 a.m. they reached camp in time to escape a storm which rose very quickly to the ferocity of a blizzard. Their report that the slope consisted of hard snow, and that in good weather the summit might be reached, went some way to lightening the mild anxiety occasioned by the wind battering at the tents. Nor could one be over-sanguine when one reviewed the condition of the rest of the party; particularly the Sherpas, who throughout the storm, which towards evening began to relent, lay ominously quiet. It would need more than ordinary bad weather to make the descent hazardous, but obviously we could not afford to stay at Camp IV too long.

The time which the first pair had taken to reach their highest point, perhaps less than half-way to the summit, inclined me to think either that they had gone very slowly or that we overestimated our height. So far the altimeters had deserved our confidence by their sober behaviour, having more than once surprised the party by their unflattering estimate of our achievements. Anyway, if we were going to take seven or eight hours to reach the top, and if it was the habit of the weather to deteriorate by midday (as on the last three days it had), the earlier we started the better. Accordingly I roused the party for a second attempt at 4 a.m. and got them off by 5 a.m. Gyalgen and Da Namgyal accompanied us. The sun had just risen in a leaden sky, or rather a pale, watery glow showed that it was doing its best, and it was very cold. Treading in deep powder snow, the aftermath of yesterday's storm, we gained the ridge and headed for the foot of the slope a few hundred yards away. On our right hand lay a vast, cold chasm, with a grey, wrinkled glacier dimly visible below.

We had not been going ten minutes when Roberts complained that the powder snow was freezing his feet. He decided to go back, and, without a word of explanation Gyalgen, too, turned back. No powder snow had been left on the slope. On the contrary the wind had packed the snow so hard that we were obliged to nick steps. The perishing cold, and the sight of Packard in the lead taking five or six blows to nick a step, persuaded me to take over from him but without any noticeable increase in our pace. Meantime, a thin wind accompanied by mist blew steadily across the slope, which was too broad to afford any cover. We struggled up for a few hundred feet, but when the wind showed no sign of dropping, nor the sun of piercing the clouds, we too turned tail. By 6.30 we were back in camp.

For the second time the mountain, or its close ally the weather, had beaten us. As we sat licking our wounds, more precisely restoring circulation to our toes—a long process—we noticed with mixed feelings a gradual mending of the weather. Before midday, when according to our notions deterioration should have set in, the day became more and more delightfully calm, sunny and clear. Packard suggested starting again but no one else thought much of that at so late an hour. Instead we basked in our snow hollow, driven by the heat from our tents, tracing imaginary routes upon distant, majestic Manaslu, and how we might make a real route up a peak overlooking the Naur valley. Of all the mountains displayed, from Manaslu to the Muktinath range, this looked least hostile.

Roberts wanted to go down and, since the spirits of the Sherpas seemed at a low ebb, I thought they had better go too before they caved in. I myself had little expectation of climbing the mountain but I hoped that Evans and Packard might, though the former admitted to feeling less fit. We three, therefore, would make one more attempt, retaining Da Namgyal to keep house for us. Leaving him in camp was, I think, a mistake, for he might have made a second on Packard's rope. Accordingly on 19 June, at a more reasonable hour, but after a poor night owing to increasingly wet sleeping-bags, we three started up while Roberts conducted three Sherpas down to Camp III, taking all the tents except the Logan.

The sun shone bleakly through a veil of high cirrus upon which it had painted, as upon flimsy canvas, an iridescent halo. Climbing even at that height, which was by no means extreme, our pace seemed fully as slow as that of a glacier; unhappily, one feared, without the glacier's inexorability. Having climbed for nearly two hours we paused at a small rock outcrop to take stock and to compare our height with that of Macha Puchare, whose fish-tail seemed to make a rude gesture at us from above a bank of cloud. It is difficult to judge by the eye alone, but the most hopeful among us dared not affirm that we were much, if anything, above it; which meant that we had risen only 500 ft. After another hour, during which we gained height quicker owing to the steeper slope, the altimeter put us at a height of 23,400 ft. Packard was going strong, Charles Evans panting a little, while the combined effect of age and altitude threatened momentarily to bring my faltering footsteps to a halt. In fact, my goose was cooked, but I was still strong enough to get down alone. Hoping they would move quicker, I persuaded them to leave me.

At midday the usual snow scurries began, yet with no threat of worse to follow. I still hoped they might do it, for I had last seen them nearing the shoulder. Alas; presently they reappeared coming down and before two o'clock were back in camp. They had climbed beyond the shoulder to an estimated height of 24,000 ft., where our candid friend, the altimeter, which I had urged them to take, registered only 23,800 ft. But Evans had shot his bolt, and Packard, who felt strong enough, was rightly loath to tackle single-handed the last 600 ft. of steep and narrow summit ridge. Thus a fortnight of hard work and high hope ended in deep disappointment.

On this third and final attempt neither adverse weather nor dangerous snow conditions could be made scapegoats for our failure; a failure accounted for only by the more prosaic reason of inability to reach the top. That three out of four picked men should fail at or well below 24,000 ft. was not only disappointing, but a little surprising. The performance of the veteran of the party, with all the advantages of experience, was no better. However well a man in his fifties may go up to 20,000 ft., I have come regretfully to the conclusion that above that height, so far as climbing goes, he is declining into decrepitude.

CHAPTER XIV

A CHANGE OF SCENE

THE DESCENT FROM OUR MOUNTAIN, carried out in swift but orderly stages, can be dismissed briefly. On many Himalayan mountains the descent has proved more arduous and perilous than the ascent, and has consequently provided the better story. One recalls the Germans descending in storm from Kangchenjunga in 1929, and the three who died with their six Sherpas on the retreat from Nanga Parbat in 1934; the benighted British pair on Masherbrum in 1938; and the desperate descent of the frost-bitten French pair from Annapurna I this same June. Such hazardous and sometimes fatal affairs are usually the result of bad weather, an attack pressed too long, or a combination of both. In ordinary circumstances the descent of a big mountain is accomplished in as many days as the ascent took weeks. Climbers and porters are eager, perhaps too eager, to get down; all that is needed is care that the descent does not become an uncontrolled one accomplished in a matter of seconds.

The Logan tent had been considered ample for four Sherpas, but we, who like room to spread ourselves, expecting to be uncomfortable, were agreeably surprised at passing a reasonable night. Da Namgyal, who lay in the middle curled round the centre pole, did not give us his opinion. The Camp III party were supposed to meet us halfway, but we got down there by eight o'clock of a dull morning to find them asleep. We had no intention of stopping, so we routed them out, packed up, and went on; of the Sherpas only Da Namgyal seemed alert and helpful, Gyalgen being a little morose.

The mist which now enveloped us made welcome the guiding willow wands to direct us to the proper place for the descent of the steep slope below the dome. Upon this more than ordinary care was needed. At the bottom the snow changed markedly for the worse. At this lesser height there had been no freezing, even at night, so that we floundered down to Camp II in typically soft, wet monsoon snow. The same evening we laid out the fixed ropes, anchoring one to the broken axe shaft and the other to a bundle of long pitons, both laid horizontally at a depth of two feet with snow trampled down on top. In the night much snow fell, and we had to dig out the loads before making all ready for lowering. Two hours passed in doing this, and then with a remorseful glance at the friendly ropes which had served us so well, we set off under heavy loads for Camp I. The ropes, of course, had to be left behind after safeguarding the descent of the last man.

Even though we were going downhill this bit exhausted us more than any other; ascending such snow would have been killing work. Constantly the legs and feet of one or other of us became inextricably wedged in the deep, wet snow and had to be patiently dug free. Below Camp I, so great had the changes been, little of the route could be recognized. Large areas of snow had vanished and the descent to the dump lay for the most part on rock. Having picked up there a few odds and ends we set off across the glacier in a drizzle, climbed the moraine, and descended to a kindlier region. Our long sojourn upon ice and snow gave a keen edge to the mere pleasure of treading upon warm earth, where hardy, diminutive plants made some slight show of colour and where small cheerful birds flew about as if in greeting. These sparrows, technically eastern Alpine Accentors, haunt and animate an otherwise bleak and lifeless belt between the last of the grass and the first snow.

As we dropped down to the trees of the Sabzi Chu the changes were less striking, our pleasure, though still great, less intense, and our languor increasingly pronounced. In theory a man coming down from a high mountain should go faster and faster; in practice he becomes slower and more lethargic, and is appalled by the slightest rise. On the short ascent of a few hundred feet to Base camp I found my movements were barely perceptible. A period spent at high levels no doubt affects the heart more or less severely, but fortunately only temporarily, according to the time spent and the age and condition of the sojourner. After a strenuous Alpine holiday the ascent even of a staircase is noticeably fatiguing.

In our absence Lowndes had been making profitable sorties to upper slopes and valleys, for there were not many flowers much below 14,000 ft. Emlyn Jones with Sher Bahadur had visited Muktinath on the Kali side of the Muktinath range. There they had learnt that the French had gone home after suffering injuries, but what mountain they had been on or whether they had climbed it no one could tell them, so vague and ignorant are the local people about their magnificent mountain environment. Our ascent had been watched through a telescope as far as Camp III, beyond which we had been hidden in the clouds.

As three of the party had to leave by mid-July we had about three weeks left in which to find a mountain and climb it. There was nothing suitable on the Annapurna range and rather than prolong the search for an opponent worthy of our slightly blunted steel, we decided to accept the challenge of the peak which we had marked down as a possible prize from Camp IV. Nevertheless it was a shot in the dark. We had seen nothing but the upper part of the mountain, and in the prevailing conditions of cloud, mist and a little rain, it was unlikely that we would see much more. We gave ourselves three days' rest and the Manangbhot Notables notice of our need for seven coolies. Meantime we learnt that the way to Naurgaon, the village nearest to our mountain, lay over a 17,000 ft. pass to the north, the route up the Naur Khola being longer and quite impassable in summer. The people of Ngawal, a village two miles down the valley, had close relations with Naurgaon so they were comparatively delighted to provide all seven coolies.

Accordingly on 25 June a mixed team of reasonably lusty Ngawalians turned up at midday, an hour which ensured their not having to go any farther than their own village that day. Emlyn Jones came with us, while Roberts, whose feet were still painful, took over the collecting of birds, for which I was very thankful. In the absence of Wolfe Tone, who had been unable to come, we had neither collector nor skinner. The skinning of birds was more of a problem than the collecting. Roberts, after a practical lesson in the anatomy of birds from Charles Evans, entered upon this messy part of the job with diffidence. Sher Bahadur came to the rescue. Having watched Toni practising taxidermy all the previous summer, he now showed his ability to turn out equally good specimens. No doubt Roberts would have seen to it that the museum got the species they wanted, but without Sher Bahadur's help they might have had a little difficulty in recognizing them.

After a pleasingly short march down the left bank of the river amidst stunted pines growing stubbornly on yellowish gravel, we

Bimtakhoti against a background of rock spires; Manaslu is out of sight to the left; the long house at the top is the salt and rice depot

Looking across the big moraine at Bimtakhoti to the Ladakh range: Himlung Himal (23,380 ft.) is the peak on the left, Cheo Himal (22,350 ft.) on the right; shrines appear in unexpected places; this one is on a shelf of the moraine, the lower part of which is ancient enough to carry a strong growth of heath and dwarf rhododendron

Very advanced photography: a not altogether contemptible effort showing a Saussurea growing at about 16,000 ft. with Himal Chuli (25,801 ft.) as a background; surprisingly enough everything is more or less in focus; de Saussure (1740–99), after whom the plant is named, was a Swiss physicist and Alpine traveller; he made the third ascent of Mont Blanc in 1787

camped near Ngawal, whither our mixed team withdrew to spend a last comfortable night. After climbing about 2500 ft. we camped at a spring well below the pass. So high above the valley, where more often than not cloud and mist lay, grass and flowers flourished, particularly a tall white primula with bell-shaped flowers and a refreshing scent. Yaks grazed everywhere untended; the kharkas of these uplands were unoccupied and consequently we got no milk. We often saw stone huts but they were never inhabited either by shepherds or herdsmen. One wondered why the yaks roamed the hillsides to nobody's benefit but their own.

To reach the pass we had yet 2000 ft. to climb, mostly over brown scree where we could just discern the faint zigzags of a track. Some unsuspecting ponies which happened to be grazing untended hard by, having been swiftly roped in by the Ngawalians, presently found themselves bound for the pass heavily laden. At 16,000 ft., where the grass fought a losing battle with the gravel, I found a bright mauve primula eighteen inches high; and on the north side of the pass at the same height, but on scree, the lovely pale blue delphinium with the ravishing scent which we had found in the Langtang—the plant which the natives use, not wholly successfully, as an insecticide.

The unnamed valley into which we dropped steeply was wide, flat, of typically glacial origin, where now only a meagre vestige of ice remains hanging high above it. A bold, uniform, grass-covered moraine ran the whole four or five miles to Naurgaon, and strolling along the top as upon a promenade we looked down upon grass flats dotted with grazing yaks. Neither trees nor juniper bushes grew in this high valley, which had an air of rich but unfulfilled promise intensified by numerous abandoned stone shelters, comparatively few yaks, and a solitary flock of sheep.

Naurgaon seemed sufficient unto itself without making much use of this fine valley. Poised high above the Naur river, the village surprised us by its comfortable and prosperous air. The houses, as usual, appeared to grow out of the brown, stony hillside, while below lay terrace upon terrace of young barley of the liveliest green where a swarm of women and children were busy weeding. We camped short of the village by a brook, its grassy bank fragrant with thyme, where the headman soon found us. This man, whose every word confirmed the shiftiness of his eyes, amused me by his anxiety to play down the obvious well-being of his village. Like Justice Shallow, fearing a call was about to be made upon it, he deprecated his goodly heritage: 'Barren, barren, barren; beggars all, beggars all, Sir John.'

'Any eggs?' we enquired, 'or a chicken?' 'No', he replied with a regretful smirk, the lusty crowing of many cocks echoing his words, 'We don't keep fowls in Naurgaon.' 'A sheep or a goat?' 'No', came the answer, almost inaudible amidst the bleating of a large flock wending its way to the village, 'They are all up the valley at a distant kharka.' 'Any milk?' Quite unobtainable', he regretted, contemplatively eyeing a nearby hillside thick with yaks and zos. However, he promised to supply seven coolies in place of our Ngawal team, for even his effrontery was not equal to asserting the death, burial or absence, of all the able-bodied when we were surrounded by a milling horde.

The peak we hoped to climb is unnamed on the map but is credited with a height of 22,997 ft.—near enough to 23,000 ft. to satisfy those who were particular about the height of mountains with which they associated. Its local name was Khangguru which merely means 'white snow'—a name so frequently heard in the Nepal Himalaya that strangers might be tempted to believe that some of the mountains were crowned with black snow. Through a cloud vista we caught a brief glimpse of the summit of our peak and of a wide, green nallah, running up to black cliffs, at its foot. Between nallah and summit lay an unshifting bank of cloud behind which any horrors might lurk. However, the nallah hinted at a break in the line of cliffs, and near the bottom we saw some terraced fields where we might have a pleasant camp. It looked close but in between lay a gorge 2000 ft. deep and our new coolies were no fliers. The team included a child and two old crones. By a display of firmness we exchanged the child for the village idiot; but over the women the headman was adamant, not caring, perhaps, to miss such a promising chance of ridding the village of them for good.

Naurgaon lies close to the beginning of an abrupt 2000 ft. drop to the river, and upon the very edge, as if defending the approach, is built a stone wall six feet high. Nor is the wall the only sign that the Naur valley may have been the scene of 'unhappy far-off things and battles long ago', for we found the river crossing guarded by a ruined stone tower on the far side. At this point the river flows through a canyon, the merest slit 500 ft. deep and seldom more than ten yards wide throughout its length of about a mile. We learnt later that Naurgaon was once the capital of a rajah whose territory included Manangbhot; hence these defences across the approach to it by the Naur valley.

Having dropped a great many stones from the bridge, timed their fall, and heard from Packard with becoming humility the answer to a difficult sum, we pushed on downstream to the deserted village. The fields were sown with wheat and buckwheat, and we were told that many of the Naurgaon folk wintered there. Next day, having added some firewood to our loads, we set off up the nallah. It was depressingly misty, the first of a succession of blind days; giant purple poppies and dainty blue corydalis did their best to lighten the drab scene until grass and flowers died out upon an interminable tongue of gravel. It grew ever steeper as we plodded up shrouded in mist, our horizon bounded on one hand by a gully backed by streaming wet cliffs and on the other by scree and boulders.

Down both gully and scree slope crashed occasional boulders. The mist turned to rain, the tongue obstinately maintained an uncomfortably high angle, and when at length we decided to call it a day we were obliged to dig platforms for the tents. Even for those with tents a more disagreeable and inhospitable spot in which to bed down could hardly have been found. For the coolies there was nothing. The friendly boulder, which in such circumstances at least provides an earnest of shelter, dripped like a gutterless roof and the ground in its lee had the high slope of a roof. Concern for the coolies proved needless, for they had their own ideas about lodgings for the night. No sooner had they straggled in and cast down their loads than they approached, their hands raised palm to palm in supplication, begging to be sent down. With the exception of two stalwarts who elected to stay one more day, I paid them off. Whereupon, with a whoop of joy, they disappeared in the rain.

Light, single-fly tents are moderately weather-proof if they start dry, but when packed wet and pitched wet they will certainly drip. After a wet night we left the tents standing to dry, only to strike them hastily when the drizzle began again. On we went up the tongue, noting with sour satisfaction that no better camp sites offered, until we were stopped by a bed of old avalanche snow, the streaming cliffs over which it had slid looming blackly above. Thus driven out on to the scree we traversed upwards, moving with the best speed we could muster across several deep runnels scoured by falling stones. On the far side, by a stream and a large boulder with a faint suggestion of overhang, we camped. While the Sherpas went back for the remaining loads, three of us followed up the stream until we found a line of weakness in the cliffs where it had carved out a gully. In this we climbed for several hundred feet until we could break out on to easy rocks. Assuming the difficulties were over we built a cairn to mark the route, if the line of least resistance which we were following merits such a description. We had no idea where it went; in such weather, upwards or downwards were the only discernible directions.

Meantime, unless conditions improved we should get no higher. Water oozed up through the floor of the tents, streamed from the walls where the platforms had been sunk, and dripped from the roof, reducing the inmates to sodden misery. Having decided to wait we were rewarded (2 July) with a fine day. A wan sun made sufficient brief appearances to dry everything, and Gyalgen, using the last of the firewood, baked a loaf. Courage was renewed.

By jettisoning fairly severely we were able to carry everything in one shift, Evans and Packard assisting by adding considerably to their own loads. It was a critical day, for the most part blinded by mist. Our reconnaissance had not been pushed far enough. No sooner had we passed the cairn marking its limit than we were confronted by a fifteen-foot rock wall topped by some slabs. Success hung in the balance. Using the rope for ourselves and the loads we got by this, and after some anxious moments in the mist, expecting every moment to be stopped, we found the ground became gradually easier. We reached a rock cirque and climbed out of it by an easy but precarious gully of shaky rock. This move landed us on a saddle of warm, dry shale with a glacier and its promise of water just below. At 18,000 ft. we seemed to be in a drier climate. It was still misty but the sun had power to penetrate and we felt that we had at last got our heads above water. Visibility, too, had improved so much that we could now see our route up the glacier to a snow dome, at the foot of the final ridge which we already knew, having seen it from Annapurna. There seemed to be nothing to stop us now unless we met with soft, deep snow such as we had experienced recently at 20,000 ft.

The glacier, seamed with crevasses, many of them concealed, had to be navigated with caution. Beyond it, helped by a long strip of scree laid bare by the sun, we made good progress towards the dome up which we were presently climbing on excellent snow. The others, including Emlyn Jones who seemed to have got over his 19,000 ft. complex, were going well; I was moving with more dignity than ease. We camped at the foot of the final ridge at just below 20,000 ft. The ridge looked steep but apart from a bergschrund about 200 ft. above us and some pale, watery looking patches which betokened ice, there was apparently nothing to prevent us carrying a light camp to the shoulder at about 21,500 ft. where the summit ridge assumed an easier angle. Encouraged by the perfect snow on which we trod, we thought the peak was in the bag.

At this moment of general benevolence Gyalgen saw fit to announce briefly that the Sherpas had resolved not to touch pemmican. Unlike most European climbers who take it under the perhaps mistaken impression that it is good for them, Sherpas as a rule eat it with the greatest gusto. Evidently there was more behind this than was natural, could philosophy but find it out. Whether they had suddenly and inopportunely discovered religious scruples, or whether they were preparing an excuse for cutting short their stay on the mountain, I never discovered. But it troubled me, much as a workhouse master would be troubled by the refusal of his guests to eat skilly. Not that they were likely to go hungry. We had plenty of satu, sugar and tea, as well as a large bladder of rancid yak fat which they had purchased for themselves at Naurgaon. So powerful was this stuff that it flavoured or contaminated our food as well, merely by its presence in the same load.

With high hopes we set out on 5 July to put a camp as near the shoulder as possible. As far as the bergschrund the snow was perfect, but then the covering grew thinner and thinner until soon we were carving large steps in the underlying ice.

Having climbed some 400 ft. in four hours we chose the softest ice we could find and hacked out a platform for the tent. Jones and Packard had crampons, so on the slim chance that they might complete the climb without having to cut steps, we left them there as a forlorn hope. The appearance of a halo round the sun did not auger well for the attempt next day, while Emlyn Jones's form on A-IV did not afford much assurance that he would go to 23,000 ft. But neither Evans nor I had brought crampons, without which one would be faced with the hopeless task of cutting steps for some 1500 ft. Wishing them luck we started down with the Sherpas. On the way there were no difficult places, nor was there any place where an ice-axe could be driven in to safeguard a slip.

A fall of snow in the night did not improve the chance of the summit party, and the dull, wintry morning which followed was not the kind one would choose for a long and difficult climb. But then so few are. From the door of our tent, for it was too cold to stay outside, Evans and I had the doubtful pleasure of both seeing and hearing them at work. Wisps of mist hid them intermittently, but we saw enough to know that they would not get far. They were laboriously cutting steps, a task imposed upon them by the steepness and iciness of the slope. Even wearing crampons, they could not descend safely without steps. Having seen them start back from a point about 400 ft. above their camp, we went up with two Sherpas to help them down. In the afternoon we packed up and withdrew down the glacier to the camp on the shale saddle to enjoy the warmth of that pleasant sun-trap. Although it makes softer lying than stones or even shale, no one sleeps on snow a night longer than necessary.

Thus, contrary to expectation and the gloomy forebodings freely announced by the experienced veteran, instead of laboriously having to hew a passage through defences of soft snow, we had been decisively halted on a glacis of bare ice. Forecasting snow conditions in the Himalaya is a task that would puzzle Old Moore.

CHAPTER XV

MUSTANGBHOT

On returning to Manang three of the party prepared to depart for home, poor in achievement but rich, one hoped, in memories and in experience. To the armchair philosopher success and miscarriage may be but empty words but the mountaineer, who in his more mellow moments may say the same, cherishes a private belief that success does mean something and he therefore attaches to it no little importance. Some there are who are satisfied with the mere looking at mountains; but to the mountaineer they are a challenge. If he ignores them he loses a little of his self-respect, if he attempts them and fails he suspects himself of incompetence or irresolution. Until age has calmed his passion that mountaineer would need to be endowed with the firmness of a St Anthony who is not inflamed by the sight of virgin peaks, who does not regret opportunities missed and lament desires unfulfilled.

On 16 July Evans, Emlyn Jones and Packard left, with two of the Sherpas, to return by Bimtakhoti and the Buri Gandaki valley. At the height of the monsoon they found this route arduous, the porters unwilling, and food scarce. Packard, who was sailing by a later boat, remained with one Sherpa near Arughat in order to devote a fortnight to studying the agriculture and economy of the lower villages. After a week there he became seriously ill with what was later found to be poliomyelitis; he had to be carried in a litter to Katmandu whence, after receiving every attention at the Embassy, he was sent to Bombay and later home by air. Of all the mischances that may befall a man in the Himalaya this must be the strangest and the most unexpected.

The day after their departure, Roberts being still fully occupied with birds, I started back to Naurgaon, taking with me two Sherpas. On our first visit we had heard something of a pass at the head of the Naur Khola which crossed the Muktinath range to Mustangbhot in the upper basin of the Kali river. This Mustang La, as the pass was called, was reported to be inaccessible during the summer owing to the impossibility of fording the Naur river, but I had set my heart on going there and trusted either to finding or forcing an alternative route along the north side of the offending river. In the matter of routes the local people are sometimes very reticent towards a stranger. It may be that they have a low opinion of a European's ability to traverse them, or think that their routes are not fit for a man of such obvious wealth and importance. Personally I should like to believe that they deliberately conceal their knowledge of remote tracks from higher motives—raiding or smuggling, for example—but in these prosaic times it is unlikely. A more probable reason for reticence is the fear that if the wealthy nincompoop traversing their devious ways gets into trouble, either by breaking a leg or drowning himself, they will get the blame.

We reached Naurgaon over an alternative pass by a most ingenious track which, when one looked back from the valley near Naurgaon, appeared an improbable if not an impossible line. In places one had to resort to using the hands, yet signs that the route had been used by sheep, goats, even yaks, were not wanting. The route followed a series of 'rakes' lying along the foot of reddish cliffs sprinkled with cushions of delicate blue or white aquilegia. Light blue poppies nestled in the crannies, and pale mauve primulas clustered over the wet gravel ledges.

I had threatened the shifty headman of Naurgaon with a second visit and now I had come, armed with a letter written by Sher Bahadur conjuring him in the name of authority to treat me with every consideration, and to send him, Sher Bahadur, an adequate quantity of ghi or butter. The headman, in his valley fastness, could well afford to laugh at notes of this kind whether or not he could read them. He stuffed this one in amongst the village archives, which he kept in his hat, and merely added ghi and butter to the list of what he had not got. Neither from him, nor from more reliable sources, tapped independently by Gyalgen, could we hear any comforting words about the Mustang La route which starts from Naurgaon. Late September was the earliest at which the river could be forded. We decided to go north to Phugaon, the last village this side of the Tibet border, where an alternative route, if any existed, must start, and where, too, we should be on the north side of the Naur river.

Instead of the three coolies asked for, we had to leave with two, and since nowadays Sherpas have rigid ideas about what they should carry when local coolies are included in the party, I carried my own sack. If I expected a startled protest at this piece of bravado on the part of master I was disappointed. Time was when rather than see their employer carry anything on a path—that is when not climbing—Sherpas would cheerfully shoulder eighty or 100 pounds; but nowadays it is fair shares for all—all except the local coolies on whom they pile as much of their own loads as they can.

Once more crossing the bridge over the 500 ft. deep rift we turned up the Naur valley, which presently bore away westwards in the direction of the Muktinath range and the Mustang La. What we could see of it looked bare and inhospitable but by no means impassable. Our route lay northwards up the valley of a river of equal size, the Phu Chu, which rises in a glacier of the Ladakh range. Our camp that night was near an abandoned village, where I estimated there were nearly 100 acres of terraced fields. Judging by the state of the terrace walls they could not have been abandoned for more than a hundred years, though according to our coolies the village had not been occupied within living memory. High above, a small glacier discharged a copious stream from which a long leat had once supplied water to the fields. Possibly its upkeep had proved too great a task for a diminishing population.

The Phu river now entered a series of gorges which were negotiated by means of stairways hewn out of the rock. Having climbed several hundred steps up one of these we had to go through a wooden gate topped with small chortens, and past a red, white and black mani wall. Dropping once more to the river we crossed at a place where it flowed through nothing more than a rock trench. An active man, not necessarily a desperate one, might have jumped it. Here there were several large coloured chortens, and above them a ruined tower high upon a rock pinnacle guarded the defile.

Puzzled by these towers and walls I asked for an explanation from Sher Bahadur who gave me the following story. In early days—that is presumably before the eighteenth century—when Nepal was divided into petty kingdoms, Naurgaon was the capital of a Ghale Gurung Rajah whose territory included Manangbhot and extended to below Thonje. His principal enemy was naturally his nearest neighbour the rajah of Lamjung, a place in the Marsyandi valley below Kudi; and these towers and walls were probably built in the course of a war

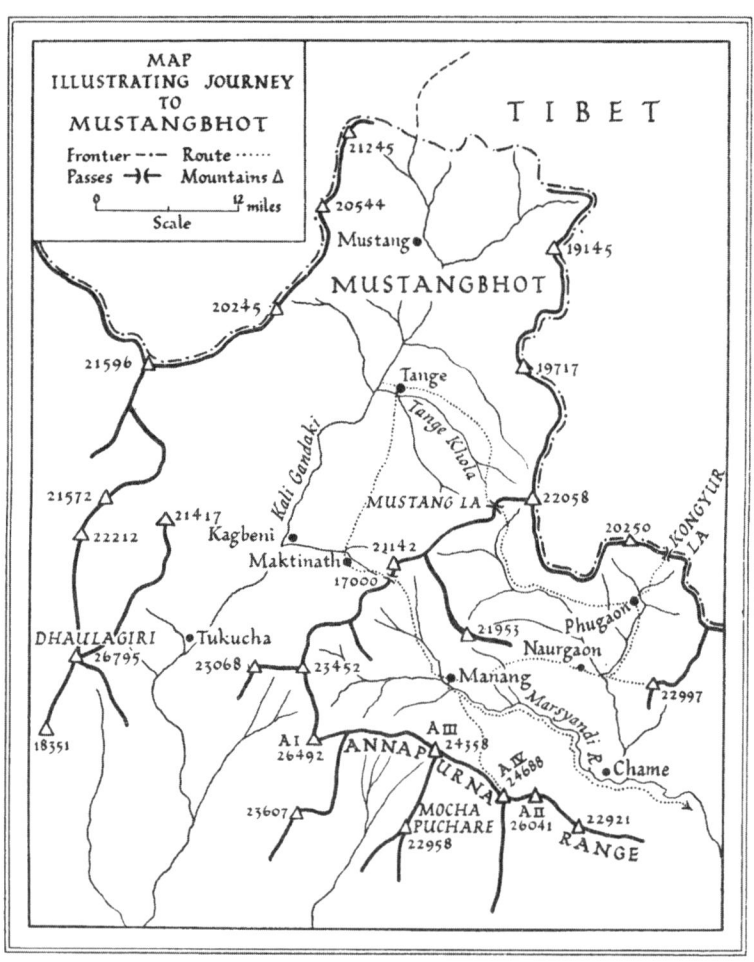

Map 5: Journey to Mustangbhot

against him. The Lamjung Rajah was decisively defeated, but subsequently he lured Ghale Rajah, on a pretence of making a peace treaty, to a village called Baman Dande in the Marsyandi valley where he had him and his followers massacred.

Half a mile beyond the gorge, on the west bank, we came to the strange village of Phugaon built on the face and top of a high cliff of boulders and gravel, the eroded remains of a river terrace. At first glance it appears to consist of nothing but narrow, clay threshing floors supported on pillars, underneath which the chaff and grain are stored when winnowing.

There are, in fact, some hovels behind these but the best houses are assembled under one roof, and surrounded by a single wall on the summit of the cliff. We had to put our tents on a threshing floor, the only other flat sites being the tiny terraced fields of 'kuru', a barley, already in ear. Phugaon is about 13,500 ft., yet there are more houses and more barley fields 1000 ft. higher up the hillside. Near the village a river as large as the Phu Chu and equally turbid emerges from the snout of a big glacier, and on the spur between the two rivers stands a small white gompa and a line of thirteen chortens. Such are the austere features of a harsh landscape where hardly a shrub grows, much less a tree; a landscape of yellow cliffs, white granite boulders, and the grey ice of the glacier which had once borne them to the valley.

The headman of Phugaon, who with a straggling beard and a maroon-coloured gown looked like a semi-venerable Chaldean, urged us to drop the Mustang La project, prophesying nothing but woe. If we were bent on seeing passes we could visit the Kongyur La over the Ladakh range two days' march to the north, and he offered a man and a woman to take us there. We accepted this earnest of goodwill but asked him to press the enquiry for men who knew the Mustang La.

With man and wife, who kept us waiting till eleven o'clock, we started on a fine morning for the Kongyur La. The woman went so slowly and rested so often that after half a mile I sent her home; whereupon the man, in spite of his burden being thus increased, went off like a scalded cat, a greater burden having apparently been lifted from his mind. After crossing the river to the gompa the track climbed for 1500 ft., and then traversed easily across barren slopes of black shale which coloured the occasional stream with the same dismal hue. We camped by a stone hut in company with some Naurgaon men who had just brought a convoy of yaks, sheep and goats over the pass. Some of the animals having foundered on top of the pass, the men themselves had to go back to fetch the loads.

Four of them set off at first light. Interpreting such keenness as an ominous sign boding a long day, we started soon after, leaving our camp standing. Indeed, it proved a hard day which I should have enjoyed more had we been able to see anything. Mist enveloped us at the start, snow fell as we climbed the pass, and a downpour of rain drenched us as we returned. When still well short of a glacier which I could dimly discern was the source of the Phu Chu we turned right-handed up a valley where very soon we came upon the ice of another glacier. Having crossed this we climbed very abruptly above its northern side to a height of nearly 18,000 ft. There was no track. It was a case of every man and animal for himself on a shifting surface of black gravel and mud. The semi-liquid state of the surface, which continued for nearly a thousand feet, showed that underneath lay remnants of ice of the retreating glacier.

At the top of this *route douloureuse* we caught the four early birds and continued in their company on a horizontal traverse over dry scree and boulders with the glacier far below. After two or three miles of this stony wilderness we turned uphill, heading for a gigantic rock curtain which ran diagonally upwards towards some ice-cliffs. The conjunction of these two seemingly impenetrable barriers was swallowed in the mist, but a more unlikely place for a pass could hardly be found. The track climbed steeply close to the foot of the great rock wall from which, I soon realized, stones fell with alarming frequency and appalling velocity. The local talent tackled this section in short, sharp rushes, pausing to draw much-needed breath as they crouched as close as possible to the foot of the cliff; while the foolish flock or the indifferent yak must perforce take its chance of being hit well out in the beaten zone. As we climbed we found that the converging ice-cliff never quite met the rock, the comparative warmth of which served to keep the ice at a respectful distance. Presently we emerged upon a wide snow plateau at about 19,000 ft.

Across this the traffic had worn a foot-deep trench which we followed for half a mile until we came to the bales of wool jettisoned by

Rice fields in the lower Marsyandi valley; the sharp peak left of centre is Macha Puchare

A last glimpse of the snows on the way home; Baudha is on the right and next to it is Himal Chuli

Dhankhuta is an immaculately clean little place; the fact that a Governor has his residence there may account for this; the roofs are of small tiles shaped like drain-pipes cut lengthwise

A family group in Bung—cheerful enough to be the family of Mr Bung the Brewer of Happy Families; the man is one of our Dankhuta escort wearing his official hat

the last caravan. In thick weather and falling snow there was no point in crossing the plateau to look at the Tibetan side, so that I cannot say what the descent was like. It could scarcely be worse than the ascent, but had we been bound that way we should have been profoundly discouraged by the news that for five marches there were no villages. The way was not littered with skeletons like some central Asian passes I have seen (we found none), but the toil and the hazards of the long ascent before they reach even this comparative oasis of level snow, and the arduous floundering at 19,000 ft. while crossing it, make the pass most cruel for animals. Surely the trader by land who launches himself and his beasts on so perilous a route, as well deserves the proud title of Merchant Adventurer as he who traffics by sea.

On a day of such horrid obscurity it was not easy to place this pass even within three or four miles of a peak of 20,250 ft. shown on the map as standing on the frontier ridge. Over rough going one inevitably overestimates the mileage. Time, or for travellers without watches the telling of beads, must be the only standard of measurement. Nevertheless, I felt convinced that the Ladakh range and consequently the frontier is several miles north of where it is marked on the map, which hereabouts becomes vague and conventional. Rivers and their tributaries are suspiciously like the conventional herring-bone, and the contours have the too-simple curves of a sea serpent. On the Tibetan side the map is a pleasing blank for a space of fifty miles until a large blue line indicates the course of the Tsangpo river. In consequence the goal to which this high and perilous pass leads remains for me only a vague name which varied every time it was uttered—a riddle to be solved by some happy traveller in less troubled and less trammelled times.

Returning to Phugaon we found that the venerable Chaldean had been as good as his word. Under extreme pressure two able-bodied men, whom we assumed were familiar with the Mustang La, had volunteered to share what might be a hungry journey. They took with them five days' food which I hoped would last until we reached some village in the Kali valley. Merlin delivered a harangue, like a priest about to sacrifice, gave us his blessing and a couple of potatoes, expecting, no doubt, to see us back in a few days. According to the map, which in its broader aspects gives a fairly true picture, we had to strike due west across a tributary of the Phu river before launching into the upper Naur valley, where we planned to keep as high as possible along its northern side. I assumed the Naur flowed in a gorge and had a theory that by keeping high enough we should avoid the gorge and find easier going. As Holmes used to tell Watson, it is a capital mistake to theorize before you have data.

Our men did not cast up until eleven o'clock—a delay which enabled us to dry out after the wet Kongyur trip—when we at once embarked upon a 3000 ft. climb to the ridge barring us from the tributary river. A thousand feet higher we came to the last fields and houses of Phugaon where the men dallied with a Siren, in less classical language, a 'floozie', who sat on a roof combing her wonderfully straight black hair. This danger past we sweated to the top of the ridge on a well-marked path. There it divided, one branch going down to a bridge, as we were told, and the other leading up the valley. Unwilling to sacrifice height so hardly won we took the latter. This led us easily across shale slopes, which though utterly void of vegetation were the home of many 'bharal' (wild sheep). A sharp fall of hail coinciding with our arrival at a spring of water, we camped there and for fuel grubbed up some roots of heath growing in the moist gravel.

The sacrifice of height had been only deferred. We dropped a thousand feet to the river, forded it with the help of the rope, and began another fierce climb which ended in 500 ft. of loose scree. A faint path had accompanied us so long that I began to think we had hit on an alternative route to the pass, until it presently petered out at a place where there was some particularly nourishing gravel for grazing yaks. From the top ($c.$ 17,000 ft.) we expected to see up the Naur valley, so Gyalgen and I made a violent but vain effort to reach it ahead of the gathering mists. The men having arrived and viewed with extreme distaste a brief expanse of gravel and a grey wall, I had to behave as though I knew where we were going; to put into practice my high theory without the least hint or guidance as to how rigidly it could be applied. Well in the lead, I alarmed my followers by taking an even higher line, no doubt giving them reason to think that the idiot in front had no lesser or more sensible goal than the eternal snows. When a line of yellow crags intervened I doubted if our coolies would stand for strict adherence to theory; a theory which no one had expounded to them and which seemed only to drive its advocates ever higher and higher.

After losing some 500 ft. by descending to the foot of the crags, we made another mile without further loss until brought to a halt by an enormously deep nallah, guarded by cliffs on the far side and in its upper reaches by a waterfall and a vague hint of ice. No principle or theory could stand in the face of facts like these, reinforced as they were by the sight of a patch of grass and some juniper bushes on the river bank nearly 2000 ft. below. 'A merciful Providence fashioned us hollow, on purpose that we might our principles swallow', so without demur but with considerable misgiving, I began plunging down the scree to commit the party to the mercies of a low-level route along the river bed.

Other travellers had evidently camped or grazed their animals on that grass by the river, and, although we could not reach it, we were cheered by the sight of a distinct track on the other bank. To our surprise and satisfaction we made good two or three miles among the boulders of the river bed before a series of rock buttresses compelled us to climb high before we could regain the river beyond. Early in the afternoon we came to a point where two rivers of almost equal size joined to form the Naur, one branch descending from the north-west and the other from the north-east. Here was a poser. The path on the other bank, which we still had in view, disappeared after crossing the north-west branch. The Sherpas thought the pass lay up that nallah, the local men were struck dumb. No one had advised them about this critical choice and, as we learnt, they had never been near the pass before. I favoured the north-east branch, not only because any fording would thus be deferred but also because of a hint from the despised map. On the Kali side of the Muktinath range only one of the many nallahs had a name, the Tange Khola, and it seemed more than likely that the way to the Mustang La followed this. Its head lay well to the north-east. But, in fact, the obvious difficulty of fording the river, although its volume had now been reduced by half, left us no choice. We went on up the right-hand branch. Cliffs soon forced us to climb high, and from the vantage point to which we were driven we picked out here and there on the far side of the river an unmistakable track; thus I led on with more confidence until we camped less than a mile below the glacier source of the river. I thought the way to the pass must lie up this glacier, but a walk upstream that evening convinced me that a small side nallah almost opposite our camp held the clue. The constant cloud canopy hovering at the 15,000 ft. level added the charm of uncertainty to the interest of new country, but I had seen enough to realize that the glacier could lead only to a peak of 22,000 ft. at the point of junction of the Muktinath and the Ladakh ranges. Moreover, up the valley there was no sign of the track which apparently petered out on a small grass flat near the entrance to the side nallah, where a few piled stones marked the remains of a stone shelter.

So far up, only half-a-mile from its glacier source, the river was fordable. Having crossed it we searched the flat and the vicinity of the stone shelter for tracks heading up the side nallah. Upon finding nothing our confidence began to ebb. Was it possible the track we had seen led merely to this diminutive grazing ground? Avoiding the stream, which emerged from a gorge, an unlikely line for a track, we climbed the slopes above it, following the natural line a track would have taken. Not the faintest trace rewarded our wide casts. A gash in the hillside caused by a landslip brought us up short, and we sat on the edge of it wondering what to do. For want of anything better I plunged down the loose earth of the slip to the stream-bed below where, to my delight, I found at first some old yak dung and then a faint but definite track in the gravel. At these tidings our coolies, now on their fourth day out becoming a little dubious about their future, brightened instantly and threw off dull care like men who hear the distant summons of a gong.

At a fork of the valley we lost the track, recovered it by a wide cast, and began to skirt a vast slab of white ice which, on the brown shale, appeared detached as a cloud, after the manner of a central Asian glacier. Presently we were standing by a cairn on top of the Mustang La on a broad shale saddle peering into the mist on the Mustang side. Its height is about 18,000 ft. We anticipated an easy run down to some hospitable village in the Tange Khola; foolishly, for it is an almost invariable rule in the Himalaya that a descent to a valley means a great deal of climbing. The valley quickly narrowed to a gorge which the track avoided by climbing back into a small lateral nallah, where we found all the amenities for a camp—fresh water and some scrub.

After hovering briefly over the main valley again the track took fright and sheered off, as well it might from a place that had the appearance of having been the epicentre of repeated earthquakes. In the next lateral nallah we surprised a party of men and women busy gathering and drying wild garlic. They were not local residents but called themselves 'Khumbas' from Tukucha well down the Kali valley; they assured us we should reach the Kali that evening. Having landed us in yet another side valley the track very wisely quitted the Tange and all its deep-cut affluents for a better world. But we went on down, unable to resist the false lure of a large but apparently deserted village on a terrace above the river. On this level shelf, where there were possibly a couple of hundred acres of abandoned fields and scores of ruined houses, the going was so good that we ignored the sinister warning that the absence of any path should have conveyed. Nemesis was at hand. A gash some 200 ft. deep, cut by a side nallah, yawned suddenly at our feet.

Even if it had promised escape from further trouble, there was no climbing down the vertical gravel walls of either this nallah in front or of the Tange on our left. We must return to the track we had long since quitted or climb 2000 ft. of scrubby hillside to reach a trickle of water above the lip of this deep trench. It was already late afternoon, so we chose the climb. Men thus frustrated, dashing at it in vehement rage, should have made short work of this paltry ascent; for us, sunk in the languor of sullen resignation, it involved several hours of moody toil. At the top, in addition to water, we found the path from which we had so foolishly strayed.

Dense mist succeeded a night of rain. As usual we began by climbing until the path reached a shoulder where we realized, in spite of the mist, that we were looking across the spacious depths of the Kali valley. Instead of descending at once the path kept well up the hillside in a northerly direction; but we had learnt our lesson and were prepared to follow whithersoever it led, even to Tibet. At intervals we bellowed in unison, like ships advertising their presence in a fog, until at length we were answered by the bleat of a sheep, a welcome sound to weary wayfarers or even to hardy mountaineers whose veneer of hardiness is at last wearing thin. Dogs barked as we approached a black tent and a line of tethered yak calves. Having got some information but nothing else, we pushed on, the path at long length trending downwards. The mist melted, revealing far below the green fields of Tange village, and a line of willows along a flume.

CHAPTER XVI

MUKTINATH

―――◆―――

THIS LITTLE GREEN PATCH betokening human activity shone like a good deed in a naughty world—a world of shocking sterility, harsh colour and violent shapes. Below 14,000 ft., that is, below the level of the kindly mist, vegetation practically ceases except for a sparse, spiny bush which I am assured, though I find it hard to believe, is a kind of honeysuckle. The plant flourished defiantly on what Cobbett would have called a' 'black, spewy gravel', emphasizing by its pervading presence the total absence of other plants of either use or beauty. The Kali river was not in sight. It runs at the bottom of a deep trench as if ashamed of hurrying stealthily by, withholding its life-giving water from so thirsty a landscape. Beyond it, on the western side, lay a similar woodless waste of yellow, grey and black hills—a barren landscape, very rarely refreshed by the green fields of a village to which the water of some side nallah had been cunningly led.

Tange occupied a terrace above the Tange Khola a mile short of its junction with the Kali. The headlong career of this precipitate river drew to an inglorious end meandering over a ridiculously capacious bed for such a pitifully small stream. Its wide gravel bed was sunk between gravel cliffs 200 ft. high scored at regular intervals with gullies. The bright sun on the cliffs and the deep shadows of the gullies gave them the appearance of giant organ pipes. Upon the terrace above these cliffs Tange had ample room to spread, but the houses, as usual, were crammed together. However, they were all on one level and not stacked like a house of cards. Apart from some donkeys, the first I had seen anywhere in Nepal, the village was remarkable for a double row of giant stupas, coloured brick red, their lower part covered by one big flat roof. The houses, with their high battlement of drying firewood, looked even more Tibetan than those of Manangbhot. The height is not much above 11,000 ft. They told us they grew two crops a year—winter wheat or barley, which is cut by June and followed by buckwheat or potatoes.

Tange could give us only essentials like rice, tsampa and buckwheat, a yellowish flour which can be turned very easily and quickly into excellent cakes. Milk or mutton seemed hardly within their scheme of life, though they had some vast herds of goats which presumably lived on honeysuckle. Having exhausted this unfruitful topic and given the Phugaon men the rather one-sided option of staying with us or going back over the pass, I walked down to the Kali river. Its thick waters rolled along a bed similar to that of the Tange, but wider and with higher cliffs. These yellow gravel cliffs have been carved from old river terraces and behind them rise wildly eroded and weirdly coloured hills of slate-blue, cobalt, mauve, chrome and orange, all blending into an inky blue over distant Tibet. It is fascinatingly ugly country, the more fascinating for being so little known. No snowy peaks broke like white waves upon the horizon of this tumbled multi-coloured sea; for across this twenty-mile-wide basin the Ladakh range dwindles to insignificance.

Mustang town or village is some ten miles north of Tange on the west side of the river which is crossed by a ford. The only explorer to visit Mustang and the upper Kali was one Hari Ram, one of the Survey of India native explorers, in 1813.

> Lloh Mantang (Mustang) [he reported] is situated in the centre of a plain 11,905 ft. above the sea... the plain is irrigated by channels. Mustang is enclosed by a wall of white earth and small stones, 6 ft. thick and 14 ft. high, forming a square with a side ¼ mile long, and having an entrance gate to the east. In the centre is the Rajah's palace consisting of 4 stories, about 40 ft. in height, and the only building to be seen from the outside. In the N.E. corner of the enclosure is a gompa containing copper gilt figures and 250 lamas. There are about 60 other houses, two-storied and about 14 ft. in height, forming streets and lanes. Drinking water is brought in by means of a canal, and this overflowing makes the interior slushy; since there is always an accumulation of filth the smell is very offensive. Since no census is taken I cannot say how many people there are but they appeared to be numerous. Besides the residents there are always a number of

traders from Tibet and Nepal who either exchange their goods here or take them to Lhasa or Nepal. The trade in salt and grain does not extend very far north. Trade is chiefly carried on by Thaklis, a class of traders of mixed origin, who have the privilege of going to Lhasa and they even go to Calcutta for the purchase of goods. The Rajah, who is a Bhot, collects a revenue from all sources of about 10,000 or 12,000 Rs a year, out of which he pays 2000 or 3000 yearly to Nepal from the land revenue, and 10% of the taxes levied on goods brought from across the northern frontier to the Lhasa government.

Hari Ram went on to Tradom in the Tsangpo valley but his account is vague, as is the map north of Mustang. The frontier is marked about ten miles north, and the Kali river, indicated by only a dotted line, appears to rise on the Tibetan side. This is very probable because ammonite fossils of the Jurassic Tethys are found along the banks of the Kali in Mustangbhot. I picked up some fragments on the way to Muktinath and found a considerable deposit at Muktinath itself, which, indeed, owes its sanctity to the abundance of these fossils, the sacred 'shaligram' of the Hindus. Hari Ram put the Tibetan frontier at the Photu La (15,000 ft.), a pass two days' march north from Mustang. The pass probably lies on the watershed of the Kali and the streams flowing north to the Tsang-po.

We walked for two days through equally arid country to Muktinath. Our party was augmented by two Sherpas who were returning to Solu Khumbu, the Sherpa district south of Everest. Seven months having elapsed since they had set out on a trading venture to Tibet, it would seem that for the Himalayan business man time is not necessarily money. We followed a broad highway some 3000 ft. above the Kali; the going, however, was pretty rough, and worn into ruts by the feet of innumerable sheep and goats. We met with many flocks, each numbering several hundred, either carrying rice or grain up to Mustang, the exchange mart, or bringing down salt.

From Muktinath the traders go down to the Kali valley to Kagbeni, or lower still to Tukucha at the foot of Dhaulagiri, to pick up their rice. There is another route on the west side of the valley, and if the traffic there is anything like as heavy the combined total must be very great.

Dhaulagiri and its huge ridges dominated that side of the valley, but clouds prevented our identifying with certainty Annapurna I, its fellow portal on the east. Through the twenty-mile-wide gap between these two 26,000 ft. summits the Kali river flows at a height of only 6000 ft. At this time, the end of July, although the monsoon was in full vigour, Dhaulagiri remained wonderfully free from cloud. I had the impression that north of the Himalayan crest-zone the Kali valley is even drier than the Marsyandi. What bad weather there was seemed to come from the north. On three of the four days we were there heavy thunderstorms gathered in the north to sweep southwards along the crest of the Muktinath range. But no rain fell below a height of 14,000 ft.

The celebrated Hindu pilgrim resort of Muktinath lies at a height of nearly 13,000 ft. at the head of a valley draining westwards from the Muktinath range into the Kali. Well watered by springs and streams it evidently enjoys a comparatively moist climate. Some pines grew in a ravine on its south side—that is, on the north-facing slope where pines and juniper always flourish best—while the slopes above the village were clothed in grass. Although Muktinath is higher than Manangbhot, where the harvest takes place in September, the earlier wheat fields had already been cut and threshing with flails was literally in full swing. We camped near the topmost house of the straggling village where our arrival created no stir. A place to which several thousand pilgrims come every year must be accustomed to strange sights; moreover, within the last two months, it had been visited by two of the French party and by our own Emlyn Jones.

Having collected about thirty pounds' weight of fossils from a rich deposit hard by I took the Sherpas to see the sights; or rather they took me, for Muktinath meant much more to them than to one for whom it was merely a name. For the Nepalese, Muktinath ranks with Gosainkund, Pashpati and Ridi, as one of the four great places of Hindu sanctity. According to Sher Bahadur, the name should be Mukti-Narayan, as it appears in old scripts, Narayan being an incarnation of Vishnu to whom the shrine is dedicated. It owes its sanctity to the presence of the thrice-sacred 'shaligram'. This is also found at Ridi and Pashpati much farther down-stream in the same valley of the Kali or 'black' Gandak. Perceval Landon in his *Nepal* says that the stones are regarded as emblems of Narayan or Vishnu and during worship before his shrines they are held in the hand to sanctify the making of a vow. In the temples they are generally contained in a small copper cup, together with some Ganges water and a few leaves of the tulsi plant. In his account of Nepal (*v. supra.*) Hamilton gives the following description of the Muktinath shaligram; but evidently his informant did not make it clear that Muktinath now stands 3000 ft. above the Kali Gandaki.

> On the banks of the Gandaki at Muktinath is a precipice from which the river is supposed to wash the Salagrams or black stones, which are considered by the Hindus as representatives of several of their deities, and which are the most common objects of worship in Bengal where images are scarce. They are of various kinds and accordingly represent different deities. On account of its containing these stones this branch of the river is usually called the Salagrami, and the channel everywhere below Muktinath, until it reaches the plains of India at Sivapur, abounds in these stones. All the Salagrams consist of carbonate of lime and are in general quite black. Most of them are what naturalists call petrifactions and the most common are Ammonites, half imbedded in a ball of stone exactly of the same nature as the petrified animal. Others, which are reckoned the most valuable, are balls containing a cavity formed by an Ammonite, that has afterwards decayed and left only its impression. Some balls have no external opening, and yet by rubbing away a portion of one of their sides the hollow wheel (chakra) is discovered. Such Salagrams are reckoned very valuable.

In the deposit which we found at Muktinath itself nearly all the stone balls contained a fossil, but in breaking them open the fossil, too, was usually broken. This deposit occurred in a sort of black shale, smelling faintly of sulphur, which the people dug out for dressing their fields.

The temple and shrine of Narayan at Muktinath does not appear to be ancient. It stands in a sunken stone courtyard surrounded by a stone wall over which flows the sacred spring through 108 metal spouts carved like gargoyles. The spring itself gushes from the foot of a cliff a few hundred feet above the temple. There were no pilgrims other than my two Sherpas. They did the necessary round of the 108 spouts,

An oil press in a village in the Arm valley; as the heavy upright beam rotates it crushes the mustard seed against the side of the hollow log in which it pivots

The village cobbler of Panga, the first Sherpa village we came to; watched by his Lhasa terrier he is making the Tibetan style felt knee-boot

Prayer flags and an inscribed boulder at the entrance to a village in the Dudh Kosi valley; as one draws nearer to the Himalaya the more frequent these symbols become

drinking from each in turn. It was certainly delicious water, what the Spaniards would call 'agua muy rica'—very rich water. The pilgrim, according to Sher Bahadur, having bathed and drunk 108 successive times and performed other ceremonies, takes a vow either to relinquish one of his evil habits or to become a vegetarian.

A far more curious thing than these 108 spouts is to be seen in a nearby Buddhist gompa. For Buddhists, too, journey to Muktinath and thereby acquire merit. As Buddhism spread northwards from India at the time of Asoka, or, as is more likely, when it later declined and approximated to the surrounding Hinduism, the Buddhists put up their own temple at Muktinath and appointed nuns to look after it. The present gompa and the present nuns are both extremely dilapidated, but neither can date from the time of Asoka. The interior of this dark and dingy gompa, into which we were admitted by an old crone, the Sherpas having discarded their boots, is almost devoid of ornament. On a rock ledge at one end sits the usual gilt Buddha with a few butter lamps burning in front of it. But underneath this natural altar are three small curtained openings, in each of which burns a lambent blue flame, presumably of natural gas; through the centre opening flows a small stream and the flame issues from a rock so close to the water as to justify the natives' stories of burning water. The Sherpas prostrated themselves before the Buddha while the old hag held up the curtain over the centre aperture for their edification. They were thus able to examine the flames at their leisure. But my examination of it was perforce perfunctory; for the Sibyl withdrew the curtain only reluctantly and briefly for one who was so obviously far from the Way and who was perhaps not even seeking it. The Sherpas, having finished their oblations, took earth from the floor and filled a bottle with this holiest of water to take back to Darjeeling. When, like an impious Yahoo, I asked them if they were going to sell it, they were genuinely shocked.

We had now to get back to Manangbhot over the Muktinath range which is crossed by a 17,500 ft. pass. This climb of 5000 ft. nearly broke my heart. Since I was carrying thirty pounds of fossils I might well liken it to the 'severely scientific' ascent of Chimborazo by Whymper with his two Swiss guides the Carrels, when Jean Antoine had to carry his twelve-pound baby, as he called the mercurial barometer. It is an easy and much-used pass. On top there was no view to detain us, so we dropped quickly down to camp in a flowery meadow by the first juniper scrub. Four hours of fast going down this Jargeng Khola, where the vegetation is almost prodigal, brought us to Manang village. In the main part there are about fifty houses built on a terrace overlooking the Marsyandi river. Just across the river and very nearly touching it is the snout of the ice torrent, already mentioned, which comes tumbling down from Annapurna III. The presence of this ice at the door of the village, so to speak, gives it a stern, almost savage air, which is scarcely merited; strange indeed is the contrast between the ice on one side of the river and the bountiful wheat-fields on the other. In an open space in the middle of the village is a long mani wall crowned with a double bank of prayer wheels, fifty-four each side, which are turned by those who tread the lustral path. Another curious item is the village smithy, the smith and his family being immigrants from lower Nepal. They had lived there for many years, but they appeared just as incongruous in their surroundings as we Europeans.

At the base camp, which we reached on 3 August, only Sher Bahadur was in residence, the two naturalists having gone up the Khangsar nallah, a stream which unites with the Jargeng above Manang village to form the Marsyandi. Of all the small valleys of the Marsyandi basin, Lowndes thought that the Khangsar was not only the richest in flowers but that the people of Khangsar village were the most friendly. Either on account of its botanical treasures or because it was the only valley where milk and butter were to be had, he spent a considerable time there. The base camp had been improved by the installation of a stone-floored sitz bath sunk in an irrigation channel which ran through it. If he had not actually done the building, Lowndes had certainly been its inspiration, for he was much addicted to soap and water, and thought it no ostentation to wash almost every day.

Baking cakes and eating them, collecting some primula seed from the Naurgaon pass, and bathing out of respect for Lowndes, occupied me for five days while waiting for the return of the naturalists and an expected parcel of mail. We had arranged for this to be dispatched at fortnightly intervals to Kudi whence we collected it at highly irregular intervals. This batch gave us our first news of the climbing of Annapurna I on 3 June by the French, a feat of daring, dash and determination, accomplished at heavy cost. The photographs of their route may or may not give a true impression, but from them one would infer that it was a route from which a mountaineer might well shrink without being suspected of timidity.

Before returning to Manang in September to collect seeds, which by then should be ripening, Lowndes wished to examine the flora of the Dudh Khola; and as Roberts had already collected some 170 birds we thought the time had now come to collect a mountain. We therefore agreed to foregather at Bimtakhoti towards the end of August. Meantime I was to go there in advance to search for some peak suited to a party of moderate powers and dwindling ambitions.

CHAPTER XVII

BIMTAKHOTI AND HIMAL CHULI

I QUITTED MANANGBHOT FOR THE LAST TIME without regret. Annapurna IV, across the valley, was a too-constant reminder of failure; and in spite of a common liking for raksi the natives and ourselves had never got on close terms. They remained content neither to help us much nor to hinder us. On my final departure, I had with me as usual a man, and a goitrous woman of advanced age who had soon to be sent back.

Thonje, as a result of the considerable rainfall which it had received, seemed less attractive. The village was a quagmire of mud, or worse, and flies abounded. But rain or no rain the traffic to Bimtakhoti up the Dudh Khola went on. It consisted mainly of long strings of zos, so that the track up the valley was in a deplorable mess. We camped half-way up at a solitary house, drawn thereto by the smell of beer and meat, for a yak had just been dismembered. The slaughtering of these animals has to be done surreptitiously in a country administered by Hindus, for a yak, in spite of its uncouth appearance, can hardly be refused the protection afforded to cows. Water buffaloes, on the other hand, are not looked upon as cows and are therefore fair game. Strict Buddhists, of course, should not take life of any kind, but Tibetans are meat eaters as, indeed, they must be to prosper in their cold climate. No Sherpa will kill a sheep if he can find someone to do it for him, but he will eat it with gusto, guts, brains and all, even cracking the bones, for the marrow. In Tibet the killing is usually done by butchers, a class who are in a low category, bound for hell anyway; and since the sin of killing for meat is very justly pooled amongst all who partake, the butcher's share is so trifling that his progress thither cannot be much accelerated nor his sojourn there greatly prolonged. According to Sir Charles Bell, if a high lama eats meat he makes a special effort on behalf of the animal slain to ensure that it will be reborn in a higher state. Thus the transaction ends agreeably for both parties.

At Bimtakhoti there was a frequent coming and going of herds of zos and flocks of sheep, to or from either the Larkhya pass or Thonje. The noise of bells was constant as troops of zos, a dozen or so together, plodded past our camp on the short-grass flat. Each animal carried a deep-toned bell, and the leaders of a troop had in addition collars of small bells from which dangled bright scarlet tassels of yak hair. The man in charge of the store, the 'subah', a relative of our rich friend at Kudi, told us that during the short season he weighed in more than 3000 animal loads. The rate of exchange was sixteen measures of rice for twenty-five of salt; but over the pass at Larkhya, where the Tibetans arrive with their salt, twelve measures of rice are enough to buy twenty-five of salt. According to the subah, what economists call the price mechanism has free play, the exchange rate adjusting itself by the amount of each commodity in sight. But when Roberts visited Larkhya he found all in confusion, the subah having been forced to flee before the wrath of Tibetan salt merchants who accused him of a preference for a planned economy—planned, of course, in his own favour.

Bimtakhoti lies in the shadow of a 200 ft. high moraine thrown up on the true left bank of a glacier descending from the Ladakh range. The path from Thonje crosses this glacier between Bimtakhoti and the snout, which is about a mile below; and the path to Larkhya follows its ablation valley for a couple of miles before turning eastwards to the pass which lies on the ridge joining the Ladakh range to the Manaslu massif. A little above Bimtakhoti this glacier divides into three branches, one descending from Himlung Himal, one from the direction of Cheo Himal, and one from the mountains near the Larkhya pass.

Himlung Himal was one of the peaks I wanted to examine, so we crossed the glacier to the right bank and continued north up the ablation valley of the Himal Chuli branch. There is no cultivation at Bimtakhoti. Apart from one man who spent his time sewing tinsel decorations (bought in Calcutta) on to cheap felt hats, the people, admittedly few, had no occupation other than that of spectators in life's battle; yet we had the utmost difficulty enlisting even one reluctant volunteer, so that in the end I had to carry my own kit. The weather was as unsuitable for reconnaissance as it could be—we had seen no mountains for some days—and the only source of pleasure lay in the vegetation which was so lush that we were soon soaked. We might as well have been back in the Langtang; for we found here in abundance purple aconite, the delicate blue codonopsis, and a heliotrope delphinium. However, we soon got on to sparse grass and better going across a series of old lake beds until we made camp in the rain not far short of the glacier head. In spite of low cloud we saw enough to rule out the approach to a high col, the only key to Himal Chuli.

On a drizzling morning we crossed this glacier arm and began to climb the ridge separating it from the Cheo Himal glacier. This mountain did not figure on our brief list of possibilities, but I thought we might as well look at it on the way back. Such an abrupt departure from the easy going along the valley floor proved too much for the Bimtakhoti man, who refused to follow. Whereupon the Sherpas divided his load between them and went on with so much ease that I began to wonder what they had been carrying before. On the way up we got separated in the mist, but met again on the descent after some desultory bellowing. The Sherpas annoyed me by having found what appeared to be a better line than mine. Sorrows shared are sorrows halved. When blundering in and out of self-imposed difficulties there is nothing more aggravating than the suspicion that superior judgement has found for one's companions a better way. If roped together one is spared such excruciating thoughts, nor will one's followers quietly submit to being led by ways of which they do not approve. Having reached the glacier we found no obliging ablation valley between mountain and moraine. We had to choose between a hillside of tangled juniper scrub and a loosely flung together causeway of boulders.

We camped on the first flat spot and next day crossed this glacier. A faint track on the far side soon brought us to a half-mile-long lake whose waters, even under a hard, colourless sky, reflected a deep turquoise blue. At the far end of the lake we found ourselves by the junction of the third glacier coming down from the direction of the Larkhya pass. We crossed, scrambled down a vast moraine some 500 ft. high, to come out on the Bimtakhoti track, thus completing a wet, blind, abortive, circular tour of the whole glacier system.

A week remained before the expected arrival of the others, and we had only one more peak to examine; thereafter I intended crossing to Larkhya to see if that valley held any climbable mountains. The peak was that which had puzzled us on our first flying visit; according to the map its 24,000 ft. summit lay immediately above Bimtakhoti about halfway between Manaslu and the Larkhya pass. Without much pause and without asking any local man to put himself out, we crossed the rippling stream of the Bimtakhoti meadow and began climbing through birch woods by a well-worn track leading to a grazing alp. Although this journey was about to prove unlucky for me it is interesting to note that no weasel crossed our path, no solitary magpie hopped menacingly alongside, and no crow croaked thrice. True, I fell into the stream when attempting to cross dryshod, but so did Da Namgyal who got even wetter.

Having won clear of the birch the track mounted straightly and steeply by way of a pleasant grass spur. Mist hung everywhere. When we had made good about 3000 ft., boulders having taken the place of grass, we decided to camp. Away in the mist in a hollow on our right, we heard the sound of water, but before descending we had to advance a short way along our spur which had now dwindled to a sharp ridge of piled boulders. Hopping from one to another with the carelessness of long use and wont I got out of balance, put a foot back to recover, found nothing, and fell backwards about fifteen feet, bouncing on three separate boulders. If one must move after a fall it is better to do it quickly before the body begins to protest. We had to find water, so with the help of the Sherpas I got down to the hollow, and a little later found myself laid stiff on my back where I remained for five days unable even to sit up without help.

Throughout it rained steadily, but the Sherpas kept a fire going and went down twice to Bimtakhoti for more food. When I felt strong enough to be carried we got two men up to take our kit while the Sherpas in turn carried me pick-a-back. I dreaded recrossing that ridge but there was no alternative. I sweated freely, and my injured back winced in anticipation as Gyalgen balanced a precarious way over the boulders, my weight threatening to bring us both down in ruin at every step.

The rest of the party arrived next day, 24 August. There was nothing they could do except sympathise. Time, the great healer, must do its work, so Roberts went over to Larkhya and Lowndes back to Manang, leaving Sher Bahadur to keep me company. As soon as I could rise without help I began to crawl, then to walk, and finally to walk uphill, every day increasing the distance, until on 3 September, when Roberts got back, I climbed to the scene of the accident to collect some flowers. On the Larkhya side, where he had spent an active but fruitless week, Roberts had seen no peaks intended expressly for climbing. Very few Himalayan peaks are so designed. It is a common fault, one which climbers will not cease to lament until the passage of a few thousand centuries mellows their jagged, angular features and smooths away their harshest acerbities. He reported having seen what he thought might be a direct route to the summit plateau of Manaslu, which we discussed with the dispassionate calm of men who have no intention of trying it.

There remained only the 24,000 ft. peak at whose foot I had lain as a cripple for five days without catching so much as a passing glimpse. Still it eluded our gaze from below. Twice we journeyed far out across the stony sea of the glacier by Bimtakhoti and each time a great cloud spread itself obstinately over the mountain. The necessary step of returning to 'Cripple's Camp' was never taken. Neither the weather nor my recent injury gave us much hope and, no doubt, four months in the field had blunted the keen edge of ardour. It is possible, it is certainly so in my own case, that after several months of such a life the body makes a less and less vigorous response to the food, fresh air and exercise it receives. Contrary to expectation the machine begins to run down. Instead of tackling a hill with exuberance, one faces it with premature exhaustion.

We therefore decided to go right down to Kudi, whence we might embark upon an entrancing ridge walk along the Bahara Pokhara Lekh to a sacred lake at the foot of Himal Chuli. We weakly imagined ourselves half-way up this great mountain prospecting a route, but I felt in my heart that serious climbing was over and that this was merely what the Tibetans call 'neko'—a journey undertaken for the purpose of cleansing from sin and sloth. I could not help feeling that Roberts and I stood in great need of it. The thought of going down to 2000 ft. and then climbing back to 16,000 ft. rather staggered us, but a powerful inducement lay in the expectation of collecting a long overdue mail.

There was little difficulty in finding coolies willing to go down to Thonje, though it is perhaps an ungrateful title for the two comely young women who carried for us. 'Coolie', as it is thus anglicised, is a horrible word; those who use it frequently, as I do, lay themselves open to the suspicion of entertaining a lofty, almost brutal, disdain for their more or less faithful followers, regarding them no more than Falstaff did his fifty tattered prodigals lately come from swine-keeping, who would, however, 'fill a pit as well as better'. Like other men, coolies will sometimes let one down and will always try one's patience, but after reading the accounts of some travellers, one is left wondering whether coolies really are men with souls, whether they have bellies that hunger and feet that feel the cold. I name no names but readers of Himalayan travels will recognise the following extracts: 'difficult to match them (the coolies) in any jail in India'—'the misery of the night was increased by the moaning and wailing of the coolies from the rocks, where they sought shelter'—'these admonitions failed to impress the coolies, who, in a most critical place, sat down to take the snow out of their boots.' (The Cissies.)

We made one march of it to Thonje, meeting on the way a man with three bags of mail. It was too late to change our plan, in which the mail had had no small part, but the news of the outside world which we now read did not make us regret our decision to start moving down. The three-day journey down the Marsyandi gorge made us understand why it had always been difficult to persuade men to fetch the mail from Kudi. The track, slimy, slippery and half overgrown after months of rain, presented the unwary with many opportunities for misadventure. One had to shuffle very quietly over the narrow planks of the 'parris' which were greasy enough to warrant the strewing of a little sand for those misguided enough to wear rubber-soled boots. A bamboo suspension bridge, frail and rickety, had been put across the river by the smallpox village, but in length, height, sag, decay and all the ingredients of peril, it was outdone by a bridge below Tagring. The landslip there, now in active eruption, was sending down a constant stream of mud and boulders. As no one would attempt to cross this, travellers had to take another route and to cross the Marsyandi at their peril by this aged bridge.

Kudi is merely a place of a few shops selling cloth. In one of these, sitting on his string-bed, and assisted by any passer-by, the postmaster transacts his rare official business. There is no proper village and consequently no headman, so that we had difficulty in replenishing our food and hiring coolies. After spending a blazing hot day in camp by the river, waiting for some maize to be ground into flour, we retraced our steps up stream for a few miles. On the eve of the wettest ten days we had ever experienced, everyone assured us the monsoon was over.

At the junction of the Musi Khola, which comes down from the south side of Manaslu, we quitted the main valley and climbed a thousand feet by a stone staircase to the remarkably neat little village of Usta. The sun was sinking as we pitched our tents in a small square in the middle of the village, the only flat space at hand. Framed between the terra-cotta walls of two houses, the Musi Khola and its pine-clad slopes lay black in the evening shadows. But beyond the trees the rocks glowed warmly, and high over all shone the still sun-gilt face of Manaslu.

Roberts was soon in conversation with ex-soldiers or with men on leave from some Gurkha regiment, of whom there are nearly always a few to be found in these villages. This district, known as No. 3 West, is one of the recruiting areas. He heard news of a former subadar-major who had served with him during the war, who was now tending both his own and the village flocks up in some kharka or ghot on the Bahara Pokhara Lekh. Apart from the pleasure Roberts might have in meeting again a man with whom he had shared some hazardous times, I looked forward confidently to the milk and butter which, I thought, would surely cement this meeting of the old comrades' association.

Two men volunteered to accompany us as guides and porters to this distant ghot. As we toiled up through the forest a sultry morning ended in a thunderstorm which broke over us in copious rain. Trusting to the local weather prophets we had discarded capes and umbrellas at Kudi. Wet and chilled to the bone we were led, not unerringly, among a maze of cattle tracks to what looked like a water buffalo wallow. It was in fact a ghot, where there was a hut. There, on a small island which promised to dry out at low water, we put our tents. It was a most repulsive spot—there seemed nothing for buffaloes to eat but leaves—but we soon drowned our sorrows in successive beakers of hot, rich milk.

Next day we reached the broad back of the lekh where we joined the main track. This was used indiscriminately not only by pilgrims, but also by sheep, cattle, and buffaloes on their way to the high

Namche Bazar with its spacious detached houses is not a bit like the huddled-up villages of Manangbhot; the deep valley between the village and the snow ridge carries the road leading to the Nangpa La, the 19,000 ft. pass into Tibet

On the march to Thyangboche it snowed all day; this was the only bad weather throughout October and November

The snow disappeared next day; the valley behind is not that leading to Everest but the valley of the Dudh Kosi which here turns northwards

pastures. To our surprise we soon came to what our guides called the Bahara Pokhara, or big lake—a poor thing, more of a pond than a lake, of a dismal pea-green colour, and overhung by dreary rhododendron trees. A small rest house for pilgrims and a shrine showed that sanctity has little to do with beauty, and we were glad of the assurance that there was a bigger and better lake, more worthy of a pilgrimage, much farther away.

We continued up the ridge against a constant trickle of buffaloes and men, carrying their mat shelters, who were vacating the higher grazings, until early rain obliged us to camp at a deserted ghot. Our guides now announced that their food was finished; but Roberts, with a prolonged burst of indignant eloquence, persuaded them to go on for one more day. We should then have to carry the stuff ourselves. After another mile or so along the ridge, whence we beheld a vast prospect of rain-swept hills of indigo blue flecked with white mist, our guides appeared to be at a loss. Instead of sticking to the ridge as they should have done, they were persuaded, like better men have been, to march to the distant bleating of sheep. I must say we were in full sympathy with this move, but it was unfortunate that these sheep must have been grazing in the Musi Khola valley 5000 or 6000 ft. below. We were obliged to follow a track which contoured below the ridge and which grew inexorably rougher and apparently more aimless. Our admiration for the pilgrims or for anyone else who used it mounted steadily, but we met neither pilgrims nor sheep. At last we camped in a drizzling mist in a hideously depressing boulder-strewn cwm.

Next day our porters departed, leaving us to shoulder our own burdens. Twice the track cheated our expectations by climbing in a very determined manner to what we expected to be the main ridge, only to drop as far down the other side of what was evidently only a spur. We were quite bewildered when we met a man, a shepherd, who told us the ghot we were looking for was quite near. But he then soured his sweet tidings by adding that he himself was bound for Usta which he expected to reach that evening. Evidently his standard of near and far differed widely from ours, for this was our fourth day from Usta. However, a couple of hours later we heard dogs barking, and through a rift in the mist we caught sight of several mat shelters. Unlike those of the Langtang sheep steadings, these shelters were so small and wretched that we put up our sodden tents to await the coming of the subadar who was up the hill with the sheep. A small, indeterminate man soon arrived. Like the other shepherds he was wrapped in a broad striped blanket, and was a man, one might think, who had never known anything other than a squalid mat hut on a dreary hillside. It was not easy to recognise in him the man of authority, the smart subadar-major, educated and widely travelled. Apart from reminiscences we exchanged very little with him. I gave him some cheroots, but neither milk, butter, nor dai, on which our thoughts had been fastened for some days, were to be had. All the ewes were dry; for their breeding arrangements are such that lambing takes place in the autumn, and at lower levels. In fact the subadar with his barren flocks was himself on the point of departure. We learnt from him that we were on the wrong side of the main ridge, the pilgrim track and the lake to which it leads both lying on the south side.

 We spent the next two days in this camp weather bound. Day and night a fine rain swept the ridge. The great moralist, whom I have frequently had occasion to quote, remarks very justly that 'the misery of man proceeds not from any single crush of overwhelming evil, but from small vexations continually repeated'. The drips inside the tent were the small vexations which by constant repetition occasioned our misery. We did our best to lighten our troubles by smoking cheroots, eating the food thrust at intervals through the tent door, and reading Captain Slocum and another book, *Over the Reefs*. The last dealt with the South Sea Islands—sunshine and soft breezes, hula-hula girls and pork—and we could not help feeling that as travellers we had come to the wrong country.

 On the morning of 17 September the rain let up for a time and with the help of two of the subadar's men we climbed the ridge, dropped down the other side, and set up our tents on the shore of a very lovely lake, clear, still and deep. With the coarse brown grass of the surrounding fells, the rocks above half-veiled in mist which hid the tell-tale sweep of snow beyond, we might well have been by some Lakeland tarn. But an examination of the shore hard by destroyed this illusion, for built in the shallow water were numerous little cairns, festooned with cords and bits of bamboo, and crowned with maize cobs, lemons, tomatoes, cucumbers, the votive offerings of pilgrims who bathe ceremonially in the shallows. To bathe ceremonially in the lake, which the locals called Memi Pokhara, is reputed to have the most gratifying effect upon those desirous of fertility. Later, when I plunged unceremoniously into its deeper parts, I concluded that I was lucky to escape permanent frigidity.

Monal pheasant haunted these lonely shores. The evening of our arrival we put up a covey and one, whose state of mind we could not guess, committed suicide by diving headlong into the lake. In vain the Sherpas hurled stones at the floating corpse, for no one was brave enough to swim for it, but in the morning it drifted to the farther shore and we supped gloriously on roast pheasant.

For three unprofitable days we tramped the brown fells, where aconite and delphinium were still in bloom, climbing to various carefully chosen vantage points where we sat for long hours waiting for chance to lift the veil from the bright face of Himal Chuli. And when at last it came, we were too close under the mountain to experience in full the breath-taking and salutary vision of a 10,000 ft. sweep of snow and ice. Sad, too, that on this side the slender and terrible spire which had so startled us on the march in, splayed out into a wide and characterless face topped by a flat ridge. Perhaps this broad face is for the most part easy, but its lower part is so guarded by ice-falls that it would be a difficult and probably dangerous climb.

On 21 September we were due to leave. A hard white frost at night ushered in a serene morning, and for the first time the placid, green water of the lake mirrored the cloudless, glittering summit of Himal Chuli. Fine weather had come; it was time for us to go.

CHAPTER XVIII

A FRESH START

Had not the day been quite so flawless we might have found the Pilgrim Way as irksome as our other route. But one seemed to tread on air. Clinging mist and grey phantom shapes had vanished and the eye ranged over warm brown fells and blue valleys to far-off, placid, white mountains. That evening from our last camp on the ridge we watched the light fade upon a wide semicircle of familiar shapes from Baudha and Himal Chuli in the east, to Manaslu in the north, and across to the Annapurna and Macha Puchare in the west. But we had now to quit this fair region of high pastures, forgo the clean fragrance of mountain plants, and begin an unwilling descent to the vapid sights and scents of the valleys below.

At Kudi we were joined by Lowndes, Sher Bahadur, and the caravan of specimen boxes, the fruits of several months of hard labour. We celebrated our reunion with a dish of curried frogs assuaged by draughts from Roberts's large water bottle from which we could always drink heartily in the comfortable assurance that it never would contain anything so dangerous as water. I should have liked the frogs better had I not seen them being shaken from wicker traps and then tied together in biliously green slimy bundles, all legs and eyes. But if one professes and practises living on the country one must take the rough with the smooth, rancid yak fat and frogs along with buckwheat cakes and raksi.

Our party then divided, the main body going direct to Katmandu and Roberts to Pokhara, the second city in Nepal, set in a plain almost as large as the valley of Katmandu, containing many large lakes. To me the marches seemed longer and hotter than those of the outgoing journey, and since the paddy through which much of the track lay was still uncut, the fields were still flooded. One was constantly made aware of this fact by being forced off the path into the mud by an oncoming tide of coolies, bowed down under huge bales of cloth. The reason for this seasonal activity in the cloth trade was the approaching festival of Dasahra, the big event of the Nepali year.

Yet even this fatiguing and singularly untriumphant return march was not without its pleasant memories; the bountiful supply of bananas, particularly that king of its kind, the succulent 'malbogue'; the lovely bauhinia trees now a mass of white and mauve star-shaped flowers; and finally a last glimpse of Baudha, seen at sunset, its snow a pale rose and the clouds which ringed the summit glowing like reflected fire.

At Katmandu, where we were lapped in comfort at the Embassy, we did not take long to wind up our affairs. I felt I could safely but perhaps undeservedly murmur; 'Now my weary eyes I close, Leave, ah, leave me, to repose.' But it was not to be. I there met Mr Oscar Houston, father of Dr Charles Houston a companion of Nanda Devi days, who had everything in train for a journey to Solu Khumbu, the district on the Nepal side of Everest and the home of the Sherpas. He invited me to join his party, and a refusal to do so would have seemed ungracious. Moreover the journey would be of supreme interest; apart from viewing the south side of Everest there was the fun to be expected from seeing Sherpas, as it were, in their natural state. Mr Shipton and I had often discussed such an unlikely happening, and here it was offered to me on a plate. In 1949 the Himalayan Committee had asked the Nepal Durbar for permission to send a party to the south side of Everest, but this had been refused and the Langtang Himal offered in its place.

One or two drawbacks presented themselves forcibly enough to prevent an immediate acceptance. As Dr Charles Houston could not arrive before the end of October, I should have to kick my heels for the best part of a fortnight in Calcutta. Furthermore we had only five weeks to spend on the journey, as both of us had to be back home by mid-December. I had already been 'bummelling' about Nepal for five months, and on this trip there would be a fortnight each way of travel leaving barely a week to spend at the foot of the king of mountains— a time so short that its value could be but small. 'Thus Belial, with words clothed in reason's garb, counselled ignoble ease.' But on the way down to Raxaul Roberts imparted some more bracing and manly thoughts. In fact he called me a fool, and so from Sisaghari I wired acceptance. After all, I thought, if Charles Houston is prepared to fly from New York for the sake of five weeks in the Himalaya, I ought not to grudge waiting a fortnight for the sake of a memorable experience in such good company.

The party met on 29 October at Jogbani, the Indian railway station for Birat Nagar, a short mile away on the Nepal side of the border—a border marked only by a cement boundary pillar. Besides the Houstons, father and son, there were two old friends of theirs, Mrs E. S. Cowles, an American climber of note, and Anderson Bakewell who was then studying at the Jesuit College of St Mary's at Kurseong near Darjeeling. Hitherto I had not regarded a woman as an indispensable part of the equipage of a Himalayan journey but one lives and learns. Anyhow, with a doctor to heal us, a woman to feed us, and a priest to pray for us, I felt we could face the future with some confidence. As the proverb rightly says, prayer and provender hinder no man's journey.

Of provender there seemed to be enough. We had eleven scientifically packed food-boxes, each of which had to be eaten in neither more nor less than four days. The highly organised food-box system of feeding a party, which many respectable and fair-minded travellers mistakenly prefer to more elastic or empiric methods, seldom gives satisfaction. Living off a food-box might be called Ordeal by Planning or the Scientific Martyrdom of Man; the victim being told not only what to eat but in what amount and when. Happily there are still problems, such as space, time, and the human soul, too immense for science; and there are a few subjects, food being one, with which the stereotyped planner's mind had better not attempt to grapple. Thus the optimum contents of a food-box—apparently a simple matter—is too complex for the limited capacity of a man's brain. No one has yet filled a box with food which will satisfy a given number of men for a given number of days with nothing wasted and nothing wanting.

Bakewell, accompanied by four Darjeeling Sherpas, met me a day in advance to make some necessary arrangements. The management of the Birat Nagar Jute Mill very kindly put their guest-house at the disposal of the party and arranged lorry transport to roadhead at Dharan. (Besides the jute mill there are sugar, cotton and rice mills, a saw-mill and a match factory, all owned by Indians and run by Indian

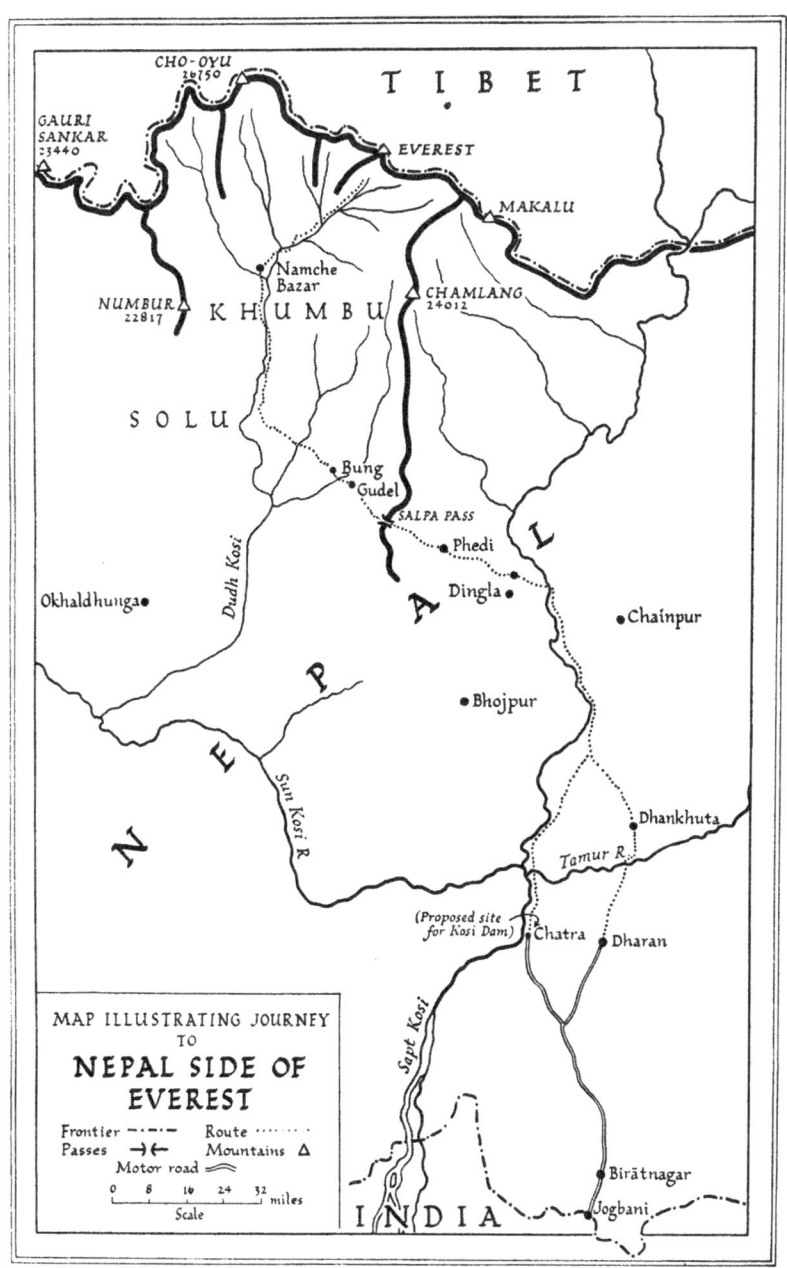

Map 6: Journey to Nepal side of Everest

labour.) We paid our respects to the Governor of Birat Nagar, who kindly arranged for coolies and ponies to meet us at Dharan, and advised the Governor of Dhankhuta district of our imminent arrival. Three of the Sherpas were our old friends Gyalgen, Da Namgyal and Pa Norbu, while Saki had distinguished himself earlier in the year with the French. Saki looked and often behaved like a genial chimpanzee, with a prognathous jaw and a menacing slouch, his long arms hanging almost to the knees. One almost expected to see him start beating his chest. They brought with them a woman who answered to the name of 'Dicky'. Her relationship to them remained obscure, but we gladly took her on the strength for the sake of her neat appearance and cheery manner. She did the party credit; but I felt sorry for Saki, alleged by some to be her husband, for she had a damnable voice and clacked incessantly. However, he that would have eggs must bear with cackling. Our party undoubtedly had in it an active principle of growth. In Delhi the Houstons had picked up yet another Sherpa, a youth who looked more like a Chinese than anything else. He was obviously too superior to be asked to carry a load but he made an admirable lady's maid.

A command car and a lorry decanted us and our baggage at Dharan, at the foot of the hills forty miles away. Here we found eighteen coolies and three ponies waiting for us. A climb of 2000 ft. on a loose stony track under the midday sun made a rather brutal first day for those new to Himalayan travel. We camped early at a village high above the Tamur valley whence, as the sun sank, we watched the huge shadow of Jannu lengthen across the white face of Kangchenjunga. The Tamur river, one of the seven tributaries of the Kosi, rises in the glaciers of Kangchenjunga, but at this season its flashing blue waters betrayed no hint of its glacier origin. Having crossed it by a new suspension bridge we began the long climb to Dankhuta on a broad track thick with coolies bound for Dharan with loads of potatoes.

As one interested in the technique of coolie travel I was struck by the almost complete absence of chautaras; but my early hopes that this might mean fewer halts and quicker travel were soon falsified. As in most parts of Nepal the load was carried in a basket tapering to the base which was strengthened by a wooden strap. The coolie carried a 'T'-shaped stick with a notch in the cross-piece which fitted the wooden strap, so that when a man wished to take the weight off his back he merely slipped the stick under the basket. It was too easy, and perfectly maddening. No one would grudge a man stopping in his tracks to scratch his head or light a cigarette but, marching as they did in close companionable order in single file, every such halt had the effect of stopping everyone else. On a narrow track no one could pass and on a broad track no one wanted to. Nor were these successive checks, caused by the whim or the need of one man, confined to one's own little bunch. If the traffic was dense, several hundreds of coolies would come automatically, and not at all unwillingly, to rest because two friends a mile away had stopped to pass the time of day.

We were all impressed with Dhankhuta—a spotlessly clean little town set on the broad, closely cultivated ridge between the Tamur and Arun valleys. The stone flagged main street is flanked by whitewashed houses with black tiled roofs and wide bracketed eaves; some have open balconies lined with window-boxes. Nearly all these were shops with open fronts in which, however, there was a mystifying absence of anything for sale. All our food had to be purchased through official channels. We were pleased by the school and by the eagerness of masters and boys to speak English, the language in which everything was taught. The tone of the school seemed to be set by a graphic phrase chalked on a nearby Hindu shrine: 'Gather courage, don't be a chicken-hearted fellow.'

We camped in a pine wood (*P. longifolia*) outside the town, and presently the Governor of Dhankhuta paid us a call. He was one of the Rana family, spoke excellent English, and provided us with an escort and an itinerary. Both were needed. Though the people in the remoter parts of Nepal are not opposed to strangers, they are not used to them; and as for the route, it was seldom that shown on the map, which is in need of revision. The usual system is that escort and coolies are changed upon entering another district. The Governor therefore sent a signal to Dingla in No. 4 East on the other side of the Arun, with which he was in touch by wireless, asking for an escort and a fresh lot of coolies to meet us at Kattekaghat, a ferry over the Arun not far from Dingla. Yet another change of escort and coolies would have to be made in No. 3 East or Okhaldhunga in the lower Dudh Kosi valley. Through the miscarriage of the first of these arrangements arose the only trouble we had, and which we overcame only by the staunchness of the jemadar and the Dhankhuta escort.

Neither the jemadar and his escort nor the coolies distinguished themselves on the first march which ended by two Sherpas and myself, who had foolishly gone on to the prearranged village, having to climb back in the dark for nearly 2000 ft. to where the rest of the party had elected to camp.

However, anyone who leaves strange coolies to their own devices on the first march, deserves all he gets. Another disagreeable event for me was the sight of an aeroplane flying south from the Everest region. That mountain was not in view but Makalu and its neighbours stood out against the calm evening sky like a marble frieze. The effect was as though some impious hand had crowned the Hermes of Praxiteles with a bowler hat.

From the broad tableland north of Dankhuta at an altitude of 5000 ft., where the scenery reminds one of the dry foothills of Ranikhet, we descended to the Arun valley, to a height of only 1000 ft. above sea-level. The Arun river cuts a deep gorge east of Makalu (27,790 ft.) and its Tibetan tributaries drain a vast area north of the Himalaya. In one place its head-waters are within ten miles of the Tsangpo. When we met the river it was nearly 200 yards broad, its greeny grey waters flowing through a wide, wooded valley. Whether because of the heat or the unhealthiness of the district, there are no villages close to the river, so that the track along its bank lies through almost deserted country.

Nevertheless, at this time of year it affords pleasant marching and camping, and frequent opportunities for bathing and fishing. Charles Houston, a man who does nothing by halves, greedy for a mahseer, had come armed with two rods and a rich assortment of flies, spoons, spinners, and other artificial baits. The continent of America, inhabited, we are told, by simple backwoodsmen, the natural dupes of smart foreigners, is apparently the home of equally simple-minded fish. One device we tried, a mere piece of wood painted white, a foot long and prickly with hooks, was, they assured me, an equally deadly lure either for bass in the Bronx river or for sockeye salmon in Alaska. But the mahseer of the Arun, if any there are, knew better.

Looking at Everest, north-west of the monastery, only the top of the mountain proper shows rising over the long Lhotse-Nuptse ridge; Lhotse is the right-hand peak, Nuptse the ill-defined peak at the left end of the ridge; the monks call the whole massif Chomo Lungma

Looking north up the Chola Khola from the slopes above Phalong Karpa; the aggressive-looking peak on the left is Taweche (21,388 ft.); the opening to the right below the light-coloured saddle is the entrance to the valley of the Khumbu glacier

Bathing in the Arun was rather too sharp a tonic. We enjoyed our most memorable bathe in one of its small tributaries, where the water ran in a long rock trough, deep, clear and blue. Despite the deliberate pace of the march—the coolies averaged one mile per hour—one became so hot and tired that plunging into this enchanting river was exquisite joy. There were fish too, in the pool, and we plied our angle with unremitting zeal and unrewarded patience. On leaving we mounted to a wide terrace, high above the river, where we walked for four miles through glowing fields of sunflowers and under mighty banyans. The ploughman busy with his oxen in a nearby field might have driven his furrow straight by directing his eyes to Makalu, looming magnificently large in the distance like the icy throne of some Hindu deity. The long white wall of Chamlang, rising at one end to 24,000 ft., effectively screened Everest which is seldom visible to travellers approaching from the south.

Having descended from this terrace to the river at Kattekaghat we were ferried across in a dugout canoe. The speed of the current, the fearful list the craft assumed, together with the rising water in which the passengers sat, made the voyage a lively one during which a weak swimmer had ample time for some solemn reflections. As we stepped ashore and stunned the ferrymen with a tip—the first paying passengers in the history of the ferry—no fresh escort saluted us and no fresh team of coolies stood by to appraise the weight of the loads they would have to carry. Dingla, which our track avoided, lay several thousand feet above the river. A sepoy we had sent there brought word back late that evening that the escort and coolies had gone to meet us at another ferry two marches down stream.

Here then was the seed of trouble which grew to give the caravan master some anxious moments. Either by waiting, or by going up to Dingla, the mistake might equally well have been put right, but our time was so short that we wanted to avoid delay at all costs. The jemadar who, of course, was now trespassing, agreed to come on with his men, while the coolies consented to go as far as Phedi, a village two marches on. Thus we postponed the day of reckoning and went on trusting to time and chance—either to being overtaken by the Dingla boys or to picking up a fresh lot of coolies at Phedi. From there we had to strike westwards to the Dudh Kosi, crossing several ridges between 10,000 and 11,000 ft. high which our Dharan coolies would be loath to tackle.

For the most part the track to Phedi followed the course of a cheerful, flashing stream, the Irkhua Khola. The stream is now marked in red on our maps, for in it Charles Houston caught our one and only fish. For reasons which defy conjecture, a bearded carp of rather less than ½ lb. in weight took one of his flies. We were still talking of this when we reached Phedi where our transport troubles came to a head. Three coolies had already departed, nine more were due to go, and here neither coolies nor rice were to be had. All hands were busy with the rice harvest which had just begun. Like many others who have trusted to careless hope and to something turning up, we had now to pay the penalty—the loss of time while someone went back to Dingla with news of our distressed circumstances. Too late we deplored the impatience which had landed us improperly escorted in a strange district; for the jemadar and the Dankhuta escort cut no ice at all with the headman of Phedi. They were mere interlopers like ourselves.

Hitherto I had regarded these men as more ornamental than useful and the jemadar as a cheerful, incompetent, slightly shifty ass. His unproductive bickering with the Phedi headman did nothing to lessen this view. But that night as I was gloomily turning in, the jemadar, heralded by a strong wave of raksi, thrust his head into my tent to announce that in spite of all we would march next day. He had accomplished the miracle of persuading four of the escort of five to carry loads; an old man and two of his grandchildren, too weak for the harvest, had offered to carry three more; several of the Dharan men agreed to follow us to the world's end and anything that remained over could be dumped. These bold hopes were no alcoholic dream. In the morning grandfather turned up with his infants, the despised escort manfully made up full loads, and only the Sherpas continued to 'work to rule'. These five, six if Dicky was included, who were in the enviable position of emigrants returning to the old country free of cost and on full pay, could have solved half our problem without unduly distressing themselves by doubling their own paltry loads. They were in fact carrying nothing but their own kit and some souvenirs with which to astonish their stay-at-home cousins, but it was not until Charles Houston and I had shouldered what remained that they were shamed into adding something to their loads. On a mountain the better Darjeeling Sherpas will not spare themselves, but they now regard themselves as a *corps d'elite* from whom coolie work should not be expected.

Above Phedi there is an 11,000 ft. pass, the Salpa Banjang. Once over this we should enter yet another district, Okhaldhunga or No. 3 East, where we should no doubt have more trouble over coolies and food. Only when we reached the Dudh Kosi valley and the Sherpa district of Khumbu might we fairly expect to leave care behind. How just this expectation was we quickly had proof. As we climbed to a camp below the pass, while I anxiously marked the progress of grandad and the escort in their unaccustomed role, we met three genuine Sherpas on their way to Phedi with salt. They were men of decision who knew a good thing when they saw it. They hurried down to Phedi, rid themselves of their loads, and rejoined us the same evening. These three men, whom we called 'The Three Musketeers', always marched, ate, and slept together. They were sterling characters, dependable and solid as rocks, who worked for us with a will and cheered us by their company all the way up and back again to the plains. The escort showed no sign of flinching from their undertaking, so grandad and the children were sent tottering back to Phedi, and we went on and over the pass with renewed confidence.

Some neglected mani walls on the way up prepared us for the big chorten which crowned the pass. Like alpine flowers these emblems of Buddhism are found only above a certain level. Descending through spruce forest to a small Sherpa village, where, contrary to some not disinterested advice, we refused to stop, we traversed a high waterless hillside covered with tall ilex to the Gurkha (Rai) village of Gudel at about 7000 ft. The presence of either Sherpa or other Tibetan-like people is governed by height rather than by locality. Their villages are seldom found below 8000 ft. while those of the Gurkha people are not seen above 7000 ft. At Gudel they would have no truck with us, so that lack of food for both escort and coolies now threatened to halt our uncertain progress. Our recent access of confidence was further undermined by the appalling prospect of the next stage, from our camp on the rice stubbles of Gudel across an appallingly deep valley to Bung, and thence to another pass over the ridge beyond. Bung looked to be within spitting distance, yet the map affirmed and the eye agreed that we should have to descend some 3000 ft. and climb a like amount to reach it. Profound emotion may find vent in verse as well as in oaths; despair as well as joy may rouse latent, unsuspected poetical powers. Thus at Gudel, uninspired by liquor, for there was none, some memorable lines were spoken:

> For dreadfulness nought can excel
> The prospect of Bung from Gudel;
> And words die away on the tongue
> When we look back at Gudel from Bung.

The village of Bung, a name which appeals to a music-hall mind, provoked another outburst on the return journey because its abundant well of good raksi, on which we were relying, had dried up.

> Hope thirstily rested on Bung
> So richly redolent of rum;
> But when we got there
> The cupboard was bare,
> Sapristi. No raksi. No chang.

(To disarm the hypercritical I might say that the 'a' in chang, a Tibetan word for beer, is pronounced like a short 'u'.)

The neat houses and terraced fields of Bung, apparently rich in promise, covered several thousand feet of hillside. In Nether Bung they grew bananas and rice, in Upper Bung oranges and wheat. A sepoy had gone on to collect rice but on arrival the whole party scattered in search of provender like hounds drawing a cover. For ourselves we acquired nothing but a goat, worth about Rs. 5, for Rs. 12, having been asked Rs. 20. In order to secure the rice we had to curtail the march and make a late start. Next morning the jemadar, with bloodshot eyes and husky voice, as became one who had attended an overnight harvest thanksgiving, led the rice procession up to our camp in swaying triumph. Thus heartened the party went with a will over the Shipki La (*c.* 10,000 ft.) and dropped 3000 ft. to a camp above the Irkhua Khola. Both this stream and that which so drastically divides Gudel from Bung are tributaries of the Dudh Kosi, but we had still another ridge to cross before reaching that valley.

However, we were now in country which our Sherpa followers knew and where we were welcome for their sake. At Panga, a village of stone houses and shingle roofs, a fat, smiling cobbler sat in the sun sewing bright coloured Tibetan felt boots, closely watched by a little Lhasa terrier. The Sherpas disappeared at once into the largest house in quest of beer where, like Brer Bull-frog, they had every right to sing:

> Ingle-go-jang, my joy, my joy.
> I'm right at home, my joy,

for this village was within the borders of Khumbu. On that account we, too, might rejoice and be thankful, but the escort and the Dharan coolies, who by this time had the air of martyrs suffering in a doubtful cause, might wonder what had persuaded them to stray from their warm rice lands into such high, benighted country.

For a day and a half we followed a rough track lying 3000 ft. above the Dudh Kosi, across two spurs of distressing height, until we dropped slowly to the large village of Chaunrikharka. The village boasts a graceful stupa of great age, but a more surprising exhibit was that of a rain gauge. It had been installed in 1948 by Dr Bannerjee of the Indian Meteorological Survey, who had also left a snow and rain gauge at Namche Bazar. We were shown the records which appeared to be correctly kept. Having descended to the river we crossed by a wooden cantilever bridge and camped; just above was the village of Gumila, the home of our Three Musketeers, who at once brought us eggs and buckwheat flour. I introduced my companions to Himalayan buckwheat cakes, which I consider not only superb in their own right but perfect for conveying large quantities of butter to the mouth. They did not think buckwheat cakes the equal of my bread which they always referred to as 'foot-bread', having noticed that after bread-making my boots were usually covered with flour. As I explained, I did not use my feet for kneading, at least not with boots on, but in baking, or indeed any cooking when empiric methods are used, some of the raw material is inevitably left adhering to the person of the cook if not to the walls and ceiling of his environment.

On 14 November we reached Namche Bazar. The track crossed and recrossed the clear, blue river, here hurrying along like a mountain torrent, by wooden cantilever bridges which in no case had to span more than twenty yards. For a river which drains what is perhaps the grandest thirty miles of the Himalaya it is surprisingly small—a stretch including, besides the Everest group, Cho Oyu (26,750 ft.), Gyachung Khang (25,910 ft.), Ngojumba Khang (25,720 ft.), and a host of lesser peaks. At this season, of course, the snows were not melting, but from the water marks on boulders we guessed the summer rise to be not more than four feet. Near the river, upon any big boulder which presented a fair, smooth surface, lama sculptors of long ago had chiselled sacred texts in deeply incised characters. Some which had recently been recarved showed up in black and white relief, but most were worn flat and were black with age. Had the original sculptor but added a date we might have had a hint as to the rate at which the river carves out its bed.

At the junction of the Bhote Kosi nallah, up which lies the road to Nangpa La (19,050 ft.), Tingri Dzong, and Rongbuk, our track quitted the deep gorge of the river. As we climbed the 1500 ft. to the village the path became wider and the going easier, and presently we were met by a Nepali official (a Gurung) and the Sherpa headman with a string of ponies. Since our first camp in the Arun valley none of the track had been suitable for riding. We were welcomed to the village by an inquisitive but friendly crowd. Namche Bazar, of course, has never ranked as a 'forbidden city'. It is far from being a city, and it has remained unvisited not because of any very serious difficulties in the way, but because no one has thought it worth the trouble of overcoming them. Nevertheless, it had for long been my humble Mecca. As we rode in I shared in imagination a little of the satisfaction of Burton, or of Manning when he reached Lhasa.

CHAPTER XIX

APPROACH TO MT EVEREST

Namche Bazar lies at about 11,000 ft. on the ridge between the Dudh Kosi and the Bhote Kosi, facing westwards across the valley to the peak of Kwangde (20,320 ft.). Unlike the Manangbhot villages where all are huddled together, the houses are detached as if the owners were men of substance. There are about thirty of these whitewashed, two-storied houses, with low-pitched shingle roofs. The ground floor serves as stables and stores, while above is the one long living room, with an open fire and clay stove against one wall, wooden shelves for fine copper ware and cheap china on another, and large trellised window frames set with five or six small panes of glass. To find glass in a Himalayan private house, fourteen days' march from civilization, is a little remarkable.

The extent of cultivation seemed small for the number of people. I imagine that more food is imported and paid for by the trade in salt and rice which the Sherpas carry on between lower Nepal and Tingri in Tibet over the 19,000 ft. Nangpa La. But there are other villages within a few miles of Namche where the acreage of cultivation is much greater in proportion to the number of houses. Kuru (a barley), buckwheat and potatoes are the crops; wheat is grown in the lower villages like Chaunrikharka and Gumila.

We went at once to our allotted house, and when the crowd had ebbed sufficiently to leave space, the tents were pitched alongside. The women accorded Gyalgen precedence at the fireplace and the headman took strong measures against the more persistent sightseers. A few privileged intruders were allowed to remain. These were mostly former porters, vouched for by their Himalayan Club service books and numerous carefully cherished 'chits' and photographs. They were considered to be sufficiently well disciplined to refrain from laughing at our strange ways and stranger faces. After a meal, fearing rightly that neither beer nor raksi was going to be offered, we went for a walk;

partly for privacy—for the Americans were a little dismayed by the attentions of the crowd—and partly in the hope of seeing something of the great mountain which was now less than twenty miles away.

A morning sky freckled with high cirrus clouds had foretold accurately a break in the weather. Low clouds were driving up from the south, and when we had climbed a hill to bring the Lhotse-Nuptse ridge into view, the upper part, over which we should have seen the top of Everest, was obscured. Even in clear weather, however, only the summit is seen. The mountain, in spite of its bulk and height, still eludes the eye of the traveller approaching from the south; who, having outflanked and passed the high white wall of Chamlang, finds himself confronted by a black and higher wall. This is the three-mile-long rock ridge linking Lhotse (27,890 ft.), or South Peak, to Nuptse (25,680 ft.), the West Peak. The south face of this ridge is too steep to hold snow. Behind it lies the West Cwm, the deep cleft which separates it from the west ridge of Everest itself.

Although my companions were in ecstasies over Namche Bazar and its friendly people, they were anxious to quit it at once and shrank from staying another night. Charles Houston and I, at any rate, had no time to waste if we were to see anything of the mountain in the six days available. We were due back at Jogbani on 6 December and had therefore to leave Namche by 21 November. Thus it was arranged that he and I should start early next morning for Thyangboche and beyond, while the others would follow later and stop at Thyangboche, where there is a monastery of whose beauty and sanctity we had already heard much.

We were astir early in pursuit of these plans and were not to be turned from them by a lowering morning with snow falling briskly. Gyalgen was in his element, chaffing the women, haranguing the men, engaging recruits for the glacier party, and cooking for us a very handsome breakfast—hot buckwheat cakes and eggs, tsampa porridge and fresh milk. With mingled feelings, greed predominating over sorrow, I noticed that their hygienic principles prevented my friends from drinking milk from such dubious sources. Only a timely exclamation of horror vetoed the proposal that it should be boiled, thus rendering it innocuous, and at the same time tasteless. After a few days of intimate life at the monastery where it was obvious that dirt, disease and death lurked pleasantly in every pot and in every corner of the room, they overcame these scruples and took to milk like cats. All except Mr Houston, senior, who was made of sterner stuff, who looked upon raw milk as more inimical to health than raw brandy and much less pleasant to take.

The glacier party had with them Da Namgyal, Saki, a Musketeer and Danu a raw recruit. Although a mere lad Danu was said to be a brother of the redoubtable Angtharkay, who had begun his climbing career in 1933; be that as it may, he certainly behaved like an Angtharkay. Short, barrel-like and solemn, he moved about in camp with the portentous tread of a bishop or a muscle-bound all-in wrestler, his hands resting lightly on an incipient stomach. But in action he carried more and went twice as fast as anyone else besides doing the work of three men in camp. He had a passion for building immense camp fires, nothing less than a holocaust satisfied him. Long before daybreak one would imagine that the sun had risen untimely, but it was only Danu rekindling the overnight bonfire, so that we could breakfast round it in comfort at first light.

A well-engineered track on which ponies can be ridden leads to Thyangboche. After traversing high it descends gradually to the Dudh Kosi which it crosses just below its junction with the Imja Khola. This river comes down from Everest, from the north-east, while the Dudh Kosi descends from the north where it rises in the glaciers of the Cho Oyu group. The track then climbs equally gradually to the monastery ($c.$ 12,000 ft.), a group of white buildings built on a grassy saddle commanding views up the Dudh Kosi, west to Kwangde, south to the fantastic snow spires of Kangtega, and east to the Lhotse-Nuptse ridge which fills the whole valley. The summit of Everest shows not very prominently over the top of this ridge, but the monks call the whole massif Chomo Lungma. It would be difficult to imagine, much more find, a finer site for worship or for contemplation. Lamas may laugh at our love for climbing mountains, but undoubtedly they themselves take great delight in looking at them. Like Christian monks they seemed to be equally lovers of the picturesque and of good living; on which two counts they have the approval of at any rate one mountaineer.

That morning we saw nothing of this noble prospect. It was snowing steadily, and the monastery yaks scuffled hungrily in the snow. The monks were a little taken aback when we walked boldly into the precincts followed by a crowd of grinning urchins or sucking lamas. However, they placed a couple of braziers in front of us, and when we heard that the rear party had been sighted we decided to lunch with them before going on to Pangboche, the next village up the Imja Khola.

At this news the interest and excitement of the lamas rose perceptibly. They realised that Charles Houston and I were merely an indifferent curtain-raiser to the coming pageant. When the newcomers rode into the courtyard below, one felt that, had they known how, the lamas would have cheered. Mrs Cowles, of course, stole the show, and soon had them all, urchins and lamas alike, eating out of her hand; nor could they fail to be impressed with Mr Houston's benign dignity—not unlike that of the old abbot of Rongbuk himself—or with Andy Bakewell's bearded gravity and manly bearing—especially as he was wearing shorts. Thyangboche is a very small counterpart of Rongbuk monastery on the Tibetan side of the mountain, not a quarter of its size and having only a handful of monks. Yet its abbot, a shy smiling youth, of reputedly great spiritual power, is held in little less reverence, and its situation is incomparably more beautiful and less austere. It is much less austere inside, too, for they produced a beaker of raksi for our lunch, and when we returned a few days later we found they had the pleasant custom of fortifying their guests with a snorter before breakfast.

Having seen our friends established in an empty house we had no qualms—none, that is, on their behalf—about leaving them in such congenial surroundings. On a fine day it is an entrancing walk from the monastery to the Imja Khola bridge; through open woods of hoary twisted juniper and of glistening silver birch, whose golden leaves were still clinging to branches hung with streamers of pale green lichen. We strolled along, past a little whitewashed hamlet, when suddenly a bend in the path brought into view the white, foaming river and beyond it a massive rock shoulder, like the grey roof of a church, from which sprang the preposterous snow spire of some unnamed, unmeasured peak. The trees ended at the river. As is generally the way, the south-facing side of the valley was bare and bore an abundant crop of stones. Few stretches of the rocky track were without mani walls and chortens, and every convenient boulder had inscribed on it a religious text.

A view of Everest from due west. The ridge in the foreground leads up to Nuptse, and the ice-fall at its foot is the entrance to the West Cwm; on the far side of the ice-fall is the west shoulder of Everest and left of this is the Lho La, the 19,000 ft. col at the head of the West Rongbuk glacier; the right-hand rock ridge is probably not the true south ridge which lies farther round; the usual climbing route lies just below the left-hand ridge; the site of 'Camp VI' is hidden by the top of the west shoulder

A party outside the monastery; Mrs E. S. Cowles is on the left; in front is Mr Oscar Houston, draped with the recently presented ceremonial scarf and charm locket; Dr Charles Houston is standing behind the excessively gross lama, and Anderson Bakewell—not quite with us—is on the extreme right

Sonam Tensing, otherwise known as the Foreign Sportsman, is in the centre of this Sherpa trio; the lad is Prometheus Danu who claimed to be brother to the redoubtable Angtharkay

Having been warned of sickness at the next village, Pangboche, we camped in a field on the outskirts where there was an empty hut for the men. A dense mist followed the heavy snowfall.

But the storm's malice was spent; after a cold night the morning broke bright and clear. Pangboche, which has few houses and a great many fields, is the last inhabited village. At Dingboche, a few miles up, there are a number of fields but no one lives there in winter. As we walked over flats of coarse brown grass by the river, we had in front of us the long Lhotse-Nuptse rock face with the massive black pyramid of Everest showing above it. One was impressed not so much by its height, for it looked rather squat, but by the suggestion it held of the immensity of its unseen mass. Three miles up, when the valley divided, we took the northern branch; the other continues eastwards, drains the south side of Lhotse, and terminates in a bay a little way south and east of the peak. Makalu, twenty miles away, beyond the head of this valley, bulked big enough, for most of it was in view, yet it was white and shapely and had not the menace of this black fragment of mountain so high above us.*

The first two miles of our northern valley consisted of broad, brown pastures dotted with stone huts and grazing yaks. One group of huts is called Pheriche and the uppermost, where we camped, Phalong Karpa. All the living huts were securely locked for the winter but we made ourselves comfortable in one which was used as a hay barn. That afternoon we climbed to about 17,000 ft. on the ridge which descends south-west from Nuptse to the fork in the main valley. The glaciers of the eastern branch seemed of no great size and terminated well above the fields of Dingboche, which we now looked down upon. On this bright afternoon with hardly a cloud in sight, we beheld a vast panorama of mountains; from Lhotse, Pethangtse and Makalu in the east, south to Chamlang and Kangtega, west to Taweche, and north to Cho Oyu and Gyachung Khang. In this galaxy, which included a host of unnamed peaks, neither the lesser nor the greater seemed designed for the use of climbers.

---

* According to a map constructed from air photographs by the late E. A. Reeves, Instructor of Survey at the R.G.S., Pethangtse (the east peak), like Makalu, lies in the basin of the Arun river.

At 14,000 ft. at this time of year, mid-November, the nights were bitter. Only a few juniper bushes thrived, yet on returning from this excursion we found Danu Prometheus tending a glorious blaze of sizeable logs. Frost soon stilled the murmur of the stream, only the faint note of a bell on some restless yak broke the deep silence. As we sat in the secure circle of the fire, our backs to the stone wall of the hut, the talk turned naturally to the Abominable Snowman. As one might expect they are found in these parts in numbers, especially around Namche Bazar in the depths of winter when the cold drives them lower. Danu affirmed that the previous year, a friend of his named Lakhpa Tensing had had his face so badly mauled by one, on the Nangpa La, that he died. By running downhill, which is, of course, the only way a man can run at these heights, one can usually get away from these creatures whose long hair, falling over their eyes, hampers them; but the unfortunate Lakhpa had apparently tripped and lying half stunned by the fall became an easy prey.

Just above Phalong Karpa is the high terminal moraine of the Khumbu glacier which comes down from the north-east, from Pumori, the Lho La and the West Cwm. The main valley, also glacier-filled, continues northwards towards the head of the West Rongbuk. They told us of a pass, now disused, at the head of this valley, but I think perhaps they were confusing it with the so-called 'Nup La' which leads from the West Rongbuk into the next valley westwards, the Dudh Kosi. I can find no account of it, but I believe this 'Nup La' was actually crossed by Mr Hazard (of the 1924 expedition) and a Gurkha surveyor. They camped just on the west side of it and then returned. We turned up the Khumbu valley where we found good going in a warm, grassy ablation valley where gentians were still in flower. As we advanced we brought into view first Pumori, and then the Lho La and the North Peak beyond it. After going for four hours we camped by a little lake beyond the last grass almost in the shadow of Nuptse. Our height was about 16,500 ft.

Our afternoon walk towards the foot of the Lho La, whence we hoped to see up the West Cwm, was very rough. Driven from the friendly ablation valley, now filled with boulders, we took to the moraine, and finally sought easier going on the glacier itself. Expecting every moment to round some corner and look up the Cwm, we were baffled by the apparent continuity of the rock and snow wall linking

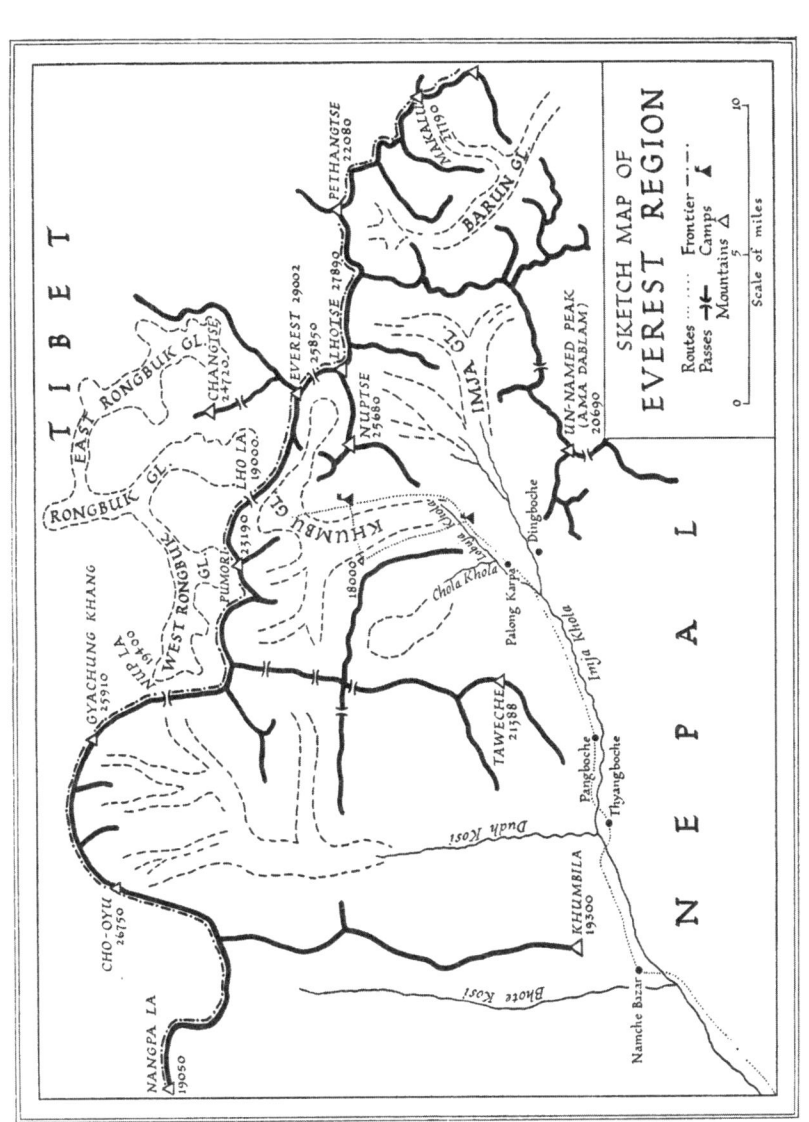

Map 7: Sketch-map of Everest region

Nuptse with the west ridge of Everest which rises abruptly from the Lho La. Before turning for home and when still a mile from the foot of the Lho La, I struck out across the glacier but still failed to see any break. Some trick of lighting must have concealed it, for we saw it readily enough next morning before we were half-way across the glacier. It is, however, the merest slit, not more than three hundred yards across, filled by a broken ice-fall which falls steeply to the Khumbu glacier almost at the foot of the Lho La.

As we had only one day left, we thought that, instead of trying to enter the Cwm, our best chance of seeing both its head and the south ridge of the mountain would be from some vantage point on the west side of the glacier. Accordingly we sent the men down to Phalong Karpa, crossed the glacier, and climbed a subsidiary feature of about 18,000 ft. to the south of Pumori. The glacier is about a mile wide and only some five in length. Its upper part is pinnacled, like the East Rongbuk glacier, though the ice pinnacles are neither so high nor so continuous. One reason for this comparatively slight glaciation—for it is only half the length of any one of the three Rongbuk glaciers—is that the southern glaciers start and finish respectively nearly 2000 ft. lower than the northern. The south aspect, too, is warmer, and the temperatures must be appreciably raised by the great expanse of bare rock on the south faces of Everest and Lhotse which are too steep to hold snow.

As we hurried across the glacier under a hard sky that seemed to hold possibilities of evil, we glanced now at the weather and now at the great mountain as bit by bit the terrific sweep of black rock rose above the West Cwm. So anxious were we to gain our point before any clouds appeared that we forced the pace—if pace it could be called—unwisely; for Houston, who had left New York barely three weeks before, found 18,000 ft. quite high enough.

In spite of our height and our distance from it—about seven miles—we could not see the high col between Everest and Lhotse of which the lowest point is 25,850 ft. A shoulder of Nuptse cut across the south ridge of the mountain, hiding the whole length of the West Cwm and this col at its head. We could see at most the upper 3000 ft. of the south ridge which looked so steep that we dismissed at once any idea of there being a route, even supposing the col could be reached.

From the map, we appeared to be due west of the south ridge and were thus seeing it in profile. On that assumption it seemed to be a waste of time discussing the possibility of reaching it; but I now think we were not looking at its true edge but merely a buttress protruding from the south-west face. For photographs of this high Lhotse-Everest profile, taken during the monsoon from the east by the 1921 reconnaissance party, show a snow-covered slope rising from the col at a much less frightening angle. They also show the east side of the col to be unclimbable. Whether snow lies permanently on the south ridge, and what, at that great height is its consistency, are additional problems. Yet with these pictures in mind, and despite our impressions from the west, one cannot write off the south side as impossible until the approach from the head of the West Cwm to this remarkably airy col has been seen. (It is a pity that the name Lho La, or South Col, has been appropriated by the col at the foot of the west ridge; but there is perhaps no need to find a name for this true south col, 6000 ft. higher than the false, until it has been reached.)

The West Cwm has been looked at several times from the Lho La. We saw it from there in 1935 and Mr Shipton secured a photograph of it. All that this shows is a short stretch of level snow above the ice-fall, the head of the Cwm being well out of sight behind the west ridge. It is a trench confined within two more or less precipitous walls, and it somehow seems unlikely that there will be a convenient snow ramp leading from the level floor at, possibly, 21,000 ft. to the col at 25,850 ft. Moreover, a trench overhung by these two tremendous walls might easily become a grave for any party which pitched its camp there.

On the whole, whatever one may think of the last 3000 ft. of the south ridge, looked at either from the east or from the west, in my opinion, the chances are against there being any way of reaching it. Of the final 1000 ft., the crux of the whole matter, we have unfortunately no experience. Certainly they cannot be assumed to be easy.

At great heights a route must be easy to be possible, not only because of the extra exertion needed to overcome difficult places but also because of the time so lost. Even in the early days of the 1921 reconnaissance Mallory was aware of this when he dismissed the west ridge as a possible route: 'If ever the mountain were to be climbed,' he wrote, 'the way would not lie along the length of any of its colossal ridges. Progress could only be made along comparatively easy ground... ' Mallory, too, had looked into the West Cwm from the Lho La and even from that restricted view drew some conclusions.

He and Bullock had hoped to reach the West Cwm from the Rongbuk glacier, but were stopped by the 1500 ft. drop to the Khumbu glacier. He wrote: 'It was not a very likely chance that the gap between Everest and the South peak (Lhotse) could be reached from the west. From what we have seen I do not much fancy it would be possible, even if one could get up the glacier' (i.e. up the ice-fall of the West Cwm glacier). Although the weather did not worsen, it remained unkind for photography.

Under a dull, hard sky, with neither sunlight nor shadow playing about its huge faces and ridges, the mountain compelled admiration only by its immensity. Mountains without snow and ice are shorn of the greater part of their splendour, and it is not always realised that in its most familiar aspect Everest is a rock mountain. Above 25,000 ft., from the northeast ridge round to the south, no permanent snow lies except in a few gullies and on odd ledges; and so accustomed are we to associate snow and ice with great height that the fact is not easy to appreciate.

The upper part of the climbing route and what looked like the Second Step were visible, but Camp VI and the route to it from the North Col were hidden by the north-west shoulder which from here appeared to be a mountain in its own right, with two snow ridges framing a face of rock banded with fluted snow. It was surprising to see the climbing route in perfect condition, free from snow, barely two months after the end of the monsoon. We still have a lot to learn about Everest. It is not yet known how soon after the monsoon the upper rocks are cleared of snow. It has been generally believed that the snow was swept away by gales in late winter, but if this rapid clearing is caused by evaporation towards the end and immediately after the monsoon, then a favourable month for an attempt might be October when the weather is more settled and when there would be no ever-present threat of an untimely 'Western Disturbance' or an early monsoon applying the closure. On the other hand, this rapid clearing may be affected by October gales which would, of course, preclude any attempt at that time. So far as we could tell there was not much wind when we were there in late November, but even if the weather then is generally fine, the intense cold and the shortening days would be deadly disadvantages for high climbing.

We descended from our little hummock and returned to Phalong Karpa by the true right side of the Khumbu glacier. From what we had seen we were convinced that the south ridge offered little hope, but of course we had not seen enough. We had not seen the true south ridge, neither had we seen the Lhotse-Everest col nor the approach to it from the West Cwm, and until this has been seen one cannot rule out the possibility of there being a route to the summit by the south ridge.* From the head of the West Cwm to the South Col must be nearly 5000 ft.; from the head of the East Rongbuk glacier to the North Col is less than half that and yet it is as steep a place as anyone would like to have to climb with laden porters. One cannot help feeling that the tendency to greater steepness on the south side of the mountain will hold good, and that there will not be any convenient ramp by which the South col will be attainable.

Next morning 'Chimpanzee' Saki went down and very nearly out with malaria, so that for the first mile or two he had to be carried. The medicine chest, a very comprehensive one, had been left at Thyangboche, but I happened to have in my pocket a few Paludrin tablets which worked like a charm. He probably lost the first dose by vomiting, but after the second he began rapidly to perk up and reached Thyangboche on his own feet.

Our friends there had taken to a monastic life with the greatest readiness. Our introduction to it consisted of a large bowl of unexceptionable dai for supper. True we were wakened at 4 a.m. by the din of horns and the clash of cymbals, but we were not expected to rouse out for prayer or meditation, or indeed to do anything beyond reaching for a wooden jorum thoughtfully left in readiness. In this, of course, lurked what we called 'lama's milk', which was raksi flavoured with cloves.

---

* Since the above was written a party has been sent out (September 1951) to discover whether the upper part of the mountain can be reached from the West Cwm.

The jemadar, the escort and the Dharan men, all of them blue with cold, were waiting to take us down, but first we had to tour the monastery and to receive the blessing of the young abbot. This ceremony resembled a school prize giving, the abbot, in the role of dumb but distinguished visitor, distributing the prizes handed to him by the business-like secretary. As we sheepishly filed past the dais where the young abbot, attired in full canonicals and a tall cone-shaped hat, sat enthroned, with his cup, copper teapot, silver 'dorje' and all the tools of his trade, so to speak, in front of him, we bowed our heads while he draped our necks with the ceremonial scarf and a small silk talisman, at the same time handing us a paper of formidable pills. The talisman consisted of a tightly folded paper of writing and pictures combined, sealed and neatly bound with red, white, blue, purple and black threads. In the end curiosity overcame my reluctance to slice open and so destroy this miniature work of art. The monastery possesses a library of 500 wood-bound books each in its own curtained pigeon-hole. Among its rich furnishings are a gilt, life-size image of the late abbot of Rongbuk monastery and some very beautiful religious paintings, temple banners or 'Thang-ka'.

Our return journey was remarkable for the size of our retinue. We had thus no transport worries. If we wanted to lengthen our marches all we did was to transfer a few more of our followers to the pay-roll and so lighten the loads of the rest. Whether they expected to be paid or whether they merely hungered after the privilege of travelling in such distinguished company, a great many Sherpas, men and women, decided to accompany us to Dharan, or to Darjeeling if they could raise the money for a ticket. Danu, of course, came, kindling young forest fires all the way. He attached himself to me, and by always having my tent up and bedding out long before any other loads had cast up, gave occasion for some pointed remarks. Another good companion and worker was Sonam Tensing, who is better known in Himalayan circles as the Foreign Sportsman, a familiar figure on a number of expeditions which we had made together in the thirties. Having always returned to his village after each expedition and never resided long in Darjeeling, he seemed quite unspoilt, a visible token of which being the pigtail he still wore. With a voice as deep as of yore, he still crooned what I imagined were prayers, going

The young abbot could hardly be expected to mingle with the mob seen in the previous picture; here he is seated in state with his tea equipage, bell, and all the tools of his trade; above his throne hang three temple banners; this picture was taken by Mrs E. S. Cowles

on sometimes for nearly half an hour without stopping—perhaps the Buddhist prayer known as 'Clearing of Obstruction from the Path', which should be a favourite one for wayfarers.

We met with no obstructions at all and only a few slight rubs to mar our felicity. Of these, apart from a few affectionate lice which I shared with Danu until I broke him of the habit of carrying his spare clothes in my rucksack, the most embarrassing was our meeting with a large escort from Okhaldhunga which had been chasing us for nearly a fortnight. It was a case of hail and farewell, for we were on the verge of leaving their district when they caught us up. It was hard to know whom their superior would blame most, us or them, but as we were not going to Okhaldhunga it hardly mattered. We solved the difficulty with a carefully worded note to him and a small cash bonus to them. Our jemadar never got over this. Perhaps he feared this diminution of the prize fund might affect his own prospects, for he never stopped talking of the folly of rewarding men for work they had not done.

To our sorrow we met with further evidence of the long if slightly inefficient arm of Okhaldhunga officialdom, stretching out this time to the detriment of our friends of Bung. It seemed that while food grains like rice might be turned into beer, the law drew the line at turning them into spirits. Accordingly a few publicans and sinners, some of Bung's most prominent citizens, had been hauled off to Okhaldhunga to answer for it. Having drunk prematurely a bottle of genuine brandy which had been earmarked for celebrating Thanksgiving Day, we were with difficulty trying to accumulate a stock of the local fire-water; a problem not unlike those set in arithmetic papers concerned with the filling of leaking tanks. With confidence well grounded on experience we had looked forward to remedying any deficiency at Bung, and now, of course, the sources of the spring were dry. The lament on this theme, which will not bear repeating, has already been given.

Nevertheless, in the Arun valley on 30 November, the pilgrims had their Thanksgiving Dinner—table decorations by Mrs Cowles, heating and lighting by Danu, solid fare by Gyalgen, fruit cake by Himal Bill, and bottled lightning from the jemadar's private cellar. For my part I gave thanks for past Himalayan seasons, few without their missed opportunities and frustrated hopes, but all of them good, and of which this, I thought, should be the last. The best attainable should be good enough for any man, but the mountaineer who finds his best gradually sinking is not satisfied. In an Early English poem attributed to one Beowulf we are told:

> Harder should be the spirit, the heart all the bolder,
> Courage the greater, as the strength grows less.

If a man feels he is failing to achieve this stern standard he should perhaps withdraw from a field of such high endeavour as the Himalaya.

APPENDIX

The Natural History of the Langtang Valley

By O. POLUNIN

THE LANGTANG VALLEY LIES at the centre of a vast area of unknown country—unknown alike to the explorer and the naturalist. From time to time, during the last 150 years, interesting details of the plants and animals of the high alpine regions of Nepal have come to light when collections made by native collectors have been sent back to Europe. Our knowledge of the adjoining countries of Sikkim and Kumaon have helped us to build up a broad picture of the flora and fauna of Nepal, but probably more than 5000 square miles of the steepest country in the world lies waiting for detailed investigation by trained naturalists.

Within this area, many hundreds of species of plants, insects and other small animals may remain unknown to the scientific world. In addition our knowledge of the distribution of plants and animals, from east to west, and from west to east, along the Great Himalaya Range will continue to be full of gaps until Nepal has been fully explored. Nepal lies roughly at the junction of two lines of migration where plants and animals from Kashmir and Afghanistan meet those from Burma and China. No plants, as far as is known, have invaded the high Himalaya from the plains of India, and few have come south from Tibet.

At the meeting place of two previously isolated groups the biologist expects interesting things to happen; hybrids may be formed and new species evolved.

The history of natural history exploration in Nepal is quite briefly related, as there are only a few scientists who have made any profound contribution to our knowledge of the plants and animals of alpine Nepal. The story opens in 1820 when the great botanist Wallich spent a year at Katmandu. He collected among the forested hills surrounding the valley of Nepal, but was not himself permitted to travel farther into the mountains. However, he was able to arrange for pilgrims who made the annual journey to the sacred lakes of Gosainkund to bring down specimens from high altitudes, and it was in this way that the first high alpine plants from Nepal were collected. Wallich's specimens, including many species new to science, are carefully preserved in the herbaria of Europe and are a constant source of reference. The original collecting ground, lying thirty miles north of Katmandu at an altitude of 15,000 ft., has still to be visited, and fuller collections of Wallich's plants have to be made. On the basis of Wallich's collection and an earlier one by Hamilton, D. Don compiled the one and only flora, *Prodromus Florae Nepalensis*, which was published in 1825.

In 1822 Sir B. H. Hodgson was appointed Assistant Resident at Katmandu and he lived for twenty-one years in the valley, spending his spare time in collecting birds, mammals and reptiles of Nepal. His collections were exhaustive and not only did he present 9512 specimens of birds, 903 mammals and 84 reptiles to the British Museum but he contributed no less than 127 papers on his observations on the natural history of the Himalaya. Like Wallich before him, he was not allowed to travel outside the valley of Nepal and had to rely on native collectors for all his specimens from the high alpine regions.

It was in 1848 that the first European, the intrepid botanical explorer Sir J. D. Hooker, made a journey in person into the Nepal Himalaya. He went into east Nepal from Sikkim during the winter and reached an altitude of 16,600 ft. at Wallanchoon on the watershed between Everest and Kangchenjunga. His travels and general scientific observations are recorded in his *Himalayan Journals*.

During the next hundred years the mountains of Nepal were completely secluded and no Europeans were allowed to travel in them, but as if to keep the appetite whetted, a number of native collectors scoured the mountains for plants and animals to send back to the British Museum. Between the years 1921–3 an Indian named Baptista collected mammals and between 1927 and 1937 two Nepalese collectors, Lai Dhwoj and Sharma, sent back interesting collections of seeds and herbarium specimens from the mountains. Some of these, like the handsome yellow Himalayan poppy, *Meconopsis regia*, were new to science and have in this way been introduced into our gardens.

The Langtang valley, or more correctly Khola, had much to recommend it, for it lay right in the middle of this unknown strip of country and not far from the historical collecting ground of Wallich at Gosainkund. The valley formed an offshoot from the main Trisuli gorge and ran into the Langtang Himal mountains on the borders of Nepal and Tibet.

It would be as well to consider the plants and animals from the lowest point of the Langtang valley and follow the changes, stage by stage, as the valley rises towards the watershed.

At the meeting of the two valleys, at 5000 ft., the little village of Syabrubensi lay perched on a narrow terrace above the watersmeet of the two glacial rivers. In August the wooden-tiled roofs of the houses were almost hidden in the tall stems of the maize; lizards ran over the hot stones along the track side; fig-trees, Euphorbias and bananas grew in the village area. A narrow strip of ground perhaps half a mile wide with a warm temperate climate penetrated in to the heart of this mountain region. Frost never came down to this altitude and even during the monsoon, a ribbon of blue sky followed the curves of the Trisuli gorge, so that it was possible for animals and plants of warmer climates to live within a few miles of the snows. Gentle breezes passing up the valley to Tibet helped to cool the fierce heat of the deep valleys and made travel bearable. On all sides rock cliffs 2000 to 3000 ft. high rose abruptly from the river banks, and on them the cheer pine, *Pinus roxburghii*, formed a sparse covering—it was the characteristic dominant plant at these altitudes. In moister pockets on these cliffs tall alders and evergreen oaks made a heavier forest, which supported many attractive flowering trees and shrubs. The dogwood, *Cornus capitata*, was one of these; it formed small trees which were covered in a showy mass of white flowers in June, while *Berberis ceratophylla* grew into thick bushes fifteen feet high, ablaze with yellow flowers. The ericaceous plant, *Gaultheria fragrantissima*, formed a handsome tree with branches lined with rows of bell-shaped flowers: *Deutzia*, jasmine, *Indigofera* and *Buddleia* were some of the other interesting shrubs which grew in the forest clearings.

At about 8000 ft., the valley sides were not so steep and here in the folds of the hills, dotted along the sides of the Trisuli valley, were situated a number of small villages. Each village was surrounded by narrow cultivation terraces, and when we arrived in early June the young summer maize was just showing through the ground—the wheat had already been harvested some weeks before. Even at this altitude two crops are grown each year.

Khangjung is one of these villages and it lies at about 8000 ft. directly above the village of Syabrubensi at the junction of the Langtang and Trisuli valleys. At this altitude the evergreen oak, *Quercus semecarpifolia*, and Himalayan blue pine, *Pinus wallichiana*, were the dominant trees—the latter usually favouring dry sunny slopes between 6500 and 8500 ft. Another characteristic plant of this zone was the tree rhododendron, *R. arboreum*, which grew into magnificent trees nearly forty feet high with gnarled and weather-beaten trunks. We were unfortunately too late in the season to see them in flower—they present one of the finest sights in the Himalaya when covered in a mass of red or pink flowers.

In contrast to life in the valley trough, Khangjung seemed an airy perch among the mountains: streams rushed down among Willow trees and red roses flowered about the houses.

In a climb of two hours we had passed into a temperate climate and, by the side of a stream, I came across a small meadow very similar in appearance to an English mountain pasture, where I collected rushes, sedges, buttercups, vetches and chickweeds.

Khangjung was rich in bird life and several fruitful days collecting were spent here in August among the grassland and forest. Himalayan greenfinches and doves were common on the cultivated terraces, but the very tame and very talkative Nepalese streaked laughing-thrush was the bird that was continually drawing attention to itself. It was about the size of a thrush, an overall reddish brown and streaked with lighter brown, and it spent all its time creeping in a mouse-like fashion among the bushes along the path side. It uttered a surprising array of sounds which were constantly misleading one to expect some other kind of bird.

Another laughing-thrush, the white-throated laughing-thrush, hunted in small parties through the thickets of shrubs surrounding the terrace cultivation. The distantly related scimitar babblers were much more secretive birds and, in the case of the Nepal rufous-necked scimitar babbler, its whereabouts was only revealed by its monotonous call note.

Among the blue pines the scaly-bellied green woodpecker and the brown-fronted woodpecker were quite common while the white-tailed nuthatch seemed to favour the oak forests more than the pine. There were several species of warblers, flycatchers and bulbuls, but two of the commonest small birds were the western dark-grey bush-chat and the little brown hill-warbler.

From Khangjung village the path follows the northern flank of the Langtang Khola at about 8000 ft. It runs across grassy slopes with scattered pine and tree rhododendron while 2000 ft. below roars the torrent of the Langtang river. Looking southwards towards the other side of the valley, the eye surveys ridge upon ridge of fir-covered hills stretching across the horizon; and, among the hills, only eight miles away, lie the lakes of Gosainkund. They were not visible from the Langtang Khola for they are situated at an altitude of 15,000 ft.—it would have taken two days to reach them from where we were over this extremely steep country—but it would indeed have been interesting to have visited this historical collecting ground of Wallich's pilgrims.

It was difficult to account satisfactorily for the local predominance of grass on the south-facing slope of the lower Langtang valley, for the hills on all sides were covered in forests of fir and pine. Perhaps better drainage or more insolation were responsible for this change. Alternatively the activity of man or beasts is far reaching, but during our visit there was little evidence of this. In general very abrupt changes of vegetation often occurred and I noticed, on more than one occasion, that the monsoon clouds would remain poised day after day in certain folds of the hills. Under the cloud covering, conditions contrasted strongly with the sunlit slopes on either hand; heavy evergreen forests of oak and fir predominated, while the traveller expects rain and leeches to accompany him on his journey through these regions. Cloud movements appeared to be fairly regular and were often restricted to certain parts of a valley system so that they undoubtedly exerted a profound influence on the extent of plant communities.

This sudden change of vegetation occurred in the narrow gorge of the lower Langtang valley a mile or so above the hamlet of Syarpagaon. From the dry sunny slopes of grass and flowering shrubs we passed, in a distance of 100 yards, into heavy jungle of fir with bamboo undergrowth where lichens and mosses seemed to cover every branch and boulder. This extreme contrast was due to the configuration of the ground, for during the day time there was a continual passage of moisture-laden clouds passing up through the narrow gorge on their way to the high alpine slopes in the upper part of the Langtang Khola.

Before passing on to a brief description of the fir zone some of the more striking plants and animals of the pine-grass community should be mentioned. The birds at Syarpagaon (9000 ft.) were much the same species as those found at Khangjung (8000 ft.) but in August the sunbirds and flower-peckers seemed to favour the scrub and forest clearings of the higher altitude. The species most frequently met with was the Nepal yellow-backed sunbird, resplendent in metallic colours, with green head and golden-yellow breast. In late August, I could be almost certain of finding it sucking nectar with its curved beak from the scarlet flowers of a bush named colquhounia—it was indeed a sparkling and brilliant sight! The flowerpeckers sought their food among the parasitic mistletoelike plants, lorantkus, which grew on the branches of tall oak trees. The species collected, the fire-crested flowerpecker, was a tiny bird of metallic green and it had a habit of flying with great rapidity from tree top to tree top. I also saw a couple of pairs of the brilliant fire-tailed yellow-backed sunbird. But I think pride of place goes to the minivets: small parties of the short-billed minivet hunted for insects in the tops of the trees, and the scarlet and black males with their bright yellow and black females must surely be some of the most striking of all birds. Against the dark background of the evergreen oaks they could be spotted perhaps a quarter of a mile away.

There were a number of interesting plants in the pine-grass zone but only a few can be mentioned. In August a handsome bush, *Desmodium tiliaefolium*, reminiscent of the cultivated wisteria, made splashes of violet on the hillsides. The flowers grow in delicate hanging clusters from the ends of branches and the hairy grey leaves make a perfect foil to them. In the shelter of these shrubs the Nepal lily, *Lilium nepalense*, sent up its two-foot stems bearing two to four large honey-coloured trumpets: the centre of each flower had a chocolate-brown patch which was very striking. There were several species of butterfly orchids with an even more exotic appearance than our British species; *Habenaria pectinata* was one of these.

The large toad, *Bufo himalayanus*, and the venomous bamboo snake, *Trimeresarus albolabris*, were collected on these grass slopes.

The evergreen oak, *Quercus semecarpifolia*, was the dominating plant between 7000 and 9000 ft. in all the damper localities. Above this the oak merged into the next regular zone of vegetation which was characterized by the large silver fir, *Abies webbiana*, with an altitude range of 9000 to 11,000 ft.

In general the main climatic-altitude regions can be distinguished as follows: temperate, between 7000 and 11,000 ft. where blue pine, evergreen oak and silver fir are the characteristic tree species: sub-alpine, between 11,000 and 14,000 ft. with birch forest and rhododendron shrub and including the highest cultivated areas: alpine, above 14,000 ft. with dwarf rhododendron and moraine scree, cliff communities, etc. From the point of view of attempting to establish Himalayan plants in our English gardens, plants growing in the sub-alpine region are likely to be the most suitable subjects. It is between these altitudes that most of the plants, common to both Nepal and England, are to be found: in the Langtang valley, shepherd's purse, cocksfoot, goose grass and marsh marigold were examples.

Above about 14,000 ft. conditions become much more rigorous. There is a shorter growing period and a long winter protection under snow-covering and it is little wonder that many plants from these high altitudes object to the mild and moist winters of the south of England. The plants from the alpine regions, as a general rule, can only be cultivated under the special conditions of an alpine house or frame. They are more at home in the north of the British Isles.

In the deep gorge of the lower Langtang Khola, the silver fir forest offers a striking contrast to the pine and oak forests. There is an almost impenetrable undergrowth of bamboo, *Arundinaria*, standing twenty feet high, and through this grow the massive trunks of the fir, rising nearly 150 ft. above the ground. Another large tree, the spruce, *Tsuga Brunoniana*, grew in this moisture-laden gorge and from its branches hung long streamers of lichens. The ground vegetation was composed largely of members of the nettle family, such as *Elatostema* and *Pilea* with inconspicuous green flowers, but a number of species of balsam added a little colour and interest with their curiously shaped flowers. Ferns like *Polypodium*, *Drynaria*, *Leucostegia* and *Athyrium* were in great abundance and mosses covered trees and ground alike.

There were few birds to be seen but occasionally one caught sight of the long barred tail of the yellow-billed blue magpie in the tree tops. The black-headed sibia was another forest bird while among the huge boulders lining the side of the Langtang river, the attractive white-capped redstart and the plumbeous redstart were constantly to be seen. The Himalayan black bear was a denizen of these dank forests and so was the 'wild pig' and they were both surprised at close quarters on more than one occasion during our journeys.

At about 10,000 ft. there was another abrupt change in the vegetation. The river quite suddenly ceased to run through a deep gorge and the valley floor became flatter so that the outline of the valley section changed from V to U, indicating the maximum point of extension of the Langtang glacier. Since that time the glacier has receded and the terminal moraine now lies about ten miles up the valley. The somewhat flattened trough of the valley was more accessible, the forests had been cleared and cultivation terraces and meadows now lay on either hand. In June, when we arrived, roses, berberis, cotoneaster and shrubby rhododendrons were in full bloom and they made a gay and colourful contrast to the sombre forest half a mile below.

At about 11,500 ft. lay the village of Langtang on an old glacial moraine. It was surrounded by small walled fields of wheat, potatoes and buckwheat, and by closely grazed meadows. At the same altitude, across the other side of the valley, extremely steep slopes were covered in forest, and it was possible to follow the transition of one zone of vegetation to another. The firs thinned out and birch took their place as one looked up the valley side. The birch, *Betula utilis*, formed a distinct zone of vegetation above the fir, and in the Langtang Khola it formed the highest forest community. Above this lay the alpine dwarf rhododendron zone.

The cultivation area was a delightful place to collect in; along the roughly made field-walls were orange wallflowers, yellow scabious and meadow rues. The meadows were bright with the wild garlic, *Allium wallichianum*—in the early part of the summer we found the young shoots of this plant a useful addition to the cooking pot, the wild rhubarb, *Rheum emodi* also served this purpose. Asters, anemones, saxifrages,

Solomon's seal and the little pink lily, *Notholirion macro-phyllum*, were but a few of the more attractive herbaceous plants to be found in these meadows.

In the surrounding thickets grew the magenta-flowered rhododendron, *R. lepidotum*, barely four feet high, while backing it to a height of fifteen feet were the robust bushes of *Rosa macrophylla*. Sometimes one would come across a rose bush which was covered all over with rich pink flowers, each flower was a good three inches across and it made a fine splash of colour. Both these shrubs were common and characteristic plants of the thickets but there were other fine species which would look well in cultivation in England, notably *Rosa sericea*, a white flowered species, *Spiraea bella* with bright pink flowers and *Berberis kochneana*. Deutzia, cotoneaster, clematis, willow and honeysuckle were well represented.

These shrub thickets had an abundance of bird life. Two closely related species of laughing thrushes, the variegated and the black-faced laughing thrush, were very common indeed. Garrulous parties of these birds would constantly be seen flapping clumsily about among the bushes in search of insects. The rufous-backed shrike was another conspicuous bird as it perched on the top of a tall bush waiting for its prey. The short tailed, brilliant metallic green Impeyan pheasant or monal was often disturbed in the long grass among the thickets. Flocks of grey and white snow-pigeons were continually passing up and down the valley in the early part of the summer and red-billed choughs came down from the high cliffs each morning to search for grubs in the meadows. Small birds, like the Indian redstart, orange-gorgeted flycatcher, martins and willow warblers, were very common.

Many of the butterflies were reminiscent of our British species and I noted among others, coppers, fritillaries, clouded-yellows and tortoiseshells. In a small pool in a flooded meadow, I found a new species of frog, *Rana polunini*, rather a small species (44mm.) with a brown granulated skin and a feebly developed dorso-lateral fold. This species is related to *Rana blanfordi*.

The flora round the area of cultivation at Langtang village was very rich in species but it is impossible to describe it adequately by normal descriptive methods. It is from localities such as this that some of the most beautiful species of our gardens have come. The herbaceous plants growing at Langtang, like *Thalictrum chelodonii*, *Thermopsis barbata* and *Delphinium coeruleum*, are certainly worthy of a place but for one reason or another have yet to be established in cultivation.

Two and a half hours up the valley, past the last fields of buckwheat at 12,500 ft., lies the first regular summer grazing or 'kharka' named Kyangjin Ghyang. Here there were perhaps a dozen stone huts roofed with bamboo matting which were used by the herdsmen for a few weeks each summer when they took their herds to the alpine pastures.

A rise in altitude of 2000 ft. had had a profound effect on the vegetation. The rough meadows at Kyangjin were surrounded by low scrub barely two feet high. A single magenta-flowered rhododendron, *R. eleagnoides*, was very common and with it, *Spiraea canescens*, *Potentilla fruticosa* and *Berberis concinna* formed a springy covering of shrubs over the rough ground. Among this grew a number of liliaceous plants such as *Polygonatum hookeri* with a head of a few pink flowers closely pressed to the ground and the rather dull-purple flowered *Lilium nanum*. The chequered brown and yellow *Fritillaria cirrhosa* managed to hold its head up above the scrub: this plant was collected by our Sherpa porters and the bulbs were eaten as a preventative against goitre. The Langtang people seemed unaware of this and many of them had large goitres. Other monocotyledonous plants like *Roscoe alpina*, *Aletris pauciflora* and *Iris kumaonensis* were frequent at this altitude on the well-consolidated moraine.

In June the herds of yak, cows and their hybrids the zos were grazing at Kyangjin but they soon passed on to the higher kharkas which were scattered along the main and lateral valleys wherever the ground was sufficiently horizontal to allow rough grassland to develop. Some of the highest grazings lay at 16,500 ft. and even at this height there were generally the foundations of one or two temporary shelters which could be quickly made habitable by throwing a bamboo matting roof over the walls. At night the animals were collected round these huts so that the ground became trampled and manured, with the result that little pockets of such world-wide weed species as docks, shepherd's purse, speedwell and plantains were conspicuous. Sometimes this manuring encouraged the growth of primulas and on more than one occasion I came across a wonderful showing of the rounded purple heads of *Primula denticulata* and round another kharka a yellow sheet of the delicately scented *Primula Stuartii*.

The birds at Khangjin Ghyang showed a marked change, for the country was now more open than at Langtang. The thicket-loving birds like laughing thrushes and flycatchers had almost disappeared and in their place came the redstarts, pipits and rose finches.

Quite the commonest bird of the grassy boulder-strewn slopes was Hodgson's pipit, a small brown-streaked bird similar in appearance and behaviour to a meadow pipit. The Indian redstart occurred in small parties among the piles of shattered rock and they were constantly catching the eye as they flew from rock to rock a few yards ahead of one, for when they alighted they bobbed their chestnut-and-black tail up and down continuously. Willow warblers, such as the grey-faced and the Nepal orange-barred willow warbler were common about the low bushes.

The rose finches were the most conspicuous birds with their bright cherry-red colouring. I came across small parties of them at this altitude but in August and September they favoured the open mountainside above the tree line. Near the herdsmen's huts at Kyangjin I collected the spotted-winged, the red-headed and the Indian rose finch.

The birch forests formed a very distinct community in the Langtang valley. They occur above the fir zone at altitudes between 12,500 and 14,000 ft. with outliers up to 14,500 ft. They grew on steep north-facing slopes and formed an almost pure forest with the mountain ash as the only other important tree. *Rhododendron campanulatum* formed a dense undershrub to a height of ten to fifteen feet in this forest. There was a rich growth of cryptogamic plants over the boulder-covered floor and on some of the tree trunks, but the bark of this birch peeled off in long streamers so that mosses and lichens could not get much of a hold. This bark comes off in very thin strips and it is used by the Langtang men to wrap butter or as cigarette papers.

Ferns such as *Dryopteris jibrillosa*, *Cryptogamme brunoniana* and *Athyrium duthiei* were common, while the number of conspicuous flowering plants were limited by the heavy shade. A robust primula, *P. strumosa*, with butter-yellow flowers, grew by the sides of streams running down through the forest, and the orchid, *Goodyera repens*, with delicately mottled leaves, was occasionally to be seen.

Once again the birds were quite distinct in the birch forest. Tits were abundant and with willow warblers they formed mixed parties which hunted through the tops of the trees. A little-known bird, the rufous-bellied crested tit, which is restricted to Nepal, was one of the commonest. Like most of the Himalayan birds that we came upon in the Langtang valley, this tit does not migrate to the foothills during the winter and consequently it is not known to European ornithologists in the field. It behaved in a typical tit-like way; its favourite position seemed to be upside down on the very end of a hanging birch branch. The Himalayan cole-tit was another common tit, while the brilliant scarlet-headed bullfinch, with scarlet body, black wings and tail, was a wonderful sight against the pale green leaves of the birch trees and a background of swirling clouds. A tail-less wren, the scaly-breasted wren, was often to be seen hopping in and out among the mossy boulders in search of food. Tree-creepers quartered the tattered bark of the weather-beaten birch trees and Himalayan nutcrackers hunted in small parties among the branches.

Above the Birch forest, soil, drainage and situation began to have a marked effect on the distribution of vegetation, and a number of distinct plant communities were found. On the gentler slopes where the soil had an opportunity of consolidating, a dark peaty soil accumulated and in it grew two species of rhododendron forming a dense springy growth about a foot high. *Rhododendron anthopogon* was the dominant plant over large areas and it sometimes grew up to an altitude of 16,000 ft. where it was no more than four inches high. It bears a close head of rather dull white flowers and its oval leaves have rusty brown hairs on the underside—the leaves were aromatic when crushed. The other species, *R. setosum*, was less widely distributed, it has bright cerise flowers with a habit reminding one of an azalea. The delicate mosslike plant *Cassiope fastigiata* was often seen in the peaty soil, the rows of small white hanging bells were constantly attracting attention. Another unusual plant was the strange pungent-smelling *Codonopsis thalictrifolia* with elongated trumpet-shaped flowers of a pale milky-blue colour.

Grassy patches often occurred among these rhododendron-covered slopes, particularly when grazed, and among them grew those striking semi-parasitic plants the louseworts, *Pedicularis*. I collected no less than twenty-two species of this genus including two new to science. Some of them are very colourful and it is a pity that they cannot be cultivated and induced to parasitise our lawns and add their colour to them. *Pedicularis megalantha* was one of the finest species; it had a loose head of twenty to thirty rich magenta-coloured flowers each three-quarters of an inch across, the whole flower head standing a foot or more high. Another species, *P. siphonantha*, had pink and white flowers and *P. sculleyana* had a large head of cream-coloured flowers. *Polygonum* was another large genus (twenty-four species collected) and a most handsome species, *P. vaccini-folium*, with small oval leaves and short spikes of pink flowers sometimes gave a pink tinge to the boulder-covered hillsides.

The Himalayan poppies, *Meconopsis*, occurred sparingly but they were always striking. *M. paniculata* was the most frequent with its six-foot stems bearing silvery-yellow leaves and clusters of large lemon-yellow flowers. Similar in colouring but lighter in build were the two exclusively Nepalese species *M. dhwojii* and *M. longipetiolata*—the former was named after its Nepalese finder Capt. Lai Dhwoj. The dark purple-flowered species, *M. discigera*, was always arresting.

A number of primulas were conspicuous along the sides of streamlets and in the damper ground. *Primula sikkimensis* which grows well in cultivation was one of these: its mealy covered stems grew nearly two feet high and from the top hung a cluster of twenty large yellow flowers. Other primulas such as *P. concinna* and *P. flagillaris* are minute and the tiny pink or white flowers are carried barely half an inch above the ground.

With increase in altitude the vegetation becomes less and less uniform. Splintered rock faces throw down wide fans of scree, and piles of boulders cover more and more of the mountainside. Between 14,000 and 16,000 ft. the dwarf rhododendron community predominates but open communities of high alpine plants are more liable to take its place as the altitude increases. Above 16,500 ft. there is little extensive vegetation but instead scattered pockets of plants growing wherever they can get a foothold. From about 17,500 ft. there are great areas of mountain debris composed of piled and splintered blocks, where no plants can grow. The highest plant seen in the Langtang valley was collected by Tilman at 19,000 ft.—its name has not yet been ascertained.

In this alpine zone, in addition to the dwarf rhododendron community there are other habitats supporting characteristic plants. On cliffs, particularly where water percolated through cracks, species of primula, like *P. sharmae* and *P. buryana*, grew on mossy ledges. The latter species has a compact rosette of hairy leaves with a cluster of white bells on a short stem and it was one of the new species found by Wollaston on the 1921 Everest Reconnaissance Expedition at a place called Nyenam in Tibet only thirty miles away from the Langtang Khola. We came upon another very beautiful species which was also found in this locality for the first time and which was named *P. wollastoni* after him. This plant has a rosette of leaves closely pressed to the ground and from the centre a slender stem bears a conical head of half a dozen thimble-shaped flowers, pale blue in colour and dusted with a snowy 'farina'. I collected some seeds of this plant in early September; they germinated well although not fully ripe, and were successfully brought to flower in England two years later. This plant was growing in one small area, at 16,000 ft., among short grass on a morainic pile of small stones and silt.

Another beautiful damp cliff plant was *Meconopsis bella* with delicate grey-green fern-like leaves above which the solitary Cambridge-blue bells were poised on thin stems. *Potentilla*, *Saxifraga* and *Lloydia* were common genera on these cliffs.

Another distinct community of plants were those colonising loose scree with good drainage. Many had their leaves covered in a thick felt of silvery hairs like the deep blue flowered *Veronica lanuginosa* or *Eriophyton wallichianum*, *Androsace* and *Leontopodium*. Quite the most arresting of all these woolly plants was *Saussurea gossipiphora* for it looked like a spherical ball of cotton-wool. There was a small hole in the top, the size of one's little finger, which allowed for the entry of bees to the completely closed interior. The compact head of flowers was never exposed and it was noticeably warmer within the plant.

But perhaps the climax to my plant collecting was the finding of *Delphinium brunonianum*. Lloyd had come upon this plant in a high scree north of the main Langtang glacier and before he left he gave me the necessary directions to find the place. On the last day of my seed collecting journey up the Langtang Khola I made a special journey to find it. After a prolonged search I found it amid a jungle of rocks at 16,500 ft. where clumps of its clear blue flowers stood out against the grey lichen-covered rocks. The leaves were rounded and hairy and they grew up from between the boulders, while above them six-inch stems carried three or four large balloon-shaped flowers. Each flower is hairy on the outside and is lined with darker blue veins, the spur is short and conical and the petal tips are a brown velvet colour. However, the crowning joy to this plant is the rich oriental scent which is given off by the mature flowers—an *embarras de richesse* on this desolate mountain side. My Sherpa porter carried down a bunch of the flowers and hung them in the shelter and for several days we enjoyed the exotic perfume. This plant is used as an insect repellent in Tibet. Hooker found the plant in east Nepal but he records that it smells strongly and disagreeably of musk. Tastes may differ but it is more likely that different races of the same species give off different perfumes. Other high scree plants of note are *Allardiaglabra, Crepisglomerata, Oxytropis melanocalyx* and *Phlomis rotata*.

Yet one further high alpine locality requires mentioning and that is where surface water runs over scree or silt. This often occurs in the ablation valleys running parallel to the glacier—where the glacier has shrunk away from the cliffs on either side leaving narrow strips of sparse vegetation. These valleys were quite rich in species, particularly of *Ranunculus*, gentians, sedges, primulas and *Cremanthodium*. This latter is a handsome genus of Himalayan plants usually with solitary yellow flowers—like an inverted coltsfoot. Several species grew gracefully along the side of streamlets, notably *C. decaisnei* and *C. plantagineum*. A beautiful sweet-scented primula with spear-shaped leaves covered with yellow 'farina' sometimes grew in extensive patches. It was *P. macrophylla* and it had a head of white or violet flowers. *Gentiana nubigena* and *G. ornata* were two late-flowering gentians with striped blue and yellow flowers.

There are many other interesting species of flowering plants in the alpine zone but it has only been possible to mention a few of the large-flowered species. In the attached list I have named a further number of these plants but the greater part of the collection now deposited at the British Museum (Natural History) has yet to be identified.

A few mammals and birds inhabiting the higher altitudes must be mentioned to complete this brief survey of the Langtang Khola. The most conspicuous mammal was the small brown pika or mouse-hare, *Ochotona*, which we often came upon unawares sunning itself on the top of a boulder in the high moraines. It is little bigger than a rat; it is tail-less and has a rounded vole-like profile. In one summer-shelter that we occupied, a mouse-hare had its home in the rough walls of the hut and we derived great pleasure from watching it as it fed on leaves not two yards away from us. Very occasionally we caught a glimpse of the tahr, *Hemitragus jemlaicus*, on the high cliffs, while on several occasions in the birch forests we saw droppings of the musk deer, *Moschus moschifer*. This animal is strictly preserved in the Langtang valley and it is the headman's duty to see that there is no poaching from neighbouring areas. The musk pods, which are glands produced on the abdomen during the rutting season, are collected and become a perquisite of H.H. the Maharajah of Nepal.

In the alpine zone there are a number of characteristic birds among which the rosefinches were perhaps the commonest, but I was unfortunately unable to distinguish the species in the field, and at an altitude of 16,000 to 17,000 ft. heavy breathing made collecting much more difficult. The rufous-breasted accentor, white and grey wagtails, and several species of rosefinch collected round the kharkas hunted for seeds and insects in the ground disturbed by herds of cattle. Small parties of snow-pigeons and choughs were often to be seen about the wastes of rock and scree. On several occasions I saw a large bird of prey, probably a golden eagle, with a dark bronze-coloured body and a paler yellow head. The large snow-cock was sometimes disturbed on the high stony hillsides, but the bird that I particularly associate with piled moss-covered boulders and desolate scree in the Langtang valley is the tiny Nepal wren. It creeps like a mouse over, and often beneath, boulders and disappears from view for seconds at a time to reappear in a quite unexpected place some yards distant. Its shrill chirrup was a pleasant reminder that there was life among these wide Himalayan wastes.

I should like to conclude by thanking all those of the British Museum (Natural History) who have made it possible for me to give full names to some of the plants and animals mentioned. In particular I should like to thank Sir N. B. Kinnear, Dr G. Taylor, Mr H. A. G. Alston and Dr M. Smith.

A List of Plants Collected during the 1949 Expedition to Central Nepal

This list is in no way complete but it includes many of the plants which are most likely to interest the gardener and alpine gardener. Seeds from some of these plants were brought back to England.

RANUNCULACEAE
    Clematis montana
    Anemone rupicola
    Thalictrum chelidonii
    Th. virgatum
    Delphinium ?denudatum
    D. brunonianum
    D. densiflorum
    Aconitum leucanthemum

BERBERIDACEAE
    Berberis ceratophylla
    B. concinna
    B. concinna var. *breviora*
    B. usteriana var. *rubicunda* (var. nov.)
    B. kochneana var. *auramea* (var. nov.)
    B. floribunda
    B. polunini (sp. nov.)
    B. angulosa
    Podophyllum emodi

PAPAVERACEAE
    Meconopsis simplicifolia
    M. horridula
    M. dhwojii
    M. paniculata
    M. longipetiolata
    M. lyrata
    M. bella
    M. discigera

FUMARIACEAE
    Corydalis cashmiriana
    C. trifiliata
    C. juncea
    C. meifolia

CARYOPHYLLACEAE
    Lychnis apetala

GERANIACEAE
    Geranium refractum

LEGUMINOSAE
    Piptanthus nepalensis
    Astragalus pychnorhizus
    Oxytropis melanocalyx
    Desmodium tiliaefolium

ROSACEAE
    Prunus cornuta
    Spiraea bella
    S. canescens
    Potentilla microphylla
    Rosa macrophylla
    R. sericea
    Pyrus pashia
    Sorbus cuspidata
    S. microphylla
    Cotoneaster microphyllum var. *cochleata*
    C. frigida
    C. horizontalis
    C. affinis
    C. acuminata

SAXIFRAGACEAE
  Saxifraga pallida
  Chrysosplenium alternifolium

CORNACEAE
  Cornus capitata

CAPRIFOLIACEAE
  Viburnum stellatulum var.
    involucratum
  V. erubescens
  V. cylindricum
  V. ?foetidum
  Lonicera rupicola

DIPSACEAE
  Morina longifolia

COMPOSITAE
  Anaphalis nubigena
  Allardia glabra
  Cremanthodium decaisnei
  C. ?plantagineum
  Saussurea gossypiphora
  Crepis glomearat

CAMPANULACEAE
  Codonopsis viridis
  C. purpurea
  C. ?dicentrifolia
  C. convolvulacea
  C. thactrifolia
  Cyananthus lobatus
  C. incanus
  C. hookeri
  C. inflatus
  Campanula colorata
  C. aristata
  C. modesta

ERICACEAE
  Gaultheria nummularioides
  G. trichophylla

  Cassiope fastigiata
  Lyonia villosa
  Pieris formosa
  Rhododendron arboreum
  R. campanulatum
  R. barbatum
  R. lepidotum
  R. anthopogon
  R. setosum
  R. elaeagnoides
  R. cowanianum (sp. nov.)
  R. nivale

PRIMULACEAE
  Primula rotundifolia
  P. denticulata
  P. atrodentata
  P. sikkimensis
  P. reticulata
  P. obliqua
  P. macrophylla
  P. stuartii
  P. pusilla
  P. muscoides
  P. tenuiloba
  P. minutissima
  P. strumosa
  P. ?gracilipes
  P. sharmae
  P. involucrata
  P. wollasoni
  P. buryana
  P. soldanelloides
  P. glomerata
  P. concinna

GENTIANACEAE
  Gentiana nubigena
  G. ornata
  Halenia elliptica

BORAGINACEAE
  Onosma bicolor

SCROPHULARIACEAE
   Verbascum thapsus
   Veronica himalensis
   V. lanuginosa
   Pedicularis siphonantha
   P. longiflora var. tubiformis
   P. sculleyana

LENTIBULARIACEAE
   Pinguicula aplina

LABIATAE
   Phlomis setigera
   P. rotata
   Eriophyton wallichianum
   Leucas lanata

POLYGONACEAE
   Polygomum affine
   P. vaccinifolium
   P. emodi

ORCHIDACEAE
   Epipactis royleana
   E. helleborine
   Goodyera marginata
   G. repens
   G. fusca
   Orchis chusua
   O. diantha
   Habenaria arietina
   H. pectinata
   H. intermedia
   Herminium pugioniforme
   H. angustifolium

   H. josephi
   Satyrium nepalense
   Cypripedium himalaicum

HAEMODORACEAE
   Aletris pauciflora
   Ophiopogon intermedius

AMARYLLIDACEAE
   Zephyranthes carinata
   Hypoxis aurea

LILIACEAE
   Polygonatum hookeri
   P. cirrifolium
   Streptopus simplex
   Theropogon pallidus
   Allium wallichii
   A. prattii
   Lilium nanum
   L. nepalense
   Notholirion macrophyllium
   Fritillaria cirrhosa
   Lloydia serotina
   Chlorophytum nepalense

GNETALES
   Ephedra gerardiana

CONFERALES
   Pinus wallichiana
   P. roxburghii
   Tsuga brunoniana
   Abies webbiana

A List of Birds collected in the Langtang Khola and the Adjacent District of Central Nepal

Numbers refer to the species numbers given in
Fauna of British India: Birds by Stuart Baker.

- 7 Himalayan jungle crow
- 23 Yellow-billed blue magpie
- 48 Red-billed chough
- 46 Himalayan nutcracker
- 59 Green-backed tit
- 64 Himalayan cole-tit
- 65 Rufous-bellied crested tit
- 68 Brown crested tit
- 77 Red-headed tit
- 108 White-tailed nuthatch
- 137 White-throated laughing-thrush
- 140 White-spotted laughing thrush
- 161 Black-faced laughing-thrush
- 162 Variegated laughing-thrush
- 171 Nepalaese streaked laughing-thrush
- 177 Striated laughing-thrush
- 214 Nepal rufous-necked scimitar babbler
- 220 Barker's rusty-cheeked scimitar babbler
- 243 Mandelli's spotted babbler
- 304 Hodgson's fulvetta
- 311 Black-headed sibia
- 333 Stripe-throated sibia
- 339 Stripe-throated yuhina
- 342 *Yuhina occipitalis*
- 345 Yellow-headed ixulus
- 386 Himalayan black bulbul
- 405 White-cheeked bulbul
- 4 Tree-creeper
- 457 Wall-creeper
- 458 Nepal wren
- 471 Scaly-breasted wren
- 476 Chestnut-headed wren
- 484 Indian blue-chat
- 491 Hodgson's shortwing
- 494 Northern-Indian stonechat
- 495 Stonechat
- 502 Western dark-grey bush chat
- 525 Little forktail
- 526 Blue-fronted redstart
- 532 Indian redstart
- 534 White-capped redstart
- 535 Plumbeous redstart
- 546 Golden bush-robin
- 549 Red-flanked bush-robin
- 606 Blue-headed rock-thrush
- 614 Himalayan whistling-thrush
- 628 Rufous-breasted accentor
- 632 Sooty flycatcher
- 636 Orange-gorgeted flycatcher
- 645 Slaty-blue flycatcher
- 649 Indian little pied flycatcher
-     Verditer flycatcher
- 699 Yellow-bellied flycatcher
- 712 Indian black-headed shrike
- 714 Rufous-backed shrike
- 738 Indian short-billed minivet
-     *Phylloscopus sp.*
- 860 *Phylloscopus reguloides*
- 863 Grey-faced willow warbler
- 864 Nepal orange-barred willow warbler
- 889 Black-browed flycatcher-warbler
- 891 Grey-headed warbler
- 923 Brown hill-warbler

1024	Hodgson's munia	1204	Upland pipit
1044	Red-headed bullfinch	1266	Fire-tailed yellow-backed sunbird
1055	Pink-browed rose-finch		
1052	Red-headed rose-finch	1274	Nepal yellow-backed sunbird
1055	White-browed rose-finch	1303	Fire-crested flowerpecker
1059	Beautiful rose-finch	1311	Thick-billed flowerpecker
1063	Spotted-winged rose-finch	1337	Scaly-bellied green woodpecker
1069	Indian rose-finch		
1076	Dark rose-finch	1370	Brown-fronted pied woodpecker
1078	Blandford's rose-finch		
1089	Himalayan greenfinch	1436	Blue-throated barbet
1102	Tree-sparrow	1451	European cuckoo
1115	Hodgson's mountain finch	1579	European hoopoe
1139	Crested bunting	1590	Swift
1165	White wagtail subsp.	1683	Spotted owlet
1169	Swinho's white wagtail	1838	Thick-billed green pigeon
1174	Eastern grey wagtail	1858	Snow-pigeon
1194	Blyth's pipit	1928	Impeyan pheasant or monal
120	Hodgson's pipit		

H. W. TILMAN

The Collected Edition

For the first time since their original appearance, all fifteen books by H. W. Tilman are being published as single volumes, with all their original photographs, maps and charts. Forewords and afterwords by those who knew him, or who can bring their own experience and knowledge to bear, complement his own understated writing to give us a fuller picture of the man and his achievements. A sixteenth volume is the 1980 biography by J. R. L. Anderson, *High Mountains and Cold Seas*. The books will appear in pairs, one each from his climbing and sailing eras, in order of original publication, at quarterly intervals from September 2015:

Sep 2015	**Snow on the Equator**
	Mischief in Patagonia
Dec 2015	**The Ascent of Nanda Devi**
	Mischief Among the Penguins
Mar 2016	**When Men & Mountains Meet**
	Mischief in Greenland
Jun 2016	**Mount Everest 1938**
	Mostly Mischief
Sep 2016	**Two Mountains and a River**
	Mischief Goes South
Dec 2016	**China to Chitral**
	In Mischief's Wake
Mar 2017	**Nepal Himalaya**
	Ice With Everything
Jun 2017	**Triumph and Tribulation**
	High Mountains and Cold Seas

www.tilmanbooks.com